RATZINGER'S FAITH

RATZINGER'S FAITH

FAITH

THE THEOLOGY OF POPE BENEDICT XVI

TRACEY ROWLAND

CABRINI COLLEGE LIBRARY
610 KING OF PRUSSIA ROAD
RADNOR, PA 19087

OXFORD
UNIVERSITY PRESS

OXFORD

UNIVERSITY PRESS

Great Clarendon Street, Oxford OX2 6DP

Oxford University Press is a department of the University of Oxford.
It furthers the University's objective of excellence in research, scholarship,
and education by publishing worldwide in

Oxford New York

Auckland Cape Town Dar es Salaam Hong Kong Karachi
Kuala Lumpur Madrid Melbourne Mexico City Nairobi
New Delhi Shanghai Taipei Toronto

With offices in

Argentina Austria Brazil Chile Czech Republic France Greece
Guatemala Hungary Italy Japan Poland Portugal Singapore
South Korea Switzerland Thailand Turkey Ukraine Vietnam

Oxford is a registered trade mark of Oxford University Press
in the UK and in certain other countries

Published in the United States
by Oxford University Press Inc., New York

© Tracey Rowland 2008

The moral rights of the author have been asserted
Database right Oxford University Press (maker)

First published 2008

All rights reserved. No part of this publication may be reproduced,
stored in a retrieval system, or transmitted, in any form or by any means,
without the prior permission in writing of Oxford University Press,
or as expressly permitted by law, or under terms agreed with the appropriate
reprographics rights organization. Enquiries concerning reproduction
outside the scope of the above should be sent to the Rights Department,
Oxford University Press, at the address above

You must not circulate this book in any other binding or cover
and you must impose the same condition on any acquirer

British Library Cataloguing in Publication Data

Data available

Library of Congress Cataloging in Publication Data

Data available

Typeset by SPI Publisher Services, Pondicherry, India
Printed in Great Britain
on acid-free paper by
Biddles Ltd., Lynn, Norfolk

ISBN 978-0-19-920740-4

1 3 5 7 9 10 8 6 4 2

*In Memory of Dorothy Davies (1912–1981)
and for Stuart Adair Rowland*

Acknowledgements

This work was written as a guide to the thought of Benedict XVI for those who are not necessarily professional theologians but who are none the less interested to follow the thought of the leader of the world's largest Christian communion.

At the time of completing the manuscript the only other work of its type available in English is that by Aidan Nichols OP, the John Paul II Lecturer in Roman Catholic Theology in Oxford. This work differs from that of Father Nichols in taking a more thematic, less chronological approach, but none the less I regard his work as the gold standard for this field.

I wish to thank my colleagues at the John Paul II Institute in Melbourne for their support for this project, especially Lieutenant-Colonel Toby Hunter and Mrs Penny Power who take care of the lion's share of the administrative work of the Institute, Dr Nicholas Tonti-Filippini who runs the Bioethics programme, Most Rev Peter J. Elliott, a former official of the Pontifical Council for the Family (1987–1997), who heads our outfit, and our Senior Tutor, Anna Krohn. Drafts of chapters were farmed out for comment and here I am especially grateful to the following: Revd Scott Armstrong, Brian Boyle MSC, Bernard Colbert, Michael Daniel, Ellen Garrett, Fr Gregory Jordan SJ, Peter Knowles OP, Robin Koning SJ, Patrick Quirk, Alcuin Reid, Revd Anthony Robbie, Marcia Riordan, James V. Schall SJ, Owen Vyner, and Glen Tattersall FSSP. Fr Fergus Kerr OP also reviewed the manuscript for Oxford University Press and made some very helpful suggestions.

Monica O'Shea was enormously helpful in chasing references for me and being our domestic goddess in residence, Louise Mitchell checked the manuscript for stylistic errors, and Maria Klepacka helped with translations.

I also benefited from the chance to study the thought of Benedict XVI with leading European and American scholars at a colloquium entitled 'Crisis and Kairos: The Philosophy of History and the Thought of Joseph Ratzinger/Benedict XVI' in June 2006. The colloquium was presented in partnership by the Lumen Christi Institute of the University of Chicago and L'Institut Catholique de Paris. My thanks are due to Thomas Levergood of the Lumen Christi Institute for the invitation to attend the colloquium and for some great dinners in Paris and Cholet.

Thanks are also due to my husband who proofread the penultimate draft and who offered many practical and creative suggestions in the process. This work is dedicated to him and to the memory of my maternal grandmother.

The Foreword has been provided by His Eminence George Cardinal Pell, a fellow Patron of the Australian Catholic Students' Association, who for ten years served Cardinal Ratzinger as a member of the Congregation for the Doctrine of the Faith. My thanks are due to His Eminence for the support he gives to our students and for his taking the time to read this work and contribute his own thoughts.

TRACEY ROWLAND

Contents

Foreword

No Pope in history has published as much high quality theology on such a variety of topics as Pope Benedict XVI. At the time of his election to the papacy few would have disputed his position as the most distinguished living Catholic theologian, although his writings have not had the same seminal importance as those of Hans Urs von Balthasar, Yves Congar, and Karl Rahner, who have predeceased him.

Other popes have made more important contributions to the development of doctrine, such as Leo the Great at the Council of Chalcedon and even Pope John Paul II, especially with his two moral encyclicals *Veritatis Splendor* and *Evangelium Vitae*; but in this second example Joseph Ratzinger's role as Prefect of the Congregation for the Doctrine of the Faith was significant.

Tracey Rowland's new volume on *Ratzinger's Faith: the Theology of Pope Benedict XVI* is an example of first-rate scholarship, further enhancing her progress towards becoming Australia's leading theologian. It is also an enjoyable read and more accessible than her earlier masterly work *Culture and the Thomist Tradition: after Vatican II* (2003) which charted the contending cultural forces in western society after the Council, our naïve optimism about the beneficence of modernity and our equally damaging overestimation of Catholic cultural strength in the meltdown (more or less) of faith and practice nearly everywhere in the First World. Before the Council, Catholic Holland and French-speaking Canada ranked with Ireland as high points of faith, piety, and missionary endeavour. Today only ashes remain in Holland, although the embers are starting to glow once again, Cardinal Ouellet is struggling manfully in Quebec, and the fate of Catholic Ireland, still with formidable strengths despite the sexual scandals, hangs in the balance.

These pockets of self-destruction, unique in Catholic history, were (obviously) not intended by the Council Fathers, nor logical consequences of the Council's teaching. They were accompanied by steady growth in most mission areas, the maintenance of Catholic strength behind the Iron Curtain, and the stabilization of Catholic life in South America through the rebuff of liberation theology. Joseph Ratzinger was an important player in all these events after his appointment as Archbishop of Munich in 1977.

When I was a seminarian in Rome during the Council, the 'peritus' Joseph Ratzinger was not widely known in my circle nor regarded as particularly radical. He became better known in the English speaking world after the upheavals of 1968 highlighted the extremist agenda of some Catholic priests and theologians from which he distanced himself and his formation in 1972 of the *Communio* journal.

In the mid-sixties, before the crisis of '68, Ratzinger wrote that 'if the Church were to accommodate herself to the world in any way that would entail a turning away from the Cross, this would not lead to a renewal of the Church, but only to her death'. There are elements in the Church even today, diminished in numbers while still vocal, who have not grasped this truth, but the cardinal, now pope, has always remained faithful to this fundamental insight.

Rowland claims, accurately I believe, that while some of Ratzinger's opponents have changed, his basic theological framework is unchanged with no fundamental U-turn even after 1968. His most important shifts of position are in liturgy and ecclesiology.

Before the conclave of 2005 I was under the mistaken impression that I had read most of what Cardinal Ratzinger had written. I was surprised to discover the range of his earlier writings in particular and Rowland has done us a big favour by clearly setting out his positions, providing a road map charting his progress through the much changed worlds of theology from the 1950s to the early third millennium.

She explains in some detail the nature of Ratzinger's attitude to Thomism, his opposition to what she describes as Leonine or Baroque Thomism, which flourished in many seminaries before the Council, and his opposition to Suarez.

Certainly most of the Scholastic manuals, written in Latin, which we studied in philosophy in the 1960s here in Australia were arid, out of date, impersonal, and mechanistic. It was this impersonalism which prompted the young Karol Wojtyla's thesis on Max Scheler's personalism and the sensitivity to human experience in his phenomenology. Ratzinger's scepticism about the Thomism of the manuals was shared almost universally among the seminarians of the sixties.

This scepticism should not be exaggerated as Ratzinger, like every main-line Catholic, is indebted to Aquinas in a thousand ways, especially in morality, and he is not hostile to classical Thomism in general or to St Thomas personally.

Rowland believes that the Holy Father takes from St Augustine his understanding of the centrality of love (as in his first encyclical) and its essential link to truth, a conviction that faith cannot be separated radically from reason ('reason has a wax nose') and his devotion to the transcendental of beauty, whether it be in art, music, literature, and especially in the liturgy.

She also goes to considerable pains to refute those who would pit the Thomist John Paul II against the Augustinian Benedict. They are different personalities with different gifts and backgrounds. John Paul II came from a church which battled both Nazism and Communism and saw both off the stage of history. He was a lay student at university, compelled to do forced labour, a natural leader and a poet, an instinctive populist, actor, and optimist. His doctoral studies were in philosophy and spirituality.

Pope Benedict grew up in the communal strengths of Catholic Bavaria, but German Catholics were unable to impede Hitler's rise to power and shared in the disasters he brought on his people. Benedict is a man of deep spirituality, genuine kindliness, and massive learning developed through a lifetime of study and writing. A theologians' theologian, he is a spectacularly successful teacher at many levels (as the crowds at his weekly audiences attest), reserved rather than gregarious, used to biding his time as he unfolds his programme.

He is not the prisoner of any school, nor is he dependent on his advisers, and it is still too early to judge how different his priorities might become from his predecessor's. The long-term engagement with Islam is still in its early stages and Benedict's attitude to the reform of religious life still unclear.

However the partnership of Pope John Paul II and Cardinal Ratzinger was one of the most brilliant and effective in papal history as they dialogued with the world of learning and confronted the culture of death. Any future initiatives of Pope Benedict are likely to be in continuity, complementary and not antithetical to the patrimony of his mentor.

Long before the Council the young Ratzinger had been interested in liturgical reform and many will find his outspoken comments about aspects of the post-vernacular liturgical developments surprising and thought-provoking.

He believes that some contemporary liturgies are forms of apostasy, similar to the Hebrews' worship of the golden calf! For him calls for open Communion reflect an unconscious deism as the Last Supper was not held with publicans and sinners. The Holy Sacrifice of the Mass is an act of worship not a fellowship meal, and reducing the Eucharist to an exaltation of the local community is a radical inversion of proper priorities. Genuine liturgical renewal has been opposed by forces that are bureaucratic, philistine, and secularist.

The Church is now moving to redress these imbalances and reaffirm the beauty and continuity of the Latin liturgical tradition. As a cardinal, Ratzinger strongly supported the publication of *Liturgiam Authenticam* which requires accurate and beautiful vernacular translations of the Roman Missal. It will be interesting to watch the reform of the liturgical reform, which will be carried forward by Pope Benedict, but certainly not completed in his pontificate.

In Tracey Rowland Pope Benedict has an enthusiastic champion and a faithful interpreter. Her enthusiasm for his theology is contagious.

It is a sign of the times and a portent of the future that this excellent volume was written by a young, married woman, who is the Dean of the Melbourne campus of the John Paul II Institute.

George Cardinal Pell
Archbishop of Sydney

Introduction

On 6 November 1992, Joseph Ratzinger was appointed an associate member of the prestigious Académie française in the section for moral and political sciences. The Académie was founded by Armand-Jean Cardinal Richelieu in 1635. Its members, known as *les immortels*, have included Victor Hugo, Louis Pasteur, and Voltaire. This honour from a completely secular institution in the capital of a country renowned for keeping God out of the public realm, at least since 1789, is some indication of Ratzinger's high standing in the world of European letters. As one of the most prolific theologians of his generation he has held positions at the University of Bonn (1959–1963), the University of Münster (1963–1966), the University of Tübingen (1966–1969), and the University of Regensburg (1969–1977). He speaks several modern languages (German, French, Spanish, Italian, English) and is quite at home with classical Greek, Latin, and Hebrew. He plays the piano and especially enjoys the music of Mozart and Beethoven. He shares this interest with his older brother Georg who has held the post of *Kapellmeister* of Regensburg Cathedral. Ratzinger was made a bishop and cardinal by Paul VI in 1977 and appointed Prefect for the Sacred Congregation for the Doctrine of the Faith (the CDF) by John Paul II in 1981. This latter post is regarded by some as the second most significant within the Catholic Church after that of the papacy itself, or at least the most significant of the nine heads of Congregations. While holding these appointments Ratzinger continued to publish substantial academic works. His doctoral dissertation, defended in 1953, was entitled *The People and the House of God in Augustine's Doctrine of the Church*; and his postdoctoral thesis, or *Habilitationsschrift*, offered an examination of St Bonaventure's theology of history.[1]

In his thirties he attended the Second Vatican Council (1962–1965) as an advisor or *peritus* to Josef Cardinal Frings of Cologne. In those years he was representative of a younger generation of scholars who were frustrated by what they called the Roman School of Theology, a form of Neo-Scholasticism which did not allow much room for the use of conceptual frameworks built on other than scholastic categories. (Scholasticism generally refers to the entire medieval Christian movement in western philosophy. It was characterized by an intense interest in logical and linguistic analysis in order to create a systematic presentation of Christian beliefs. The framework was held together by tightly defined concepts.) The proponents of late nineteenth- and early twentieth-century versions of Thomism (a philosophical and theological academic tradition based on the works of the thirteenth-century Dominican, Thomas Aquinas, who dominated the pontifical academies in Rome prior to the Second Vatican Council) tended to steer clear of any entanglement with the historical dimensions of issues. The ahistorical character of Thomism was seen as a virtue. Those in the pre-conciliar era who wanted to understand how it is that grace is mediated in history were often suspected of the heresy of Modernism. Although difficult to pin down and define precisely, Modernism has been described by Aidan Nichols as a tendency to rely exclusively on historical science so as to determine the theological meaning of biblical and other texts, without acknowledging any role for tradition in the hermeneutical process.[2] As a caricature one might say that the Modernists wanted history without tradition, while the Roman School types wanted tradition without history.

Ratzinger was never enchanted by pre-conciliar Thomism and he has been quite frank about this in several interviews given later in life while he was Prefect for the Congregation of the Doctrine of the Faith (1981–2005). He acknowledges that 'Scholasticism has its greatness', that it is not without merit, but as a student he found it to be too dry and impersonal. In contrast, he found that within the works of St Augustine, 'the passionate, suffering, questioning man is always right there, and one can identify with him'.[3] Alfred Läpple, a seminary prefect from Ratzinger's student days, presents this disposition in the following excerpt from an interview given soon after Ratzinger's election to the papacy:

[According to Ratzinger] God is not recognized because He is a *summum bonum* that is able to be grasped and demonstrated with exact formulas, but because He is a You who comes forward and gets Himself recognized . . . In the dialect of Bavaria we would say: it [scholasticism] wasn't his beer ... He's not interested in defining God by abstract concepts. An abstraction—he once told me—didn't need a mother.[4]

At the theology faculty in Munich, Läpple introduced Ratzinger to the thought of the French Jesuit, Henri de Lubac. Läpple gave him a copy of de Lubac's *Catholicism*, which Ratzinger was later to describe as 'perhaps de Lubac's most significant work' and for him a 'key reading event'. In his *Memoirs, 1927–1977* Ratzinger stated that this work gave him 'not only a new and deeper connection with the thought of the Fathers but also a new way of looking at theology and faith as such'. He then looked around for other books by de Lubac and 'derived special profit' from his *Corpus Mysticum*, in which he found a new understanding of the unity of the Church and the Eucharist, and this in turn helped him 'enter into the required dialogue with Augustine'.[5] Läpple also introduced Ratzinger to the work of John Henry Cardinal Newman (1801–1890). This included Newman's famous *Letter Addressed to His Grace the Duke of Norfolk*. Läpple reminisced that for him and Ratzinger Newman was their passion.[6] Newman's choice of motto was the very Augustinian *Cor ad cor loquitur* (Heart speaks to heart) and it was to this very Pascalian respect for the 'reasons of the heart' that Ratzinger was drawn.

While emphasizing that God is the eternal *logos*, or reason in creation, throughout his career in his many addresses to scholarly audiences, Ratzinger has been at least as interested in the theme of God is love, and the relationship between faith and love, as he has been interested in the relationship of faith and reason. He would argue that for Catholic theology it is necessary to consider both relationships and that the Augustinian–Bonaventurian emphasis on love provides an antidote to the tendency of some scholastics, particularly the late nineteenth-century Neo-Scholastics, so heavily influenced by the intellectualism of Aristotle, to neglect this dimension.

In various interviews Ratzinger has described himself as a 'decided Augustinian' and 'to a certain extent a Platonist'.[7] In relation to the first he follows the Augustinian *credo ut intelligam* maxim, according to which belief is a necessary prerequisite for the pursuit of understanding: 'just as creation comes from reason and is reasonable, faith is, so to speak, the fulfillment of creation and thus the door to understanding.'[8] In relation to the second, Platonic influence, Ratzinger has written that he believes that 'a kind of memory, of recollection of God, is, as it were, etched in man, though it needs to be awakened'.[9]

In one interview Ratzinger claimed that St Augustine interested him very much 'precisely insofar as he was, so to speak, a counterweight to Thomas Aquinas'.[10] He describes Augustine's epistemology as 'much deeper than that of Aquinas, for he is well aware that the organ by which God can be seen cannot be a non-historical "*ratio naturalis*" [natural reason] which just does not exist, but only the *ratio pura*, i.e. *purificata* [purified reason] or, as Augustine expresses it echoing the Gospel, the *cor purum* [the pure heart]'.[11] Ratzinger further commends Augustine for his recognition that the 'necessary purification of sight takes place through faith (Acts 15: 9) and through love, at all events not as a result of reflection alone and not at all by man's own power'.[12] None the less, his first work was a German translation of the *Quaestio disputata* of St Thomas on charity, put together in 1946, and throughout his studies he makes reference to the stance of St Thomas whenever he thinks there is a valuable insight. He is not shy about using Aquinas as a source. His need for a counterweight, so to speak, would seem to stem not from a fundamental hostility to theoretical propositions taken from classical Thomism but from the tendency of more contemporary Thomists, certainly those who dominated seminary faculties prior to the Council, to bifurcate philosophy and theology into completely separate disciplines and then present the Catholic faith as something consistent with scientific reason, as if that is the most important thing about it. He thinks this kind of treatment really diminishes the splendour and internal coherence of the faith. In the essay 'Faith, Philosophy and Theology' he wrote:

With a terminology still inchoate in St Thomas' works, the domains of inquiry belonging to philosophy and theology were distinguished, respectively, as the natural and supernatural orders. These distinctions reached their full rigor only in the modern period which then read them back into St Thomas, thus imposing on him an interpretation which severs him more radically from the preceding tradition than is warranted by the texts alone.[13]

In the same essay, Ratzinger concluded:

The exclusion of ontology from theology does not emancipate philosophical thinking but paralyzes it. The extinction of ontology in the sphere of philosophy, far from purifying theology, actually deprives it of its solid basis. Contrary to the common hostility toward ontology, which is apparently becoming the sole link between contemporary philosophers and theologians, we held that both disciplines need this dimension of thought and that it is here that they find themselves indissolubly linked.[14]

In his Angelus Address of 2007 on the Feast of St Thomas Aquinas Benedict spoke of St Thomas offering an 'effective model of harmony between faith and reason' with his charism as a philosopher *and* a theologian, and then he concluded that 'faith presupposes reason and perfects it, and reason, enlightened by faith, finds the strength to rise to knowledge of God and spiritual realities'.[15] For Ratzinger, faith and reason, theology and philosophy, are symbiotically, and not extrinsically, related. Faith without reason ends in fideism, but reason without faith ends in nihilism. For Ratzinger 'pure reason' à la Immanuel Kant simply does not exist. He has said this many times over several decades. Some Thomists, eager to defend the faith at the Bar of eighteenth-century philosophy, have taken on board elements of Kant's epistemology. Many Neo-Scholastics influenced by these projects may find this statement shocking but it is none the less true that Ratzinger and Friedrich Nietzsche (1844–1900), the father of post-modernism, are united in their opposition to the Kantian belief in 'pure reason'. The way that Ratzinger often expresses the principle is by saying that 'reason has a wax nose'. Its shape is determined by theological convictions. Those in European universities who continue to defend the faith by reference to eighteenth-century notions of rationality are using ammunition that was declared obsolete several decades ago. Anyone who tries to defend pure reason around the Sorbonne in the twenty-first century might find themselves laughed out of the Latin quarter (though it must be conceded that in some of the British universities the Continental post-modern turn is still regarded as something 'foreign', and therefore not to be taken too seriously). None the less, Ratzinger's Augustinian epistemology, with its emphasis on the theological presuppositions of philosophies, gives him a very contemporary intellectual profile and a bridge to the post-moderns who are much closer to Augustine than they are to Aristotle or Kant.

The young Ratzinger was also frustrated by an academic climate or culture which was fearful of engaging what he was later to describe in *Principles of Catholic Theology* as 'the fundamental crisis of our age', namely, 'understanding the mediation of history within the realm of ontology'.[16] In short, if the fundamental crisis of our age is a 'Heideggerian problematic' (understanding being in time), a Thomism which prides itself on being 'above history' will never be able to resolve the crisis from solely within its own resources. It may have part of the solution, but what Pius X called Modernism could not be resolved by a head-in-the-sand 'history is irrelevant and only heretics think about it' sort of response. If one reads the works of pre-conciliar Thomism, and even some contemporary Thomism, one gets the impression that the world is filled with non-believers because of their intellectual defects, because there is some part of a theoretical framework they have failed to comprehend. Ratzinger, and many others of his generation, found this almost infuriatingly myopic, and this frustration fed into the Conciliar debates. They understood that what the Church was contending with was not so much poor philosophy, but competing humanisms, competing visions of the meaning of human life, and the nature of human dignity, which had grown out of the Romantic reaction to the very mechanical anthropology of the Enlightenment(s). After World War I when Christian soldiers killed one another in the trenches of the Somme, albeit under orders from leaders who had lost their Christian conscience, if they ever had one, Christianity was in the midst of a credibility crisis and a vacuum was opened for what were, in effect, alternative religious frameworks. The arrival of Marxism in the 1920s, Fascism in the 1930s, and New Ageism in the 1960s came with their own eschatologies (the Communist Utopia, the Third Reich, the Age of Aquarius), their own ecclesiologies (the authority of the Communist Party, the Nazi Party, and the enlightened pot-smoking gurus), and their own anthropologies (the Communist Man, the Master Race, the Flower Children), and so on. In such social contexts the Neo-Scholasticism of Arnold Wilmsen, the young Ratzinger's philosophy professor, was an inadequate response to the spiritual crises raised by these substitute religions and by mid-twentieth-century French and German Existentialism.

Perhaps because so many of the questions raised by the Existentialists and the so-called Modernists were products of the nineteenth-century Romantic movement in Germany, Ratzinger, Karl Rahner and Hans Urs von Balthasar, and other German-speaking theologians of their generation were able to see that something more than Neo-Scholasticism was needed to address what were fundamentally Romantic movement issues in a period of European history when Christianity appeared to have run its course. To put this point another way, if the central interests of the Romantics were history, tradition, beauty, individuality, and self-development, a Catholic response to this tradition needed to address these themes. Many Thomists who taught in seminaries in the first half of the twentieth century did not go near these topics, either out of a lack of interest or because of a fear of being suspected of Modernism. For seminarians like Alfred Läpple and Ratzinger, the writings of Newman and the Fathers of the Church provided a refuge and a treasury wherein one could safely reflect upon these topics.

Alfred Läpple also claims that Ratzinger was influenced by a view of Revelation according to which Revelation is first and foremost the historical action of God, in the progress of the history of salvation, rather than the communication of some truths to reason through concepts, as claimed in the Neo-Scholastic view. Here one can detect resonances of Newman's work on the development of doctrine, St Bonaventure's theology of history, and the nineteenth-century Tübingen School's account of tradition. In *Answering the Enlightenment: The Catholic Recovery of Historical Revelation* Grant Kaplan encapsulated the spirit of the Tübingen project in the following paragraph:

Through Romantic and Idealist lenses, the Tübingen School re-envisioned tradition as a living truth instead of the transmission of old ideas, the church as an organism instead of a *societas perfecta*, Christ as the incarnate *logos* rather than as a mere teacher, and the Holy Spirit as an active participant in human life instead of a departed entity who last engaged in the world's affairs during Pentecost.[17]

In the course of preparing his *Habilitationsschrift*, Ratzinger was attracted to St Bonaventure's more personal and historical perception of Revelation as an action whereby God shows himself in a definite historic moment. According to this view, while Revelation is certainly reflected in Scripture, it preceded it and was not identified with it. Here Ratzinger's criticism of the 'theoretical propositions' account of Revelation, derived from the thought of the Spanish Jesuit Francisco Suárez (1548–1617), drew opposition from one of his examiners—Michael Schmaus—who regarded Ratzinger's thinking as Modernist. Having found himself in a position where his thesis would fail because of the section on Revelation, Ratzinger simply decoupled the risqué section from the rest of the document, and submitted the remaining uncontroversial sections. It is said that at the oral defence of his thesis Ratzinger sat mute while his two professors—Michael Schmaus and Gottlieb Söhngen—argued about the Suárezian understanding of Revelation. Läpple distinguishes their positions by saying that 'according to Schmaus the faith of the Church was to be communicated through definitive and unchanging concepts that set out perennial truths; [whereas] for Söhngen the faith was mystery, and was communicated through a history'.[18]

Ratzinger's Augustinian pedigree has also been manifest in the attention he gives to beauty and his understanding of the catechetical importance of language and symbols and the relationship between matters of form and substance. In philosophical parlance beauty is classified as a transcendental property of being, along with unity, truth, and goodness. Scholarly opinion varies over the issue of whether Aquinas regarded beauty as a theoretically separable transcendental from the good, however John of La Rochelle and St Bonaventure, following a strong Augustinian line, clearly identified beauty as a transcendental in its own right.[19] Armand Maurer argues that Aquinas did play down beauty relative to truth and goodness and that this tendency reveals his basic Aristotelianism and his lukewarmness to Platonism.[20] Although Ratzinger has not directly addressed the issue as an academic question, implicit within everything he writes on beauty is a preference for the line that follows St Augustine, John of La Rochelle, St Bonaventure, and, in contemporary times, Hans Urs von Balthasar.

These different emphases given to each of the transcendentals in the works of the Fathers and Scholastics may relate to primary choices between Plato and Aristotle, but they may also simply reflect different spiritual dispositions. The American Franciscan psychologist, Benedict Groeschel, believes that many people have a strong primary attraction to one or another of the transcendentals, and that this can be discerned in the lives of the saints. For example, he suggests that for Aquinas truth was his primary transcendental, for St Francis of Assisi it was goodness, and for St Augustine it was beauty. After Augustine's prayer 'O God, make me chaste and celibate, but not yet', the phrase for which he is most famous is the lament: 'late have I loved thee, O beauty, so ancient, so new'. Ratzinger's focus on the transcendental of beauty is therefore part of his Augustinian heritage and also one of the many points of convergence between him and Hans Urs von Balthasar and John Henry Newman. The latter had to contend with Evangelical Protestants who believed that a concern for beauty and matters of form is the mark of the Pharisee. Whereas in the works of von Balthasar there is a focus on the beauty of Revelation in general, in the works of Ratzinger discussions about beauty most often arise in the specific context of liturgy. Here Ratzinger stands in sharp relief from John Paul II who, while acknowledging that there were problems with contemporary liturgical practices and particularly with liturgical music, none the less focused his attention on other fronts.

Whereas John Paul II was concerned that a culture of death was being fostered through a range of practices which treat the human body as a commodity, and offered his theology of the body as a positive corrective for this, Ratzinger can be seen to be contributing to the critique of the culture of death with his positive work on the theology of culture. In this his liturgical works are the centre point. While in no way intending to suggest that either pope is a dualist, another way to present the difference is to say that John Paul II was focused on practices which completely destroy the human body or at least undermine its dignity through a severance of the good from the true, while Ratzinger has focused on practices which diminish the possibilities of the soul or the self, for its own transcendence. The marketing of vulgar art, music, and literature and the generation of a very low, even barbaric, mass culture is seen by Ratzinger to be one of the serious pathologies of contemporary western culture. By this reading, clerics who think that they will win young people to the Church by adopting the marketing strategies of public relations firms and attempting a transposition of the Church's cultural patrimony into the idioms of contemporary mass culture are only further diminishing the opportunities of youth for an experience of genuine self-transcendence. The projects of the papacies of John Paul II and Benedict XVI are not therefore antithetical but complementary. Benedict has taken on board his predecessor's accounts of what went wrong with contemporary conceptions of truth and goodness and he adds to them an account of the contemporary predicament of beauty.

It is therefore in his epistemology, and especially in his emphasis on the heart or the relationship between truth and love, and in his interest in history and the transcendental of beauty, that Ratzinger is at his most Augustinian and Bonaventurian. Contrary to many hastily prepared editorials at the time of his election to the papacy, Ratzinger's Augustinian dispositions should not be construed as having anything to do with wanting the Church to retreat from the world, or wanting her scholars to close down conversations with the rest of non-Catholic humanity. Unfortunately, in popular parlance the adjective 'Augustinian' has often been tarred with a Calvinist brush. By this anachronistic reading Augustine is seen to represent an extremely negative attitude toward human nature and to have no time at all for the achievements of pagan civilizations. This is in fact a Lutheran gloss, as Luther wanted nothing to do with Platonic notions of beauty or Aristotelian reason. Ratzinger could not be further from this *mentalité*. He is very much at home at places like the Sorbonne, even though it is no longer staffed with Franciscans and Dominicans. He is not afraid to engage in academic discussions with atheist proponents of the Enlightenment project like Jürgen Habermas or self-described 'secularists' like Marcello Pera, the president of the Italian senate. The promotion of a puritan-style retreat from the world is based on an interpretation of the spiritual standing of the world in the thought of St Augustine which flows from the Reformation branch of this tradition. Ratzinger belongs to a different branch with people like the great Jesuit Erich Pryzwara (1889–1972), for whom Augustine, steeped in classical culture, and rejoicing in its achievements, none the less recognizes the necessity of Christ's Revelation to transcend its limitations and breach its *aporia*, or doubt.

The contemporary works of Robert Dodaro, vice-president of the Augustinian Patristic Institute in Rome, are helping to rehabilitate Augustine from the charge of not caring about the world.[21] Dodaro makes the point that such readings of Augustine are usually based on a few isolated passages from *The City of God*, but if one reads Augustine's letters to laymen occupying high offices in the Roman bureaucracy one gets an entirely different picture. Ratzinger's reading of Augustine is on this point consistent with Dodaro's. There is thus no fundamental difference between the more Thomist John Paul and the more Augustinian Benedict on the question of the relationship of the Church to the world. They both agree that she is the 'light of the gentiles' or in the language of Vatican II, 'the universal sacrament of salvation' and that there is nothing in the scriptures which warrants a policy of retreat into a ghetto.[22] Often the faithful are persecuted and forced to struggle for survival on the margins of society as in pagan Rome, Elizabethan England, Republican France, Bismarck's Prussian-dominated Germany, and contemporary Communist China, but it is one thing to be coerced into a ghetto, quite another to walk in meekly as if one deserves to be there.

None the less there is likely to be a difference between the papacies of John Paul II and Benedict XVI with respect to the theological trouble spots which draw their attention. While anthropology and the meaning and purpose of human sexuality and human dignity might be regarded as key themes in the papacy of John Paul II, with Benedict XVI it is more likely that the key themes will be ecclesiology, liturgy, and Revelation. In shorthand terms one can say that while *Gaudium et spes* (The Pastoral Constitution of the Church in the Modern World) and *Dignitatis Humanae* (The Declaration on Religious Freedom) were the Vatican II documents closest to the heart and mind of John Paul II, for Benedict XVI they are *Lumen gentium* (The Dogmatic Constitution on the Church), *Sacrosanctum concilium* (The Constitution on the Sacred Liturgy), and *Dei verbum* (The Dogmatic Constitution on Divine Revelation). His first encyclical, *Deus Caritas Est* (God is Love) (2006) begins with a reiteration of the account of Revelation in *Dei verbum*, and his first apostolic exhortation *Sacramentum caritatis* (The sacrament of charity) (2007) offers corrections of false interpretations of *Sacrosanctum concilium* and further develops the ecclesiology of *Lumen gentium*.

Given his antipathy to the theological establishments of his youth, the question which is often posed about Ratzinger is whether he has been a Vicar of Bray, a tergiversator who tacks to and fro with changes in the theological breeze in order to advance his position within the hierarchy. At the Vatican Council he was popularly regarded as one of the leading radicals—a close associate of Karl Rahner (1904–1984) and Hans Küng—though by the early 1970s he was clearly sailing in a different race. His own contention is that he has not fundamentally changed his positions:

> My basic impulse, precisely during the Council, was always to free up the authentic kernel of the faith from encrustations and to give this kernel strength and dynamism. This impulse is the constant of my life. I have never deviated from this constant, which from my childhood has molded my life. I have remained true to it as the basic direction of my life.[23]

The problems within the Church that attract his attention may have changed, but not his fundamental theological orientation. This is not only Ratzinger's own self-judgement, but it is a judgement shared by Francis Schüssler Fiorenza of the Harvard Divinity School, a former student of Ratzinger's who now resides in a very different theological stable.[24] Fiorenza believes that Ratzinger has from his earliest days stuck to a consistent theological vision. He has consistently opposed the pre-conciliar theological establishment, or what is often called 'baroque theology', he has been constant in his sensitivity to the Protestant criticism that Catholics care more about philosophy than Scripture, he has consistently opposed the heavy reliance of Catholic ethics on elements borrowed from the Stoic tradition, preferring a more scriptural and Christocentric approach, and he has demonstrated a constant interest in the themes of the relationship between Scripture and tradition, and liturgy and ecclesiology. He has never made a U-turn on any of these fundamental orientations. It is really only in the last of these, the territory of liturgy and ecclesiology, that there have been apparent 'shifts' of position at the level of particular questions, though not at the macro level of a fundamental theological framework.

Thus, whereas in his early works he was critical of pre-conciliar liturgy for being too baroque—a theatrical work of the priest in the presence of laity whose minds were elsewhere—and whereas he complained of 'ritual rigidity in need of defrosting', in his more recent works he has shown sympathy for those who are critical of contemporary liturgical practices, and he has gone so far as to say that many contemporary liturgies are acts of apostasy, analogous to the Hebrew's worship of the golden calf.[25] Ratzinger may none the less argue that his liturgical *principles* have remained constant. What have changed are liturgical *practices*, and in particular some contemporary practices are so totally contrary to everything he believes liturgy is about that the direction of his criticism is now targeted on the contemporary Rite. What he calls 'parish tea party liturgies' are a much greater problem from the point of view of his liturgical principles, than laity silently reciting their favourite litany while the priest whispers the words of the Canon of the Mass. In the second instance, the laity still understands that liturgy has something to do with worship of God, whereas the focus of the parish tea party liturgy is on the participants' relationships with one another.

In the context of ecclesiology there has been a similar shift of concern about what is happening in practice. Whereas at the time of the Council Ratzinger was eager to foster the horizontal dimensions of the Church, to loosen centralized curial control, by the late 1970s he was more interested in strengthening the Church's vertical dimension, the authority of the hierarchy, including the papacy. Here again Ratzinger may well argue that the change is not one of principle, but one of what needs to be emphasized in a dramatically changed ecclesiastical landscape.

All commentators agree that the watershed year marking the divide between the apparently more radical 'theological teenager' and the more sober mature theologian is 1968. This was also of course a watershed year for the whole of the western world. Jean-François Lyotard has suggested it was precisely in this year that modernity as a cultural project was finally abandoned by the intellectual elite of the great universities.[26] In the biographies of Ratzinger much is made of the fact that in 1968 his faculty in Tübingen suffered the same turmoil as other universities across Europe, Britain, the United States, and countries of the British Commonwealth. However, in interviews Ratzinger has rejected the suggestion that these student riots prompted him to change the direction of his theological compass and he is always keen to emphasize that the demonstrations at Tübingen were not directed against him personally. What seemed most to disturb him, in addition to the student rebels' lack of urbanity and failure to observe the normal academic courtesies, was the fact that at the barricades around the Sorbonne, Jesuits and Dominicans were to be found giving out inter-denominational Communion. There is nothing in his early ecclesiology or Eucharistic theology which could be squared with the practice of inter-communion. In both his ecclesiology and Eucharistic theology he strongly follows Henri de Lubac's emphasis on the link between the two. The Eucharist makes the Church, and only those who are members of the Church can legitimately share in her Eucharist. Nor was he ever sympathetic to the view that political activism can bring about the Kingdom of God. Thus, while inter-communion among student rebels on the Sorbonne picket line was for some a milestone in the liberation theology movement, it also marked a point at which Ratzinger became self-consciously aware of the difference between his own theological orientations and those of former associates such as Rahner and Küng. Their theological works were in various ways adapted and used by liberation theologians in the 1970s and 80s, but no liberation theologian ever tried to apply Ratzinger's theological reflections. Again, Francis Schüssler Fiorenza agrees that the shifts in Ratzinger's thought were not due to any traumatic event (such as students deriding the cross as a symbol of sadomasochism) but rather to the ambiguities inherent within the movement for theological renewal itself.[27] One could find baroque scholasticism problematic from more than one perspective.

Fiorenza's interpretation is also endorsed by Joseph A. Komonchak, another high-profile commentator from outside Ratzinger's own theological stable. Komonchak claims that 'from Ratzinger's *Introduction to*

Christianity (1968) down to the homily he delivered on his installation as Pope Benedict XVI, a distinctive and consistent approach has been visible'.[28] Komonchak describes it as a 'Bonaventurian theological vision' according to which only the gospel will save us, not philosophy, not science, and not scientific theology. In a period of disillusion with modernity the Church can make her appeal to the world by 'presenting the Christian vision in its synthetic totality as a comprehensive structure of meaning that at nearly every point breaks with the taken-for-granted attitudes, strategies, and habits of contemporary culture'.[29]

The analysis in the following chapters is broadly sympathetic to Komonchak's assessment. In his Christmas message of 2006 Benedict XVI stated unequivocally that 'without the light of Christ, the light of reason is not sufficient to enlighten humanity and the world'.[30] As James V. Schall wrote in his commentary on this message, Pope Benedict believes that the 'depths of reason are discovered more under the stimulus of revelation than by science or human reflection, however legitimate and valuable these are'.[31] However, while the Bonaventurian motif is undoubtedly strong it is important to note that Ratzinger is always working with a larger score. Ratzinger needs to be understood with reference to a variety of motifs in Augustine, Bonaventure, Newman, von Balthasar, Romano Guardini, Henri de Lubac, and Josef Pieper, to name only the most prominent scholars to have influenced him. There may be inner affinities at work within this list but they none the less each contribute their own variations. It would also be wrong to regard Ratzinger as fundamentally hostile to either philosophy or science (though he may be hostile to many projects which market themselves as a scientific theology).[32] His basic principle is that reason needs to be informed by faith and that cultures and cultural practices need to be judged with reference to Revelation, but this does not mean that he sees no value in philosophy or science. The point is that alone, cut off from Revelation, not only can they not save us, but they have a tendency to turn into oppressive ideologies. Further, it would be wrong to think that only those who operate along the Augustinian and Bonaventurian line come to these conclusions. In 1964, at the very height of the conciliar enthusiasm for the modern project, the Italian Thomist Cornelio Fabro (1911–1995) published his magnum opus *God in Exile*. In this he concluded that the best hope for the Church lies in the possibility that Christian revelation might appear radiant to modern man as a way out of the 'holocaust-mottled dead end in which he sees the *cogito* consuming itself'.[33] Meanwhile on the contemporary international academic horizon it is difficult to find anyone more hostile to the project of modernity, including the epistemology of Kant, than the Thomist Alasdair MacIntyre. He has even complained of the tendency of people to label him a communitarian because he says that communitarianism is a project to fix liberalism and not only has he *not* offered remedies for the condition of liberal modernity, it has been part of his case that there are *no remedies*.[34]

It is thus one thing for the Thomist tradition to pride itself on its achievement of plundering the spoils of Aristotle, of its openness to the best of pagan thought, but quite another for its proponents and theologians generally to treat the synthesis of St Thomas as a kind of all-purpose garbage-recycling unit which has the capacity to pick up any rubbish and repackage it as something useful. The degree of openness of the Thomist tradition to external traditions can be exaggerated. St Thomas did not think he was building a cultural sewage treatment plant. Thomists like Fabro and MacIntyre acknowledge that there are limits to what can be baptized and assimilated. One does not have to be a follower of Augustine or Bonaventure to be wary of elements of the culture of modernity. Some Thomists, Frankfurt School atheists, Nietzschean post-moderns, Barthians, Anglo-Catholics, Evangelical Protestants, the current Archbishops of Canterbury and York (Dr Rowan Williams and Dr John Sentamu), Mormons, New Age therapists, and members of the Glastonbury Order of Druids, to name but a few, have their own catalogues of criticism of the 'taken-for-granted attitudes, strategies, and habits of contemporary culture'. In taking a critical stance toward contemporary western culture Benedict XVI is not living an ivory tower existence in an exclusive club for Augustinians and Bonaventurians. His whole scholarly approach eschews such an exclusive vision. He does, however, operate with certain understandings about the nature of Revelation, the relationship between Scripture and Tradition, faith and reason, nature and grace, and the role of the Church in the economy of salvation, which all feed into his critique of contemporary western culture. Thus while Komonchak is right to conclude that for Ratzinger the Church can make her appeal to the world by 'presenting the Christian vision in its synthetic totality as a comprehensive structure of meaning that at nearly every point breaks with the taken-for-granted attitudes, strategies, and habits of contemporary culture', the position to be taken in the following work is that it is too much of a broad brush approach to explain this solely or even primarily by reference to Ratzinger's preference for Augustine and Bonaventure over Aquinas.

In each substantive chapter which follows the plan is to present key themes in the thought of Ratzinger, now Benedict XVI, with reference to the problems within the tradition of the Catholic Church and the cultures of modernity and post-modernity he is trying to resolve. For the sake of clarity reference will only be made to 'Benedict XVI' or 'Benedict' in the context of statements which he has made since his election to the papacy. Before proceeding to the key themes, however, Chapter 1 is an attempt to situate Ratzinger in the context of late twentieth-century and contemporary theological circles. In doing so it is also hoped that the precise contours of his Augustinian and Bonaventurian presuppositions will be clarified and brought into sharper relief.

I

Ratzinger and Contemporary Theological Circles

The Second Vatican Council (1961–1965) is often presented as a historic battle between 'progressive' bishops and their theological advisors who wanted to change Catholic teaching to more closely harmonize it with the social movements of the 1960s and 'conservatives' who remained wedded to the spirit of the Counter-Reformation era and who, at their most extreme, wanted no engagement at all between the Church and the world beyond her cloisters. According to a popular reading, both Karol Wojtyla (John Paul II) and Joseph Ratzinger (Benedict XVI) started out on the progressive side but had second thoughts after the cultural revolution of the late 1960s. They began bravely but did not have the courage to carry through the progressive agenda. According to this reading, these two pontificates therefore reflect a kind of neo-conservatism in the sense of the bon mot that a neo-conservative is a liberal with a teenage daughter.

More pejoratively, it is suggested by some that Wojtyla, the son of an army officer, who grew up in provincial Poland, was badly infected with the piety of the Polish peasantry and spent the most formative years of his life in a backwater cut off from the intellectual currents of the avant-garde in places like Paris, Louvain, and Tübingen. Though he showed some moments of creativity in the late 1950s and early 1960s, when faced with the materialism and sexual libertinism of the 'free' western world, he quickly lapsed into an affirmation of the comforting certitudes of the peasants of the Carpathians. The equally pejorative reading of Ratzinger, popularized by his former supporter Hans Küng, is that of an ambitious and intellectually precocious son of a Bavarian policeman who changed theological allegiances for the sake of promotion within the Catholic hierarchy. A far deeper reading, however, is one which situates the thought of both popes within the intellectual history and academic circles of their times.

At the beginning of the Second Vatican Council there were three significant intellectual groupings identified most strongly by their stance on the relationship between nature and grace, but also by what they understood to be the most impressing intellectual problems in the life of the Church. Broadly, these groups could be described as: (i) the Neo-Thomists, that is, those who belonged to the second and third generations of Thomist scholars following the revival of Thomism by Jesuits such as Joseph Kleutgen, who influenced Leo XIII, culminating in 1879 with his publication of the encyclical *Aeterni Patris*; (ii) the French *Ressourcement* scholars, antagonistically labelled as marketeers of a *nouvelle théologie* by some of the Neo-Thomists, and represented at the Council by Henri de Lubac SJ (1896–1991) and Jean Daniélou SJ (1905–1974); and (iii) the German and Belgian Transcendental Thomists, so named because of the centrality of Immanuel Kant's transcendental idealism in their work, represented above all by Karl Rahner SJ (1904–1984).[1]

One of the greatest leaders of the Neo-Thomists was Réginald Garrigou-Lagrange OP (1877–1964), Professor of Dogmatic and Spiritual Theology at the Angelicum from 1909 to 1959. The French writer François Mauriac described him as the *monstre sacré* of Thomism.[2] Another common description is that of a 'strict observance Thomist'. Though he did not attend the Council and died early in 1964, he had certainly influenced the thinking of many who did attend. The 'Leonine' or generation of 1879 Thomists, and the Neo-Thomists who followed them, were strongly influenced by the theology of the Counter-Reformation, especially by the works of Cajetan (1469–1534), Suárez (1548–1617), and Bellarmine (1542–1621). As one might expect, the Dominicans were more strongly influenced by Cajetan, while the Jesuits were steeped in the thought of Suárez and Bellarmine. The Leonine Thomists produced many translations of the works of St Thomas, including the famous Leonine critical editions under the direction of the Dominican Tommaso Maria Francesco Zigliara (1833–1893), and under their impetus Désiré-Joseph Cardinal Mercier (1861–1926) founded the Higher Institute of Philosophy at the University of Louvain which produced *Le Revue néo-scolastique de Philosophie*.

Since at least as far back as the 1940s, however, the Leonine and Neo-Thomists have been criticized for their heavy reliance on the sixteenth- and seventeenth-century commentaries on St Thomas. They had a tendency to present the teachings of St Thomas in a simplified propositional format suitable for rote learning but not conducive to serious scholarship. Their attempts at an anachronistic reading of Aquinas as an interlocutor of Descartes or Kant have also met criticism. They are remarkable above all for their general ahistorical temper.[3] They were focused on defending the faith to Rationalists and had little to say to those who represented the Romantic reaction to Rationalism and for whom historical and cultural particularity and individuality and the reasons of the heart were key themes. The French intellectual historian Etienne Gilson (1884–1978) referred to the scholarship of the Leonine era as a 'brew of watered-down *philosophia aristotelico-thomistica* concocted to give off a vague deism fit only for the use of right-thinking candidates for high-school diplomas and arts degrees' and he described the works of Cajetan as 'in every respect the consummate example of a *corruptorium Thomae*'.[4] His contemporary the Dominican Marie-Dominique Chenu (1895–1990) agreed, and described Leonine Thomism as a *misérable abus* of classical Thomism.[5]

In recent times Alasdair MacIntyre has similarly criticized leading Leonine Thomists for 'deforming central Christian positions for apologetic purposes' and in particular for reworking Thomistic themes in Kantian terms.[6] In order to defend Aquinas and, more broadly, Christianity at the Bar of the Enlightenment, they tacitly or even wittingly accepted the Kantian account of rationality and tried to squeeze Thomist thought into its parameters. To these criticisms are added the complaint that the typically Leonine presentation of St Thomas's thought was often quite off-putting. The Thomist tradition was treated as an architectural model which had to be taken apart piece by piece with the smallest conceptual components subjected to rigorous analysis. It was precisely the presentation of the faith in this manner which led Ratzinger, von Balthasar, and others of their generation to complain that they found Thomism dry and unable to convey a sense of the glory of Revelation. It was a much contracted presentation of the *kerygma*.

The *Ressourcement* scholars (so named because they created the series *Sources chrétiennes*, a collection of bilingual critical editions of patristic texts) led the charge against the pre-conciliar Thomists. They argued that the Thomism which had flourished since the publication of *Aeterni Patris* not only represented a distortion of classical Thomism, but that it had unwittingly fostered the secularization of western culture with its 'two-tier' theory of the relationship between nature and grace. The two-tiered theory was especially strong in pre-conciliar Jesuit thought. By this reading, Cajetan and in particular Suárez, who fostered the theory in the post-Reformation era (in an attempt to defend the intrinsic goodness of human nature against the Protestant emphasis on its depravity), were partly to blame for the Modernist crisis at the turn of the twentieth century and the intense secularization of western culture which followed in subsequent decades. The two-tiered approach became very popular with Catholic scholars in Protestant countries who were trying to build bridges between the Liberal tradition and Catholicism. The idea was that Catholics and non-Catholics could find common ground on the territory of 'pure nature', while the more socially contentious supernatural beliefs and aspirations of Catholics could be relegated to the privacy of the individual soul. In a lecture delivered on a tour of the United States in 1968 de Lubac concluded that the cumulative effect of this strategy and this construction of the nature and grace relationship was 'a total secularisation that would banish God not only from social life but from culture and even from the relationships of private life'.[7] However, Garrigou-Lagrange and other leading Dominican scholars such as Marie-Michel Labourdette (1908–1990) of the *Revue Thomiste* could not accept that so eminent a member of their Order as Cajetan could have misinterpreted Aquinas, albeit unwittingly, and led the Church along the paths of a secularizing dualism.

Fergus Kerr OP, in his *Versions of Thomism*, described the battle between Henri de Lubac SJ and Réginald Garrigou-Lagrange OP in the late 1940s over the nature–grace relationship as the most 'bitter theological controversy of the twentieth century'.[8] With the publication of *Humani Generis* by Pius XII in 1950, which appeared to take the side of Garrigou-Lagrange, it looked as though de Lubac's whole intellectual project would be suppressed, much to the anger of Gottlieb Söhngen, the young Joseph Ratzinger's academic supervisor. However, after living through a decade under a cloud, in 1960 de Lubac was appointed by John XXIII to the preparatory commissions organizing the Council. Paul VI later named him a theological consultant to the Council and invited him to concelebrate Mass on the day of the solemn adoption of the Conciliar text *Dei verbum*. In 1983 his rehabilitation was completed when John Paul II named him a cardinal deacon. Fergus Kerr OP concludes that 'few now doubt that when Thomas taught that human beings have a natural desire for the vision of God he meant what he said'.[9] In other words, de Lubac was right about what Aquinas actually taught. None the less, some Thomists continue to defend the tradition of Cajetan and Garrigou-Lagrange on this point. Romanus Cessario OP, for example, recently counselled younger scholars not to assume that 'one eminent French Jesuit and 100,000 *Communio* scholars can't be wrong'.[10]

The reference here to *Communio* scholars is a reference to the international network of scholars who are associated with the journal *Communio* and intellectual circles of the same name of which there are several hundred throughout the world. The journal was founded in 1972 under the inspiration of Hans Urs von Balthasar and is published in fifteen different language editions. Von Balthasar broadly fits into the camp of the *Ressourcement* scholars since he published many translations of patristic works and was influenced by de Lubac under whom he studied; however, his own project, described as a theological aesthetics, can stand alone as one of the greatest theological achievements of the twentieth century. The heart of it may be found in his trilogy written between 1961 and 1987. It includes the *Glory of the Lord*, a seven-volume work of theological aesthetics, *Theo-Drama*, a five-volume work on the relationship between the human person and God, especially in relation to the Easter mysteries, and *Theo-Logic*, a three-volume work on the relationship of Christology to ontology.

Unlike so many of the great names in twentieth-century Catholic theology, von Balthasar was not chosen to be a *peritus* at the Second Vatican Council. In the early 1960s he was in a kind of ecclesiastical no man's land, having chosen to leave the Society of Jesus in order to start his own lay institute, the Community of St John. He spent the conciliar years writing and establishing his institute and only emerged into the foreground in the 1970s with the formation of the *Communio* journal in 1972 and the publication of *Der Antirömische Affekt* on the Petrine Office in 1974 which was something of a counterfoil to the anti-papal thought of Hans Küng.[11] Aidan Nichols has judged it to be 'theologically the profoundest book on the papacy ever written'.[12] De Lubac famously described von Balthasar as the most cultured man in Europe of his times. He was multilingual and musical and from a family of high achievers. His father was a church architect, his mother an office-bearer in the Swiss League of Catholic Women, his sister a

Superior-General of a Franciscan order of nuns, his grandmother Baroness Margit Apor, a friend of the Austrian imperial family. Other more distant distinguished relatives included a Hungarian bishop martyred by soldiers of the Red Army, an eighteenth-century Jesuit missionary who was sent to work on Native American missions in California, a couple of founders of significant municipal libraries, and an officer who died fighting for the liberty of the Swiss Catholic cantons in the Sonderbund war.[13] It is popularly believed that the only other twentieth-century Catholic theologian who comes anywhere near von Balthasar's stature is Karl Rahner from the circle of the Transcendental Thomists.

The Transcendental Thomists agreed with de Lubac's criticisms of Cajetan and the whole baroque account of the nature and grace relationship, but they offered their own alternative account from that presented by de Lubac and also from the account of von Balthasar, which, though not in complete accord with de Lubac, was closer to de Lubac than to Rahner. Rahner pointed out the oddity of trying to force grace on to a nature that was deemed to be fundamentally not receptive to it; however, in developing his own account of the relationship he allowed his theory of knowledge, which was heavily Kantian, to serve as the foundation. For Rahner, nature is linked to grace through a supernatural existential, a theological a priori in the very nature of our way of knowing. This approach tends to view the continuity between human experience and grace as belonging to the same ontic plane by stressing the continuity between *ens* [being] and *esse* [existence].[14] With this method the difference between being and existence is played down in such a way that historical and social experiences and even the events of salvation history simply make explicit something that was already present in the beginning. John Milbank has described this as a tendency to naturalize the supernatural.[15]

In his examination of Rahner's notion of 'anonymous Christianity', Aidan Nichols compiled the following list of what von Balthasar regarded as problematic Rahnerian theological tendencies:

In *fundamental theology*, the belief that a transcendental philosophy can anticipate the distinctive content of Christian revelation; in *soteriology*, the idea that the life, death and resurrection of Christ are exemplary rather than efficacious in force; in *theological ethics* the notion that the love of neighbour can be a surrogate for the love of God and Christological confession no longer necessary for Christian existence; in the *theology of religions* the idea that other faiths are ordinary means of salvation alongside the Christian way; in *ecclesiology* the idea that the Church becomes simply the explicit articulation of what is equally present (though only implicitly so) wherever the world opens itself to the Kingdom; and finally, in the *theology of history*, the fact that the universal openness of the human spirit to divine transcendence in its supernatural offer of salvation is already deemed to be *Gnadenerfahrung*, 'the experience of grace', even without any further intervention of the redeeming God in the special history of revelation.[16]

Nichols notes that this list has been dredged from Balthasar's more polemical pieces and that his chief target was 'vulgarized Rahnerianism', the kind of mindset which flourished in seminaries after the Council among those who had taken in large doses of Rahner, often hastily prepared. None the less, the list does provide a flavour of Rahner's Transcendental Thomism, and goes some of the way toward explaining how different in effect was Rahner's critique of Cajetan from de Lubac's. As a result of this tendency to naturalize the supernatural, Rahner tended to take a more positive stance toward the culture of modernity than either de Lubac or von Balthasar.

In strategic terms one could say that the great losers at the Second Vatican Council were the Neo-Thomists. They were defeated by a loose alliance of the *Ressourcement* types and the Transcendental Thomists. However, this alliance was short lived and did not survive the 1960s. By the early 1970s a definite cleavage had developed between the first group, centred around the *Communio* journal founded in 1972 by von Balthasar, Henri de Lubac, M. J. Le Guillou, Louis Bouyer, Jorge Medina, and Ratzinger, among others, and the Rahnerian group, centred around the journal *Concilium* and the Concilium Institute in Nijmegen, Holland. Along with Rahner, founders of *Concilium* included Hans Küng, Johann Baptist Metz, Yves Congar OP, Edward Schillebeeckx OP, Paul Brand, Franz Böckle, and Gustavo Gutierrez. Ratzinger was also for a time a member of the *Concilium* board. He has described it as an attempt to establish itself, on the model of the ancient rights of the Sorbonne, as the true centre of teaching and teachers of the Church.[17] He believes that this aspiration was buried at the fifth anniversary congress in Brussels in 1970 when divisions began to appear between Rahner, Congar, Schillebeeckx, and Küng.

One person who straddled both the Thomist and *Communio* circles was Karol Wojtyla. On the one side his doctoral dissertation was written at the Angelicum under the supervision of Garrigou-Lagrange, but as a postdoctoral scholar at the Catholic University of Lublin (KUL) in the years (1954–1958) he developed a version of Thomism which sought to incorporate themes in mid-twentieth-century European existentialism and phenomenology, which is precisely the project from which the young Ratzinger's philosophy professor Arnold Wilmsen had recoiled. He broadened the classical Thomist anthropology by developing the distinctions between the transitive and intransitive dimensions of human action, the internal and external effects of each human choice. In doing so he provided an opening for the Thomist tradition to what is called 'the dimension of relationality'—that dimension of the human personality which is determined by the concrete relationships of an individual's life. Like Ratzinger and von Balthasar, Wojtyla was interested in the drama of the relationship between God and each individual person. He shared their passion for theo-dramatics, but he came to it from a foundation in Thomism and phenomenology. Ratzinger's concern for matters of the heart finds an analogue in Wojtyla's interest in the 'theatre of the inner self'; and Wojtyla shared Ratzinger's interest in St Augustine's notion of participation and incorporated the theme into his major work of philosophical anthropology, *The Acting Person*.[18] Whereas Ratzinger has examined St Augustine's contribution to the notion of the person and what in contemporary terms is called the self and its interiority, Wojtyla developed Thomist philosophical anthropology in the direction of mid-twentieth-century French personalism.[19] Again we can see in the works of the two pontiffs a dovetailing of two agendas: in general terms both were interested in Christian personalism, but Wojtyla was working on the Aquinas–Mounier–Scheler line, and Ratzinger on the Augustine–Newman–Przywara–Guardini line.

At the Council Wojtyla was introduced to de Lubac and invited him to write the Preface to the Polish edition of his work on sexuality entitled *Love and Responsibility*. He also assisted the *Communio* scholars with the establishment of a Polish-language edition of *Communio*, and later as pope raised both de Lubac and von Balthasar to the status of Cardinal (though, famously, von Balthasar did not live to receive his red hat). John Paul II's quarter-century pontificate ended up being supported intellectually by an alliance of a new generation of Thomists and *Communio* types of whom Joseph Ratzinger was the most significant in the second category.[20] While John Paul II never directly entered into the dispute about nature and grace but concentrated his intellectual energies on other fields such as the theology of the body,

Aidan Nichols has argued that the *Communio–Ressourcement* tradition became the dominant theological influence on his pontificate.[21] The Italian journalist Gianni Valente has also observed that in the 1980s and 90s 'almost all the members of the numerous squad of theologians whom Pope Wojtyla appointed to the episcopate—of whom he then co-opted many into the Sacred College of Cardinals—came out of the *Communio* nursery'.[22] These included the Swiss Eugeno Corecco, the Brazilian Karl Romer, the Belgian André Mutien Léonard, the Italian Angelo Scola, the Canadian Marc Ouellet, and the Austrian Christoph von Schönborn.[23]

Today the difference between the Thomist and *Communio* types is not a difference over official magisterial teaching. Both reach the same conclusions about the immorality of contraception, the impossibility of ordaining women and of marriage between persons of the same sex, and the need for a sacerdotal hierarchy. However, they have different readings of the causes of contemporary theological crises, that is, different readings of where and how things went wrong. They therefore have different prescriptions for remedying the post-Conciliar crisis. The *Communio* scholars are firmly of the view that the problem of secularization was fostered by the intellectual errors of the Church's own scholars, in particular by the two-tiered or extrinsicist accounts of the relationship between nature and grace which came to prominence after the Council of Trent (1545–1563), by extrinsicist accounts of the relationship between faith and reason fostered by Leonine and Neo-Thomists who muted the patristic heritage of Thomism in order to defend the faith (or more usually Catholic moral teachings) within Kantian parameters, and by extrinsicist accounts of the relationship between the world and the Church, sometimes called the distinction between the secular and sacred realms, fostered by Catholic scholars dedicated to a synthesis of the Liberal and Catholic traditions.[24] In short, the *Communio* scholars argue that, at least since the Reformation, Catholic theology has been set on several dualist trajectories. Nature and grace, faith and reason, the secular and the sacred, Scripture and Tradition, have tended to be isolated and analysed in separate compartments. Whereas some Thomists have a tendency to read the post-Conciliar decline in the practice of the faith as a consequence of the demise of Thomism in seminary curricula and the subsequent intellectual inadequacy of the Church when faced with the cultural crisis of the late 1960s, the *Communio* scholars look to older problems within the tradition. They tend to regard the most important causes of the post-Conciliar chaos as the dualist trajectories of the pre-Conciliar theological establishment for which corrections were sought in the Conciliar documents. None the less, along with some Thomists they acknowledge that numerous different hermeneutical frameworks were promoted for the interpretation of these documents, the cumulative effect of which retarded the reception of the deeper theological synthesis of the Council.

In the contemporary era new schools of Thomism are emerging which are sensitive to the criticisms of Leonine and Neo-Thomism, especially to the charge that it muted the Patristic and non-Aristotelian heritage of St Thomas for reasons of rhetorical efficacy. The most interesting in the context of Ratzinger's thought is the 'Biblical Thomism' fostered by Servais Pinckaers OP, a Belgian Dominican who was from 1973 to 1997 Professor of Fundamental Moral Theology at the University of Fribourg in Switzerland. Pinckaers' early academic formation was at the Dominican priory of La Sarte, in the town of Huy in the Walloon zone of Belgium. Here (as in Leuven, where Schillebeeckx and other Flemish Dominicans were based) the theologians were in contact with members of the French *ressourcement* movement, including Marie-Dominique Chenu and Jean Daniélou. In 1952 Pinckaers completed his licentiate thesis on the topic of de Lubac's *Surnaturel* (the work which got de Lubac into so much trouble with Labourdette and Garrigou-Lagrange). Pinckaers was sympathetic to de Lubac's side in this dispute. He then went on to write his doctorate under the supervision of Garrigou-Lagrange at the Angelicum, on the comparatively safe topic of 'The Virtuous Nature of Hope, from Peter Lombard to Thomas Aquinas', which was subsequently published with an Introduction by Chenu. In the post-conciliar era Pinckaers opposed both manualist Thomist and the various proportionalist and consequentialist theories which became fashionable. Both of these approaches to moral theology shared the property of treating morality merely as a theory about human actions which are obligated, permitted, or banned. In contrast, as John Berkman has noted, while Pinckaers' work did not deny the Church's proscriptive teachings on acts in any way, he was 'ultimately oriented neither to understanding the demands of the natural law, nor to elucidating the nature of acts and virtues, but to articulating an understanding of the *telos* of the human person'.[25] A key element of this was the response of the believer to the call of the Triune God as revealed in the Scriptures and tradition. This approach is the heart of what Thomas O'Meara OP called Biblical Thomism and what Matthew Levering, a leading Anglophone Biblical Thomist, has said could also be described as '*Ressourcement* Thomism' or 'Augustinian Thomism'. It is not a 'Thomism of the strict observance', since the study of scripture and the early Church Fathers sets the tone rather than a straight repetition of Aquinas's ordering. It does not try to synthesize Aquinas with Kant, Locke, Hegel, Heidegger, or Adam Smith, and it involves an insistent critique of the nominalist shift in Scotus and Ockham. The journal *Nova et Vetera* is committed to the Biblical Thomism project which Levering also says is in broad sympathy with other ongoing theological movements, such as Radical Orthodoxy (RO).

The Cambridge and Nottingham-centred ('Nottingbridge') Radical Orthodoxy scholarship has produced one monograph specifically on Thomist thought. In *Truth in Aquinas* John Milbank and Catherine Pickstock argued, against many received readings, that Aquinas's philosophical account of truth falls apart when separated from his theological framework. In general, without descending to the details, this is how Ratzinger would prefer to read the Thomist tradition, as a composite whole informed and infused by Revelation. Scholars associated with the Radical Orthodoxy circle also share Ratzinger's deeper interest in Augustine. John Milbank has described at least part of his project as a 'post-modern critical Augustinianism'.[26] He notes that much of this perspective is in profound continuity with the French *nouvelle théologie*, especially the works of de Lubac in which he attempts to overcome the 'modern bastard dualisms' of nature and grace, faith and reason. The Radical Orthodoxy scholars are at the forefront of the provision of theological critiques of the cultures of modernity and post-modernity, often with reference to Augustinian insights. They do not see liberalism as the logical outgrowth of classical Thomism, as the self-described 'Whig-Thomists' do, but rather as a heretical mutation of the synthesis offered by Aquinas. When one considers the works of John Ruskin, Matthew Arnold, William Morris, and John Henry Newman one discovers a seam within the Anglican tradition which is hostile to Whiggery, and the Radical Orthodoxy scholars are heirs to this aspect of the tradition.

The dominance of the liberal reading of *Gaudium et spes* among Catholic scholars notwithstanding, a significant convergence is emerging between the critiques of modernity and post-modernity in the works of the predominately Anglican Radical Orthodoxy scholars and those to be found in the publications of the Catholic *Communio* scholars. David L. Schindler, Stratford Caldecott, and Javier Martinez (the Archbishop of Granada) may present their arguments in a different theological dialect from Milbank and Pickstock, but their studies on the question of where liberalism stands in relation to creedal Christianity are reaching the same conclusions as the Radical Orthodoxy set. Paul Richardson, the assistant Anglican Bishop of Newcastle, recently observed that the theology of Benedict XVI has much in common with the school of Radical Orthodoxy, led by John Milbank and heavily influenced by Rowan Williams, that finds inspiration from Augustine in the past and from Henri de Lubac in more recent years. He concedes that most of the members of the Radical Orthodoxy circle (at least the Anglican ones) do not draw the same conclusions as Benedict XVI about the ordination of women, or about the meaning of sexual difference in general, but he concludes 'it is remarkable how close their base positions really are'.[27] The proximity is due in no small measure to the fact that the common neuralgic point is an opposition to the 'bastard dualisms' brought into the tradition by baroque scholasticism. Kevin Lee has argued that 'healing the wounds caused by the distortion of St Thomas Aquinas in the hands of late medieval Thomists like Cajetan and Suárez is a goal of this pontificate as it has been for the Holy Father throughout his life'.[28] If this is so, then the Radical Orthodoxy project and the theology of Benedict XVI share a common core, and a very similar reading of the cultures of modernity and post-modernity, with differences emerging in ecclesiology and anthropology. At the centre of this core is de Lubac.

While the above may seem like a rather long preamble to an understanding of the place of the key themes in the thought of Ratzinger, now Benedict XVI, it is important to understand the broad intellectual contours and fault lines of the groups outlined in order to have any capacity to situate his theological positions within the contemporary theological landscape. If, for example, one's theological stance is that of a Leonine or Neo-Thomist, Ratzinger was and remains a radical, but if one is more of a Rahnerian type, he looks decidedly conservative, even reactionary. If one is a Biblical Thomist he is a sympathetic ally. From a Radical Orthodoxy perspective he appears as a rare breed of educated Roman clergyman who can meet

Rowan Williams as an intellectual peer and who has a profound understanding of what has gone wrong in post-Tridentine Catholicism. None the less, from the Anglican 'RO' perspective, his anthropology still looks a little too 'essentialist'.[29] Finally, if one is a member of the *Communio* school, (other than Walter Kasper or one of those sympathetic to him who have a different interpretation of the *Communio* ecclesiology from Ratzinger), he is a scholar pope charged with healing intellectual wounds in the life of the Church without wrecking the tradition from its base. His mission above all, is, in Komonchak's words, to 'present the Christian vision in its synthetic totality as a comprehensive structure of meaning'. To do this he needs to know where the tradition got de-railed and the causes of the 'transmission failure' in the presentation of the vision to the post-conciliar generations. Some acquaintance with the above schools of thought is therefore necessary to understand how he is re-setting the points.

2

Gaudium et spes and the Importance of Christ

At a conference in Cambridge in 1979 Karl Rahner drew an analogy between the Christian community before and after the Council of Jerusalem (traditionally dated to AD 49) and Catholicism before and after the Second Vatican Council. He used the language of a 'decisive break' to describe the two transitions, and went so far as to assert that the break experienced after the Council was of such a magnitude that the only possible comparison is with the transition from Jewish to Gentile Christianity at the Council of Jerusalem. He added that such transitions 'happen for the most part and in the final analysis, unreflectively; they are not first planned out theologically and then put into effect.'[1] Likewise, some Catholic traditionalists have seen the pre- and post-Vatican II eras in this dualistic way—almost a pre- and post-lapsarian view propped up with various conspiracy theories and in extreme cases leading to schism.

In various publications Ratzinger has agreed with Rahner's position that a lot of theological work begins to happen only after the end of a Council—'the texts of a Council are not meant to save work for theologians. Rather, they should stimulate such work and open new horizons [and] if necessary they should also mark off boundaries between solid ground and quicksand.'[2] Ratzinger is aware that there is a limit to what can be achieved by promulgations. At best they can serve as lines in the sand, as flagpoles to warn the faithful of danger spots, but they are no substitute for a deeply spiritual, internalized understanding of a tradition.

In sharp contradiction to Rahner and some traditionalists, however, Ratzinger wants to avoid any pre- and post-Conciliar dichotomy. He has stated that 'there are no leaps in this history, there are no fractures, and there is no break in continuity. In no wise did the Council intend to introduce a temporal dichotomy in the Church.'[3] In his Preface to the *Theological Highlights of Vatican II*, published in 1966, Ratzinger was already trying to transcend the divisions between what he terms the clichés of progressive and conservative interpretations. He described his reflections as an attempt to 'delineate the inner aspects, the spiritual profile of the Council'.[4] He went on to say that the idea of 'renewal' had a twofold intention—'its point of reference is contemporary man in his reality and in his world, taken as it is. But the measure of its renewal is Christ, as scripture witnesses Him.'[5]

The enduring problem of Vatican II remains the fact that the interpretation of the Conciliar documents all depends on the hermeneutical lens one chooses to use. In legal terms a positivist or literal reading does not resolve the inner complexities in the documents. In his reflection on Paul VI's opening address to the second session of the Council, Ratzinger emphasized its Christocentrism: 'You had to hear it to fully appreciate how movingly it integrated theological considerations with personal spiritual testimony. The accents, can, of course, be variously placed. What most impressed me was how Christ-centric it was.'[6] This Christocentric reading of the Council only came to prominence some two decades later when bishops met together in Rome in 1985 to assess the reception of the Council. In the 1960s and 70s it was the more Rahnerian school of interpretation that dominated the popular Catholic imagination. The Council was popularly construed as a mandate from the Holy Spirit to accommodate the Church's practices (and for some even her teaching) to the norms and rapidly changing mores of contemporary society. The Conciliar call to discern the signs of the times was received as a call to adopt and assimilate them. In his *Principles of Catholic Theology* Ratzinger was later to devote a whole section analysing the Rahnerian contribution to this way of thinking. The 'accommodation to contemporary culture' interpretation of the Council was so strong that even the great Protestant theologian Karl Barth was prompted to ask Paul VI during an audience in 1966: 'What does *aggiornamento* [the Conciliar buzzword] mean? Accommodation to what?'[7]

For some the accommodation was interpreted as restricted to matters of expression; for others it was taken as referring to both expression and content. The latter became the archetypically liberal Catholic intellectual's position, while the former position was more commonly found among clergy who remained doctrinally orthodox but who otherwise pursued pastoral strategies of repackaging Catholic doctrine and liturgical practices into contemporary styles and language. The extent to which such projects of linguistic transposition are possible and effective is now a major philosophical issue to which Cardinal George of Chicago drew attention in his doctoral dissertation on the treatment of culture in the thought of John Paul II.[8] With the emergence of a theology of culture, these issues are only just beginning to receive scholarly examination.

The document which was most often cited in support of the strong accommodationist reading of the Council was *Gaudium et spes*. Ratzinger has described Schema 13, which became *Gaudium et spes*, as 'the most problematic of all the Conciliar texts simply because the theological thought needed to achieve a fully satisfactory statement was still lacking'.[9] He has also written that the lack of clarity that persists even today about the real meaning of Vatican II is closely associated with analyses of this particular document.[10] As John O'Malley wrote in *Tradition and Transition: Historical Perspectives on Vatican II*: 'At the time of the Council we did not think to ask from it any consistent theoretical foundation for *aggiornamento*, because most of us were not aware of the importance of having one.'[11]

This need for some substance for the concept of *aggiornamento* was finally addressed at the 1985 Synod. At this meeting both John Paul II and Ratzinger emphasized the importance of article 22 of *Gaudium et spes* as a hermeneutical lens for the rest of the document, and as one of the key motifs of the Council. It is the most Christocentric article in the entire document and, as the English theologian Paul McPartlan has noted, it appears to have been taken word for word from de Lubac's book *Catholicisme*, a copy of which had been given by Alfred Läpple to the young Ratzinger back in 1949. The central point of the article is that the human person only understands his or her identity to the extent that he or she is open to a relationship with Christ. Christology is deemed necessary for any adequate anthropology. Christ is the eschatological Adam to whom the first Adam already pointed, the true image of God who transforms man once more into a likeness to God. By emphasizing this paragraph, John Paul II and Ratzinger attempted to undercut any secularizing potential of the document. If Christology is a necessary component of any adequate anthropology, secular humanism is always inadequate. This was Henri de Lubac's thesis in *The Drama of Atheistic Humanism*.[12] According to this reading, the point of *Gaudium et spes* is not to accommodate Catholicism to the culture of modernity, but to affirm certain aspirations of the moderns, such as the longing for human freedom and self-fulfilment, and to argue that only a Christocentric anthropology has any hope of realizing these legitimate aspirations. The Christocentric accent, which Ratzinger had detected in the address of Paul VI to the second session of the Council, and which he had praised in his commentary of 1966, finally started to overtake the earlier accommodationist interpretation during the papacy of John Paul II (1978–2005). It is perhaps no coincidence that John Paul II's first encyclical, *Redemptor hominis*, was his Christological masterwork.

Consistent with the position he took at the 1985 Synod, Ratzinger remarked in 1968 that the whole Pastoral Constitution might be described as 'a discussion between Christian and unbeliever on the question of who and what man really is'.[13] He further suggested that this general theme may be found foreshadowed in Pascal's *Pensées*, especially Fragment 434: 'The knot of our condition draws its twists and turns from this abyss, so that man is more inconceivable without this mystery [of original sin] than this mystery is for man.' For Ratzinger this insight that faith provides the key to the meaning of our human experiences is a presupposition of dialogue between faith and unbelief—'only if faith throws light on experience and proves to be the answer to our experiences, can talk about man's humanity lead to talk about God and with God.'[14] He concludes that the chapter of *Gaudium et spes* in which dialogue with unbelievers is pursued around the notion of *humanitas* culminates in 'a new type of completely Christocentric theology' which 'dares to present theology as anthropology'.[15]

None the less Ratzinger has been critical of the manner of presentation of this anthropology in the document. Like other commentators since, including Walter Kasper and David L. Schindler, he has noted that there is a significant difference between an understanding of the human person as 'merely theistically coloured', that is, in some sense made in the image of God according to the account of creation in Genesis, and an understanding of the human person which takes into account the Trinitarian anthropology of the New Testament.[16] In the earlier sections of the document the Old Testament vision predominates. For Ratzinger, the starting point of anthropology has to be the notion of Christ as the new Adam: a merely theistically coloured account of the human person is both an inadequate anthropology and an inadequate theology of creation. A full theology of creation is only intelligible in eschatology. As he puts it: 'the Alpha is only truly to be understood in the light of the Omega.'[17]

Ratzinger suggests that this ambiguity arose because *Gaudium et spes* did not offer a 'radical enough rejection of a doctrine of man divided into philosophy and theology'—'the text was still based on a schematic representation of nature and the supernatural viewed far too much as merely juxtaposed.'[18] It took at its starting point 'the fiction that it is possible to construct a rational philosophical picture of man intelligible to all and on which all men of goodwill can agree, the actual Christian doctrines being added to this as a sort of crowning conclusion'.[19] The Christian part of the puzzle of the human person becomes a special 'take' on anthropology which 'others ought not to make a bone of contention but which at bottom can be ignored'.[20] This is the de Lubac charge against where the dualist tradition leads. Ratzinger complained that *Gaudium et spes* prompted the question: 'why exactly the reasonable and perfectly free human being described in its first articles should suddenly be burdened with the story of Christ?'[21]

In stark contrast to Kantian projects, Ratzinger asserted that 'there is, and must be, a human reason *in* faith; yet conversely, every human reason is conditioned by a historical standpoint so that reason pure and simple does not exist'.[22] On the other hand, 'it must be admitted that the various concrete forms of dialogue can take place in a number of ways and that here there is much to be said for an advance from outside inwards'.[23] Thus, while it is not always necessary to begin with Revelation, dialogue must always be open to Revelation, and even that which passes for pure reason, if subjected to scrutiny, will turn out to be dependent on theological presuppositions, even if the theology is some new brand of paganism. This position, first argued by Ratzinger in the 1960s, was strongly reiterated in his speech to the bishops of Mexico in Guadalajara in 1996.[24] In 'Truth and Freedom', also published in 1996, Ratzinger wrote that 'there is no great philosophy which does not draw life from listening to and accepting religious tradition. Wherever this relation is cut off, philosophical thought withers and becomes a mere conceptual game.'[25]

The daring new Christocentric anthropology had been poorly presented. Instead of it being emphasized that the Incarnation is a radical irruption in human history, an event which changes everything, a literal reading of sections of *Gaudium et spes* can give the impression that belief in the Incarnation is a kind of Christian gloss on an otherwise perfect secular humanist canvas.

An extrinsicist account of the relationship between philosophy and theology was not, however, the only extrinsicist position detected in *Gaudium et spes* by Ratzinger. He was also critical of the document for drawing a dichotomy between the human person and the Church—'the Church herself is part of the *genus humanum* and cannot therefore be contradistinguished from it.'[26] He suggested that the lack of understanding of this point shown by those who drafted the document is evidence of a 'deep-rooted extrinsicism'.[27]

By far the most often cited example of an extrinsicist position in *Gaudium et spes* is paragraph 36 which refers to the 'autonomy of earthly affairs' in the following manner:

If by the autonomy of earthly affairs we mean that created things and societies themselves enjoy their own laws and values which must gradually be deciphered, put to use, and regulated by men, then it is entirely right to demand that autonomy. Such is not merely required by modern men, but harmonizes also with the will of the Creator. For by the very circumstance of their having been created, all things are endowed with their own stability, truth, goodness, proper laws and order.

The last sentence in this paragraph, 'for by the very circumstance of their having been created, all things are endowed with their own stability, truth, goodness, proper laws and order' is taken directly from St Thomas. It is in part because of this that those who read *Gaudium et spes* as the Church's embrace of the culture of modernity claim the authority of St Thomas to support their position and suggest that those who oppose this reading must be operating on an Augustinian or at least some other non-Thomist line. However, this reading ignores Thomas's starting point of creation and emphasizes only the secondary clause, which exudes, when severed, a radical autonomy. Read in this way, in extreme cases, it can be used as a basis for the creature to turn his or her back on the Creator while pursuing autonomous or 'natural' ends. This clause is commonly taken to mean that there is no relationship between theology and politics, economics, and the other social sciences. For example, Walter Kasper has said that *Gaudium et spes* was the 'Church's recognition of the autonomy of secular fields of activity', that the Council had accepted the 'fundamental concept of the modern age', that 'secular matters are to be decided in a secular fashion, political matters in a political fashion, economic matters in an economic fashion'.[28] Paradoxically, without further qualifications, such a reading requires a kind of extreme severance of the Church from the world, even though the document is regarded as a general call to Catholics to be more engaged in the life of the world. More significantly, it is inconsistent with the Thomistic understanding of the hierarchical arrangement of goodness in the universe such that individual goods are ordered toward their final good in God.

An alternative, non-secularizing reading of this section, proposed by David L. Schindler, relates it to the analogy of being based on the descent of the Son of God into the world in such a way that worldly realities find their true meaning, precisely as worldly—or indeed 'natural'—in their character simultaneously and intrinsically as epiphanies of God's glory.[29] Support for this reading can be found in question 85 of the *Summa Theologica* of St Thomas where he not only mentions the notion of all things being by virtue of their creation endowed with their own stability, goodness, and order, but he explicitly makes mention of the fact that there are 'varying degrees of proportion, species and order corresponding to varying degrees of good':

One good is intrinsic to the very substance of human nature, having its own proportion, species and order; this can be neither taken away nor lessened through sin. Another good having its own proportion, species and order is that of the natural inclination to virtue; this can be lessened through sin but not entirely taken away. Again, there is the good of virtue and grace, having its own proportion, species and order; this is wholly destroyed by mortal sin. Finally there is the good which is the rightly ordered human act itself, with therefore its own proportion, species and order; the lack of this good is essentially sin itself.

In other words, the understanding of the stability and goodness of creation makes sense only within an architectonic framework which includes such fundamental Christian beliefs as human nature being made in the image and likeness of the Trinity and indeed of creation being marked by the form of the Trinity. This is not, however, a peculiarly Thomist position. Similar passages can be found in Augustine's *De Trinitate*, VI. 12:

Therefore all these things which are made by divine skill (*arte*), show in themselves a certain unity (*unitatem*), and form (*speciem*) and order (*ordinem*) . . .

when therefore we regard the Creator, who is understood by the things that are made (Rom. 1: 20), we must needs understand the Trinity of whom there appear traces (*vestigium*) in the Creature, as is fitting.

What these passages by Augustine and Aquinas emphasize is the notion of the analogy of being and of a related hierarchy of goodness. They do not suggest some kind of extrinsicist separation of grace and nature, the secular and the sacred. Extrinsicism is consistent with the accounts of some Thomists but by no means all. Anyone influenced by de Lubac as Benedict has been would not accept that an extrinsicist reading is possible on a proper reading of Thomas. Further, those who wish to read *Gaudium et spes* as endorsing a simplistic 'accommodation to the culture of modernity' pastoral strategy are relying on the same account of nature and grace as defended by Garrigou-Lagrange. This only illustrates de Lubac's somewhat provocative point that the turn of the century Modernists and Garrigou-Lagrange were operating from the same nature and grace first principles. With the rate of change in contemporary culture, and the end of, or at least disenchantment of, western elites with the modern project, the pastoral strategy of an accommodation to the culture of modernity becomes unwieldy. With a radical autonomy of the world itself from the Church the dialogue ends in each sphere speaking to itself.

In the following passage from *The Spirit of the Liturgy* Ratzinger clearly understands autonomy differently from those who insist on an extrinsicist account or who follow the Rahnerian alternative of 'naturalizing the supernatural':

[In the Christian vision of *reditus*,] the creature, existing in its own right, comes home to itself, and this act is an answer in freedom to God's love... The being of the other is not absorbed or abolished, but rather, in giving itself, it becomes fully itself... This *reditus* is a 'return', but it does not abolish creation; rather, it bestows its full and final perfection.[30]

Similarly, in *The End of Time*, Ratzinger wrote:

The act of being on the part of God that affects being is an act of freedom... The *exitus*, or better, the free creative act of God, does in fact aim at *reditus*, but this does not mean that created being is revoked. Rather, it means the coming-into-its-own of the creature as an autonomous creature answers back in freedom to the love of God, accepts its creation as a command to love, so that a dialogue of love begins—that entirely new unity that only love can create. In it the being of the other is not absorbed, not annulled, but rather becomes wholly what it is precisely in giving itself.[31]

Such an interpretation of the meaning of the autonomy of earthly affairs in the thought of St Thomas is from a different planet from those who read *Gaudium et spes* as the Church's endorsement of the idea that Catholics should embrace the theoretical presuppositions of secular liberalism. If Christ himself is the measure of what it means to be human, then humanity only finds itself and is truly at its best, when it freely enters into a dialogue of love with its Creator.

Flawed conceptions of the meaning of autonomy in paragraph 36 inevitably lead to flawed understandings of the treatment of freedom. Here again Ratzinger is critical of the presentation in *Gaudium et spes* because the Christocentric accent is missing. The treatment of freedom unrolls on the plain of natural theology and recourse is made to notions of a natural ethics in Old Testament wisdom theology without any reference to the criticisms of this approach in other sections of the Old Testament, including the Book of Job. Ratzinger complains that the tearing of quotations from Chapter 15 of *Ecclesiastes* in support of a 'colourless doctrine of freedom, represents not only an unhistorical reading of Scripture but also an unhistorical and therefore unreal view of man'.[32] He concludes with the strong statement that 'the general doctrine of freedom developed in the Conciliar text cannot therefore stand up either to theological or to philosophical criticism':

Philosophically speaking, it by-passes the whole modern discussion of freedom. It simply takes no account of that overshadowing of freedom of which psychology and sociology at the present time inform us in such a disturbing way. Consequently it shuts itself out from the factual situation of man whose freedom only comes into effect through a lattice of determining factors. Theologically speaking, it leaves aside the whole complex of problems which Luther, with polemical one-sidedness, comprised in the term *'servum arbitrium'*. The whole text gives scarcely a hint of the discord which runs through man and which is described so dramatically in Romans 7: 13–25. It even falls into 'downright Pelagian terminology' when it speaks of man *'sese ab omni passionum captivitate liberans finem suum persequitur et apta subsidia . . . procurat'*.[33]

This Pelagian flavour of some sections of the document comes not only through the choice of language, but also through the tendency to play down the battle between good and evil, grace and despair in order not to put off non-Christian readers. By muting these more theo-dramatic elements one can get the impression that better civic education is all that is needed for peace and harmony to abound in all its fullness. For this reason *Gaudium et spes* was not only criticized in

Catholic circles thoroughly conversant with the tradition but also in evangelical Protestant circles. Against this tendency, as early as the mid-1960s Ratzinger wrote that 'if the Church were to accommodate herself to the world in any way that would entail a turning away from the Cross, this would not lead to a renewal of the Church, but only to her death'.[34]

Later, in an essay published in 1989, Ratzinger contrasted the false neo-Pelagian optimism of the modern age with the Christian theological virtue of hope and distinguished between three different types of false optimism: (i) optimism as a cover for despair, (ii) optimism as a way of reassuring the faithful in order to create the climate in which one could dismantle the Church as quickly as possible and gain power over it, and (iii) optimism as the bourgeois substitute for the lost hope of faith.[35] The first takes concrete form in the attitude of pre-conciliar generation Catholics who remark that younger generations who no longer participate in the sacramental life of the Church have simply found different ways of expressing their spirituality, as if the sacraments are nothing more than customary traditions. The second takes concrete form in the behaviour of those found mostly in Catholic Church agencies who do their best to muddy the waters about what the Church actually teaches in order to promote their own agenda. And the concrete form of the third is found in the attitude of those upwardly mobile Catholics who believe that nothing is wrong with contemporary culture because they are doing well within it. Ratzinger came to the conclusion that in places like Holland in the 1970s, where the rate of decline for practising Catholics was the highest in the world, all three were at work. After reading *The Principle of Hope* by the German Marxist, Ernest Bloch, it dawned on him that 'optimism' is the pseudo-theological virtue of deified history and thus of the great god of modern ideologies and their promise.[36]

Moving from the macro level of anthropology to the more specific territory of ethics, *Gaudium et spes* has also been cited as authority for the principle that an individual's conscience is a higher tribunal of ethical judgement than the magisterial teaching of the Church. In this context Ratzinger has pointed out that *Gaudium et spes* never set out to offer anything more than a most general outline of a Christian doctrine of conscience. He notes that all manner of epistemological, psychological and sociological factors relevant to this topic are left untreated, and in particular the issue of how conscience can err if God's call is directly to be heard in it is unexplained. He also notes the highly popularized teaching of fellow German theologian Johann Baptist Metz that Thomas Aquinas was the first to teach the obligatory force of an erroneous conscience, but he argues that this is historically and objectively the case only to a certain extent and with considerable qualifications. In practice, Aquinas's thesis is nullified by the fact that he is convinced that error is culpable. Guilt lies not so much in the will which has to carry out the precept laid down upon it by the intellect, but in the intellect itself. According to Ratzinger the doctrine of the binding force of an erroneous conscience in the form in which it is propounded by Metz and a whole raft of contemporary Catholic ethicists belongs entirely to the thought of modern times not to Thomas Aquinas.[37]

Ratzinger concludes that 'in this essential kernel' [the affirmation of the primacy of conscience] the schema is certainly right and not vulnerable to critical thought. What is unsatisfactory is simply the way the concrete form of the claim of conscience is dealt with, the inadequate view of the facts of experience, and the insufficient account taken of the limits of conscience.[38] Contrary to the interpretation of liberal theologians, the Conciliar fathers were in fact 'anxious not to allow an ethics of conscience to be transformed into the domination of subjectivism, and not to canonise a limitless situation ethics under the guise of conscience'.[39]

Notwithstanding all the above criticisms, Ratzinger does not regard *Gaudium et spes* as an entirely problematic document. In addition to offering a daring new Christocentric anthropology, however inadequately expressed, *Gaudium et spes* at least has the virtue of having eliminated the Stoic categories for analysing the sacrament of marriage. Marriage manuals no longer speak of marital dues and rights and reduce the whole reality of marital fidelity to parental responsibilities. In *Gaudium et spes* 'neither the concept of the prime end of procreation nor the concept of marital behaviour according to nature has any place'.[40] This elimination of Stoic categories marked a radical turn toward new modes of moral teaching, especially to mid-twentieth-century French personalism. It is well known that it was the young Archbishop Karol Wojtyla from Cracow who was largely responsible for this development. It laid the foundations for what was to become John Paul II's Theology of the Body—an overtly scriptural presentation of the meaning of human sexuality with reference to a fundamentally personalist ontology, not narrowly focused on any particular faculty of the soul but on the entire person. As a consequence of this shift in *Gaudium et spes*, Paul VI's 1968 encyclical *Humanae vitae* spoke of contraception with reference to 'the person of the woman' and 'mutual personal perfection', rather than with reference to principles of contract law.

Regrettably for Ratzinger, however, the young Karol Wojtyla's personalism did not carry through to articles 15–17 of *Gaudium et spes*. These expound human spirituality under three aspects: intellect, conscience, and freedom. Neither the concept of the person nor the idea of love was mentioned here. The philosophy of interpersonal love, the whole set of I–Thou questions, are practically absent from the treatment of spirituality within this section of the document, and Ratzinger was quite appalled that anyone could attempt to speak of spirituality without thinking that Christian love might have something to do with it.[41] The first encyclical of his pontificate, *Deus Caritas Est*, can thus be read, in part, as a long-awaited remedy to what he saw as the lopsided intellectualism of the treatment of spirituality in *Gaudium et spes*.

In 2004, the fortieth anniversary year of the promulgation of *Gaudium et spes*, numerous reflections on the document were published. One of the most penetrating was that by Lieven Boeve of Leuven. He began by noting that while the dialogue partner of the Church in *Gaudium et spes* was modernity, its projects of progress and emancipation have lost their plausibility and 'one must now admit that the neo-conservative analysis of the crisis of modernity closely resembles the theories of specific postmodern authors such as Jean-François Lyotard and Wolfgang Welsch'.[42] He further observed that the neo-conservative theologians are not very upset about the crisis of modernity since they regard the fall of modern master-stories as the final proof for the validity of their opposition to the general optimistic tone of *Gaudium et spes*.[43] In their opinion it is only now that a fruitful reception of the Council, and especially of *Gaudium et spes*, can take place. Boeve presents Ratzinger as a prime example of such a neo-conservative. He then suggests that while the diagnosis of the neo-conservatives and the post-moderns is the same, their remedies differ: 'Neo-conservative thinkers hope to re-establish the theoretical framework of pre-modern times, going back before modernity and trying to forget about modernity. Post-modern theorists, on the other hand, suggest new ways of coping with the acknowledged and irreducible ambiguity of modernity.'[44]

While accepting the post-modern critiques of modernity, and concluding that they mean that the significance of *Gaudium et spes* as an attempt to reconcile Christianity and modernity is in real danger, Boeve none the less wants to preserve what he calls the method of *Gaudium et spes*, which he defines as entering into the critical consciousness of an era. Although he does not offer an ecclesiology to go with his call for an engagement of the Church with post-modern thought, implicit in much of what he writes is a rejection of the magisterium as 'operation ground control', as Ratzinger calls it. Boeve appears to have more faith in the expert opinions of scholars than the judgements of the magisterium. In this he is very much in the *Concilium* tradition.

An alternative reading which defends the 'pro-modernity' interpretation of *Gaudium et spes* from the charge of being passé has been offered by Nicholas Boyle, Professor of German Literary and Intellectual History at Cambridge.[45] Boyle notes that *Gaudium et spes* identified globalization as one of the defining features of modernity and suggests that this makes it more of a tract for our times than for the time it was written. He further praises the fundamental evolutionism of *Gaudium et spes* and aspects of the theology of Teilhard de Chardin which inspired at least some of those responsible for its drafting. He warmly endorses the European Union, describing it no less than as a 'prophetic sign for the future of humanity'.[46] He holds that *Gaudium et spes* contains the belief that 'you can teach only those whom you are willing to understand and that you can understand only those whose position you are willing to share'.[47] Unlike Boeve, he thinks that the culture of modernity still holds quite a lot of promise and that the flagship of the modern project is now the European Union.

Boyle's hope for the modern project is shared by Joseph A. Komonchak, one of the leading historians of the Council. He notes that Ratzinger seeks to occupy a middle position between ecclesial liberals and traditionalists by adopting a stance of praising the Council itself while being critical of many of its popular interpretations. However, for Komonchak this position tilts too much in the traditionalist direction, in so far as it restates the basic traditionalist hostility to liberalism in culture and society.[48]

At the turn of the twenty-first century there are thus at least five different positions taken by Catholic scholars on *Gaudium et spes* and the general 'spirit' of the Council. First, there is the position that *Gaudium et spes* was a mandate to accommodate, or at least correlate, the Catholic faith with the culture of modernity and that this is a good thing. The articles published by Nicholas Boyle in the *Tablet* may be read as occupying this position. Secondly, there is the inverse position of Catholic traditionalists: that *Gaudium et spes* was a call to accommodate or at least correlate the faith to the culture of modernity, and, as such, they want nothing to do with it. In France, in particular, it is precisely the notion that '*Gaudium et spes* represents an attempt at an official reconciliation with the new era inaugurated in 1789' (as even Ratzinger has described it) that is most disturbing.[49] For Catholic traditionalists, for whom the most outstanding leader has been Archbishop Marcel-François Lefebvre (1905–1991), modernity means the bifurcation of the self into private and public halves, liberal sexual ethics, rationalism, the undermining of social and cultural hierarchies (including the sacerdotal hierarchy), and the wholesale abandonment of tradition as a worthwhile dimension of life. For French traditionalists the concept of modernity also evokes memories of the murder of at least three-quarters of a million Catholics during the Revolution, including what is now conceded by all sides to have been nothing less than genocide in the Vendée. Anyone who has visited the Mémorial de la Vendée at Les Lucs-sur-Boulogne and read the lists of names and ages of women and children murdered for simply living in a devoutly Catholic and royalist part of the countryside would realize that a significant proportion of French Catholics would have difficulty with a document which was interpreted as tipping a bucket of holy water over the French Revolution. Third, there is the position of Johann Baptist Metz (1928–) and Juan Luis Segundo (1925–1996), that *Gaudium et spes* was the manifesto of a bourgeois revolution in modern Catholicism, which was a movement forward from Pius IX's aristocratic stance of unmitigated opposition to modernity, but it did not go far enough. What is now required is a proletarian revolution. Indeed some of the Latin American theologians became so influenced by Marxism that they actually regarded Hans Küng, arguably the most liberal of all European theologians in the immediate post-conciliar era, as a middle-class reactionary. Hugo Assmann, the author of *A Nomad Church*, is notable for taking this position. Fourth, there is the position of Lieven Boeve that the idea of hooking Catholicism up to the modern project just a few short years before leading European intellectuals were declaring the project a failure was not very far-sighted and, as a project itself, a failure, but the more basic orientation which underpinned it, of keeping the Church in a constant dialogue with the best of contemporary thought, is still worthwhile pursuing. Finally, there is Ratzinger's position.

Against the first position Ratzinger would say that *Gaudium et spes* was never intended to be a call to accommodate the Catholic faith to the culture of modernity as it is defined by sociologists; though with the proponents of positions one and four, he would agree that it is a good idea for the Church's scholars to keep themselves abreast of the best of contemporary scholarship coming from non-Catholic academies. With the proponents of the traditionalist position he would sympathize with their concerns about the secularizing interpretations which have been given to the document, and he would concede that the drafting of certain sections of the document lent itself to being given this kind of spin, but he would not concede the point that the Council itself was a bad idea or that the Conciliar fathers ever intended or even imagined that the document would be given some of the popular interpretations of the 1960s and 70s. With the proponents of the third position, the leaders of the liberation theology movement, he would probably concede the point that the document reads as though it were written for middle-class Americans and Europeans and that it lacks a critical edge when dealing with liberalism. He would also be sympathetic to those who are concerned about the problem of poverty in the Latin American countries. He acknowledges that the 'liberalism and capitalism fostered by Anglo Saxon powers [in Latin America] had become an even more painful slavery [i.e. *than Spanish colonial rule*]'.[50] He would not, however, go along with any Marxist-derived theories about progressive stages in human history. With Lieven Boeve's postmodern position, he would agree that the post-moderns have accurately identified problems with the modern project and he would acknowledge the virtue of keeping up to date with contemporary critical consciousness, but his ecclesiology is different from Boeve's in that he regards Christianity as the ultimate master-story and the Church as its guardian.

Given such a reading Ratzinger is not aptly described as a neo-conservative, because there is no evidence that he was ever enchanted with any form of liberalism and his passion for Newman would have inoculated him against it. In particular, at no time has he ever endorsed the Anglo-American neo-conservative tradition of mixing laissez-faire capitalism with social conservatism. He has also written in defence of his early patron, Cardinal Frings, against the charge of his being a liberal (as if being a liberal is something negative from which one might want to be defended) and there is rather a large amount of evidence that he consistently opposed the interpretation of *Gaudium et spes* as a call to transpose Catholic teaching into the forms of contemporary western culture, whatever they might happen to be. In the following paragraph he completely ridicules this interpretation:

Need we only call on the *aggiornamento*, take off our makeup, and don the mufti of a secular vocabulary or a demythologised Christianity in order to make everything all right? Is a change of intellectual costume sufficient to make people run cheerfully up and help to put out the fire that according to theology exists and is a danger to all of us?[51]

For many the only logical alternative to not being for modernity or post-modernity is to be for some kind of medieval or baroque restoration. However, there is no evidence of support for these alternatives in Ratzinger's works either. He explicitly rejects the baroque alternative in theology and he is not so facile a character as simply to want to replay Augustine and Bonaventure over and over until the Second Coming. He is deeply influenced by Newman's notion of the development of doctrine and by the Tübingen interest in the relationship between history, memory, and tradition. His basic orientation is for an organic development of a tradition with reference to the Church's magisterium. He tends to see both positive and negative aspects in every era and follows a methodology very similar to that of von Balthasar in the essay 'The Fathers, the Scholastics and Ourselves'. Here von Balthasar wrote that we need to 'press on past all external and superficial features of each epoch, to focus on its innermost structural law, and then to measure each respective formal law according to the structural law of what is essentially Christian as we encounter this norm in the Gospel'.[52] Von Balthasar also suggested that we need to keep a bird's perspective on the whole tradition, rather than that of a frog; and, further, that it is important to understand that the essential idea of Christianity does not 'hover like some abstract universal law over history and its changes, but rather expresses itself in the level of history in ever-new forms without our being able thereby to call any one of these forms the absolute one'.[53] This is essentially the approach that Ratzinger takes. Like a post-modern he will praise and adopt elements from many different cultural expressions of his tradition in order to foster the best of each period. However, in doing so he is sensitive to considerations of the internal order and coherence of a tradition. He does have a sense that any new cultural expression needs to have more clarity, proportion, and harmony than one normally associates with post-modern architecture. If one was to label him it would seem that neither the paleo-conservative nor neo-conservative labels are adequate to the complexity of his thought. The tags left and right are even less precise and are worse than useless in this context.

His strong preference for Augustinian and Bonaventurian over Kantian epistemology places him comfortably at the point of intersection between the pre-moderns and the post-moderns. With the post-moderns he agrees that we should not pretend that reason is theologically neutral. With the pre-moderns he agrees that there is something called Truth which the human intellect has the capacity to discern. If one accepts Komonchak's reading that he is basically anti-modern in his hostility to liberalism and adds to this his criticism of Kantian epistemology and his love of Augustine and Newman then a more appropriate label might be Adam Webb's 'cosmopolitan anti-liberal'. He believes that there is more than one expression of an authentic Christian culture, he is open to new manifestations and developments, and in this sense he can be called a cosmopolitan. However, he does believe that Christianity is *the* master-story and that the Catholic Church is a sacred institution, founded by Christ, to hand on the narrative from generation to generation. He further believes that it is not up to clerics and academics to recreate the narrative each time there is a major tremor in the academies of the world. This is not to say that he is opposed to entering into dialogue with other traditions, merely that he does not believe that he or anyone else within the hierarchy can change the plot they have received. He is not therefore a reactionary in the sense of wanting to go back to some pre-modern expression of the faith, but he does believe that as the Church moves through time and new expressions of the faith emerge, they carry within them a constant core of infrastructural beliefs. He would agree with Nicholas Boyle that 'you can only teach those whom you are willing to understand' but he would disagree with Boyle's corollary, that 'you can understand only those whose position you are willing to share'.

For Ratzinger, the whole point of *Gaudium et spes*, correctly interpreted, is that a 'daring new' Christocentric theological anthropology is the medicine that the world needs, and that it is the responsibility of the Church to administer it. He is critical of interpretations which would transform Christianity into what he provocatively calls a 'poorly managed haberdashery that is always trying to lure more customers':

the Christian faith is rather . . . the divine medicine that would never adapt itself to the wishes of its clientele and to what pleases them, for that would be to destroy them utterly. Its role must be to require them to turn away from their imaginary need, which is in reality their sickness, and to entrust themselves to the guidance of the faith . . . [54]

In his McGinley Lecture at Fordham University, Avery Cardinal Dulles SJ concluded:

Undeniably there have been some shifts in Ratzinger's assessment of Vatican II. Still finding his own theological path, he was in the first years of the Council unduly dependent on Karl Rahner as a mentor. Only gradually did he come to see that he and Rahner lived, theologically speaking, on different planets. Whereas Rahner found revelation and salvation primarily in the inward movements of the human spirit, Ratzinger finds them in historical events attested by Scripture and the Fathers. [55]

3

Revelation, Scripture, and Tradition

At the Second Vatican Council the theme of the relationships between Revelation, Scripture, and Tradition (which were topics in the jettisoned section of Ratzinger's *habilitationsshrift*) reappeared as the central issue of the Dogmatic Constitution on Divine Revelation, otherwise known as *Dei verbum*.[1] The preparatory schema for this Constitution initially reflected the Suárezian approach to Revelation which had been promoted by Michael Schmaus at the young Ratzinger's oral defence, in opposition to the approach of Gottlieb Söhngen and Ratzinger himself. In the post-Tridentine era Francisco Suárez (1548–1617) had underscored the propositional character of Revelation—a statement of faith became an occasion on which some aspect of Revelation is made clear. The study of these theological propositions then formed the sub-discipline of dogmatic theology. Just as Cajetan's account of nature and grace came to be regarded as a baroque deviation from classical Thomism, at least according to de Lubac and those who followed him, Suárez's account of Revelation came to be seen as similarly distortive of the classical Thomist position. Whereas Aquinas looked at faith from the 'inside' and focused on the change that faith brings about in the human being, Suárez looked at faith 'from the outside' and described the way we can see it working. Gerard O'Shea has presented the difference between the two in the following paragraph:

For St Thomas, the symbolic apprehension of divine truth conveyed by Revelation implied at the very least a desire for intimacy with God as a means of entering into the perception of this truth. But by the sixteenth century language was largely cut off from its participatory role, and was reduced to simply pointing at objects . . . [Suárez] no longer sees faith primarily as a supernatural habit (virtue) by which human beings participate in the very life of God. For him, faith is concerned with the *knowability* and *believability* of an object. In using these categories, he has accepted a rupture between *intelligibility* (the way in which an object is known) and *assent* (whether what is presented to the intelligence is to be believed).[2]

John Montag SJ has suggested that the overcoming of Suárez's account would involve a reversal of his divorce between words and things, as well as a reversal of the order of assent and Revelation.[3] Such a reversal can be found in the works of Ratzinger, and also in the publications of his *Communio* colleague, von Balthasar. For Ratzinger, Revelation is not a collection of statements—Revelation is Christ himself. He is the *logos*, the all-embracing Word in which God declares himself.[4]

Early in the conciliar debates Cardinals Liénart, Frings, Léger, König, Alfrink, Suenens, Ritter, and Bea opposed the very Suárezan preparatory schema and both Karl Rahner and Joseph Ratzinger were among the *periti* appointed to the subcommission for its redrafting. Although Ratzinger worked closely with Rahner on *Dei verbum* and even co-published a work titled *Revelation and Tradition* with him in 1965, his views on this topic are more in line with those of Jean Daniélou SJ, another Conciliar *peritus* associated with the French *ressourcement* school. Daniélou was critical of the Suárezian account for allowing no place to history in the development of dogma and locating reality so exclusively in essences that the dramatic world of persons was ignored.

While the Vatican I (1869–70) document on Revelation, *Dei filius*, was focused on combating the errors of rationalism and naturalism (the latter included three subcategories of pantheism), by the time of the promulgation of *Dei verbum*, almost a century later, a far greater problem was the Modernist challenge to the authority of Scripture, and the strength of the Protestant criticism that the Catholic tradition was obsessed with metaphysics and the gods of Greece to the neglect of salvation history and the Trinity, and that Catholic scholars tended to overlook the radical discontinuity of Christian Revelation with every myth that had preceded it. As a consequence the central issue of *Dei verbum* became the relationship of Scripture to Tradition and the way in which faith is related to history. Also under discussion was a proper understanding of inspiration and of the historicity of events narrated in the Scriptures. In a commentary published in 1969 Ratzinger describes the document as an 'attempt to overcome the one-sided emphasis on the Greek concept of God as a pure and changeless being of whom, consequently, no action could be predicated; and to restore the focus on the biblical God for whom it is precisely relationship and action that are the essential marks'.[5] If there is no real activity of God in the world, no Revelation in the full sense, then religious experience is reduced to fragmentary reflections and intuitive feelings of a reality that lies beyond the world. Ratzinger is especially critical of the notion that Christ's experience is a mere fragment and that alongside it there are experiences and illuminations from which one may pick and choose something meaningful. Like von Balthasar, he holds that Revelation can only be mediated from a standpoint of 'engraced' participation within the horizon of faith. Otherwise, 'there are lights, but no Light; words, but no Word'.[6]

Moreover, Ratzinger underscored the principle that *actio* (action) is an antecedent to *verbum* (speech), reality to the tidings of it. For him it is important to understand that the level of reality of the Revelation event is deeper than that of the proclamation event, which seeks to interpret God's action in human language. It is precisely because the Revelation of God is received by humanity in words *and* signs (not just words) that sacramentality holds such a central position in the life and practice of the Catholic faith.[7] This principle is embodied in article 2 of *Dei verbum*: 'This plan of Revelation is realized by deeds and words having an inner unity: the deeds wrought by God in the history of salvation manifest and confirm the teaching and realities signified by the words, while the words proclaim the deeds and clarify the mystery contained in them.' Von Balthasar makes the further point, which is strongly taken up by Benedict XVI in *Deus Caritas Est*, that 'the divine figure at the centre of Revelation is to be deciphered not simply as a word, but as absolute love' and that such love is the 'form of the virtues' and the 'form of Revelation'.[8]

In his Conciliar commentaries Ratzinger is clearly in favour of the approach taken to Revelation in *Dei verbum* and in various places contrasts it with the approaches taken at Trent and Vatican I. He notes that whereas Vatican I starts from the natural knowledge of God and considers 'supernatural' Revelation only in close connection with this idea, in order to proceed immediately to the question of its transmission in scripture and tradition, in *Dei verbum* the question of the natural knowledge of God is put at the end and God's revealing activity described within a comprehensive survey of salvation history.[9]

The starting point is now the notion of God as a person whose Revelation is personal. Further, whereas Vatican I used the expression 'the eternal decree of his will', which carries strong juridical overtones, Vatican II spoke of 'the sacrament of his will': '[I]nstead of the legalistic view that sees Revelation largely as the issuing of divine decrees, we have a sacramental view, which sees law and grace, word and deed, message and sign, the person and his utterance within the one comprehensive unity of the mystery.'[10]

Such an understanding of Revelation gives priority to the dialogue which takes place between God and the human person and in turn feeds into the Trinitarian anthropology of *Gaudium et spes*, of which Ratzinger strongly approved. It is no mere 'theistically coloured' account of Revelation, but one which pays due regard to the significance of each of the processions within the Trinity. The movement of Revelation proceeds from God (the Father) to humanity through Christ, and admits the faithful into the fellowship of God in the Holy Spirit. The purpose of this dialogue between God and the human person is not so much the transmission of information but rather the transformation of the person in the life of the Trinity. For Razinger this is not a matter of removing the intellectual component of faith but understanding it as a component in a wider whole.[11] He believes that 'the act of faith is an event that expands the limits of individual reason' and 'brings the isolated and fragmented individual intellect into the realm of Him who is the *logos*, the reason, and the reasonable ground of all being, all things, and all mankind'.[12]

In article 7 of *Dei verbum* an attempt is made to mediate between the Suárezian and more classically Thomist positions. The Second Person of the Trinity is described as both 'promulgating' and 'fulfilling' the Gospel. Here Ratzinger warmly endorses the use of the language of gift and communication to describe the preaching of the apostles. Proclamation is presented as part of the giving activity of God and this provides an essentially new starting point for the question of Tradition. He notes that 'if the origin of tradition is not a promulgated law, but communication in the gift of God's plenitude, then the idea of "passing on" must mean something quite different from before'.[13] Whereas at the Council of Trent the idea of handing down the Tradition is seen as beginning with the preaching of Christ and that of his apostles, at Vatican II the notion of handing down is broadened to living with Christ and seeing what Christ did:

A comprehensive view of Revelation, precisely because it is concerned with the whole man, is founded not only in the word that Christ preached, but in the whole of the living experience of his person, thus embracing what is said and what is unsaid, what the Apostles in their turn are not able to express fully in words, but which is found in the whole reality of the Christian existence of which they speak, far transcending the framework of what has been explicitly formulated in words. And finally, the guidance of the Paraclete promised to the disciples is not a '*dictatio*' [dictation] but '*suggestio*' [suggestion], the remembering and understanding of the unspoken in what was once spoken, which reaches down to the depth of a process that cannot be measured by the terms '*praedicatio oralis*', and the transmission of which cannot therefore be merely a process of the handing down of words.[14]

Ratzinger also observes that whereas Trent had used the idea of Tradition only in the plural—as traditions—Vatican II, except for one quotation from Scripture (2 Thess. 2: 15), uses it only in the singular as Tradition. He suggests that this makes clear a significant difference in the two positions, never consciously realized by the Fathers and their *periti* at the Second Vatican Council. Whereas at Trent the question of tradition was associated with the Protestant assault on existing ceremonial and institutional practices of the Church, at Vatican II the problem which prompted the treatment of Revelation in *Dei verbum* was the Modernist quest for historical justification for each dogmatic principle, each statement to be found in the catechism.[15]

What Ratzinger does not notice, however, at least in his 1969 commentary, is that it was precisely what he called 'the concrete phenomenon, the actually existing traditions', which became the subject of a cultural revolution after the Council. For a complex array of reasons Vatican II did come to be interpreted by many parish priests and people in the pews as a call to overhaul completely the actually existing traditions in the name of *aggiornamento*. It is now a commonplace observation that no guidelines, no theology of culture, was offered by the Council for doing this.

While on the one hand Vatican II broadened the notion of Tradition when studied in the context of its relationship to Scripture to include actually existing practices, on the other hand it offered no analysis of how these lower-case 't' traditions or practices might be transposed into new cultural registers. This was notwithstanding the fact that for many Catholics the jettisoning of these traditions was seen to be at the very centre of the Council's agenda. John XXIII had opened the Council by calling for a distinction to be made between doctrine which does not change and the manner of its presentation which can change and, by implication, ought to be changed, in order to meet the pastoral needs of so-called 'modern man'. One very interesting question raised by Ratzinger's analysis of *Dei verbum* is therefore the degree to which its understanding of the role of Tradition in the transmission of the faith was in tension with presumptions made by John XXIII about the relationship between doctrinal propositions, and the linguistic cultures in which they have been embedded, and the liturgical and social practices which have arisen in their wake.

While Ratzinger sees the broadened notion of Tradition as an advance, and one that bears the influence of the Tübingen school of theology, he is concerned that Catholic scholars should not make the same errors as many of the Romantics (French and English as well as German) in holding that tradition(s) are always good per se. They need to be received and practised critically. Here he endorses the view of Albert Cardinal Meyer of Chicago expressed in a speech to the Council on 30 September 1964 to the effect that not everything that exists in the Church must for that reason be a legitimate tradition. There may be distorting traditions requiring purification.

Ratzinger laments that Cardinal Meyer's concerns were never addressed at Vatican II and that neither Trent nor Vatican II offered a positive account of the criticism of Tradition. Trent merely suggested that only traditions which had been received by the whole Church or were of apostolic provenance were important for faith, while Vatican II more or less ignored the whole question of the criticism of tradition altogether and by so doing missed an important opportunity for ecumenical dialogue.[16] Here one may add that not only did the Council miss an ecumenical opportunity, it missed an opportunity to consider the question of how one can follow the call of John XXIII to transpose the faith into new idioms and practices without actually risking a loss of faith through transmission failure. Ironically, the Council did not consider the very theme which was so central to John XXIII's vision. If one is purifying and transposing a Tradition one needs some criteria by which so to do. At best all that Vatican II achieved in this context was the dismissal of the idea of Tradition in the thought of Vincent de Lérins (Lérins was a fifth-century monastery near Cannes, on the French Riviera). De Lérins held that faith is based on the authority of divine law, which must be interpreted in the light of the tradition of the Church, and that the only reliable standard for orthodoxy was what has been believed in the Church everywhere, always, and by all.[17] According to Ratzinger, 'he [de Lérins] no longer appears as an authentic representative of the Catholic idea of tradition, but outlines a canon of tradition based on a semi-Pelagian idea'.[18] Presumably here Ratzinger is disturbed by an account of faith linked to a notion of law and Tradition without any reference to Scripture.

While neither Trent nor Vatican II provided an adequate account of how a Tradition is developed and purified and the principles to be applied when encountering rival traditions and plundering their spoils, this theological problem continues to dog the Church's pastors. In his 1982 work *Theologische Prinzipienlehre* Ratzinger spoke of the need for a 'kind of spacesuit' the faithful could wear in order to sustain the cosmic tempo with which they are fleeing faster and faster from the gravitational pull of Tradition and, further, for 'ground controls' which could prevent 'our burning out in the vast expanse of the universe, our bursting asunder like a homunculus of technology'.[19] Ratzinger notes that, in modern times, Tradition has come to be regarded as binding a person to the past and thwarting any orientation to the future. Since the Enlightenment's 'discovery' of critical rationality, Tradition is seen as an unwarranted assumption of authority from pure rationality alone. To the concept of Tradition as the basis of a person's humanity there is now opposed the concept of an emancipated rationality that is hostile to Tradition.[20] Using a metaphor that may resonate with many in New Labour Britain he says that the structure of the general intellectual situation has been fundamentally altered: '*techne* (technical reason) is no longer banished to the "House of Commons" of learning, or, to be more accurate, there, too, the "House of Commons" has become the decisive element in the constitution; in comparison with which the "House of Lords" now seems only a collection of aristocratic pensioners.'[21] *Techne* has become the real potential and obligation of man. *Traditio* has been demoted. What was previously at the bottom is now on top.

In this context, Ratzinger's concern that Tradition has been outflanked by technical rationality is in part derived from the principle found in A. Rüstow's essay '*Kulturtradition und Kulturkritik*' which was also adopted by Josef Pieper (1904–1997) in his *Über den Begriff der Tradition* that the quality of humanity which is lacking in animals is *not* intellect, which is in some sense shared by humans and animals, but Tradition, the possibility of passing on to others the product of the intellect and thus augmenting and enriching it as it is preserved from generation to generation.[22] Ratzinger concludes that 'tradition is the precondition for our humanity, and whoever destroys tradition, destroys *humanitas*—he is like a traveler in space who himself destroys the possibility of ground control, of contact with earth'.[23] Given this constitutional crisis in the order of being, and the 'full-fledged space flight of the spirit', Ratzinger emphasizes that the Church must be, as it were, 'something of a "ground control", the seat of tradition, even though she is, properly and under other circumstances, the heavenly terminal that draws man from the closed world of his traditions and teaches him to be self-critical'.[24] He further describes as 'absurd' the projects of those who 'seek to destroy the bearer of tradition as such, to undertake an ecclesiastical spaceflight with no ground station, to attempt to produce a new and purer Christianity in the test tube of the mere intellect'.[25] He concludes that 'a Church which is nothing but a manager is nothing at all; she is no longer tradition, and, as an intellect that knows no tradition, she becomes pure nothingness, a monster of meaninglessness'.[26]

In addition to those who attack the whole notion of Tradition there are those who to some degree accept it but who do not allow it to develop organically. They want to cut off its validity at some particular point. Here he speaks of the problem of liberal and conservative archeologisms. For the liberals it is often a case of no longer being satisfied with limiting Tradition to what can be dredged out of the Scriptures. They regard with suspicion everything that comes after St Paul.[27] For traditionalists the cut-off is often the papacy of Pius X (1905–1914), or even the Council of Trent (1545–1563).

Against the full frontal assault on tradition from eighteenth-century philosophy and the additional complications created by liberal and conservative archeologisms, Ratzinger suggests that Scripture is the criterion for the indispensable criticism of tradition: 'Jesus wants us to know tradition from the perspective of the Father, and to know the Father from the perspective of tradition.'[28] In this context he has opposed the projects of those who lobby for the Scriptures to be rewritten in line with contemporary themes in class and gender politics. He argues that we have no right to reconstruct the Scriptures which have been consigned to us: 'we are not authorized to change the Our Father into an Our Mother: the symbolism employed by Jesus is irreversible; it is based on the same Man–God relationship that he came to reveal to us.'[29] Here he strongly endorses the position of *Dei verbum* (10) that Sacred Scripture and Tradition form one sacred deposit of the word of God, committed to the Church. With reference to the principles to be employed when studying Scripture the Pontifical Biblical Commission under the chairmanship of Ratzinger has produced two significant documents: 'The Interpretation of the Bible in the Church' (1994) and 'The Jewish People and their Sacred Scriptures in the Christian Bible' (2001). These build on the principles set out in *Dei verbum*, as well as the encyclical *Providentissimus Deus* of Leo XIII and *Divino afflante Spiritu* of Pius XII. *Providentissimus Deus* sought to defend Catholic interpretations from the attacks of rationalists and to this end encouraged Catholic scholars to acquire genuine scientific expertise, especially by studying the languages of the ancient East. *Divino afflante Spiritu*, however, was concerned to defend Catholic interpretations from attacks that opposed the use of science and that wanted to impose a non-scientific, so-called 'spiritual', interpretation of sacred scripture.[30] Here Pius XII argued that there exists a close relationship between both the scientific and spiritual approaches. This was affirmed in *Dei verbum*. The scientific 'historical–critical' method has its place but is not sufficient on its own.

None the less, in the post-conciliar era, the scientific 'historical–critical' method continued to be the subject of criticism, especially as it was presented in the theories of Martin Dibelius (1883–1947) and Rudolf Bultmann (1884–1976). Bultmann combined form-critical studies with a biblical hermeneutic inspired by the existentialist philosophy of Martin Heidegger, and his theory of knowledge was influenced by the neo-Kantianism of the Marburg School.[31] Ratzinger has been critical of the method of Bultmann but not entirely opposed to it. It at least has the virtue of 'allowing the polyphony of history to be heard again, rising from behind the monotone of traditional interpretations'.[32] The major problem with it is that faith is not a necessary component of the method. This is another area where Ratzinger finds fault with a 'pure reason' approach. He notes that the real philosophical presupposition of the whole system lies in the Kantian judgement that the voice of being-in-itself cannot be heard by human beings, and as a consequence there lies in modern exegesis a reduction of history into philosophy, or a revision of history by means of philosophy.[33] He believes that the whole area is so complex that it will take the 'attentive and critical commitment of an entire generation' to bring about a genuine renewal in the field of exegesis, and that 'the form of this renewal can neither be a retreat to the medieval or patristic frameworks alone, nor some other framework founded on the principle that the history of thought seriously began only with Kant'.[34] As components of this renewal, exegesis must no longer be studied in a unilinear, synchronic fashion, as in the case with scientific findings which do not depend upon their history, but must recognize itself as a historical discipline, and, while philological and scientific literary methods will remain critically important, an understanding of the philosophical implications of the interpretative process itself will be required.[35] In all of this exegetes must realize that they 'do not stand in some neutral area, above or outside the history of the Church; rather the faith of the Church is a form of *sympathia* without which the Bible remains a closed book'.[36] Here there are strong resonances with the work of Alasdair MacIntyre on the relationships between reason and Tradition, in particular the way in which Traditions prescribe their own hermeneutical frameworks in which reason can operate. MacIntyre argues that the genius of Plato's Academy and the medieval universities and mendicant orders was that they provided a culture which facilitated the transmission of the Tradition in their institutional relationships and practices. Plato had the culture of the Academy, Augustine the episcopacy, and Aquinas the Dominican Order. Further, each of these institutional cultures embodied four principles:

1. a conception of truth beyond and ordering all particular truths;
2. a conception of a range of senses in the light of which utterances to be judged true or false and so placed within that ordering are to be construed;
3. a conception of a range of genres of utterance, dramatic, lyrical, historical, and the like, by reference to which utterances may be classified so that we may then proceed to identify their true senses; and
4. a contrast between those uses of genres in which one way or another truth is at stake and those governed only by standards of rhetorical effectiveness.[37]

The International Theological Commission under the direction of Ratzinger in a statement entitled 'Memory and Reconciliation: The Church and the Faults of the Past', encapsulated much of the above four principles in the following statement: 'Bringing to light the communality between interpreter and the object of interpretation requires taking into account the questions that motivate the research and their effect on the answers that are found, the living context in which the work is undertaken, and the interpreting community whose language is spoken and to whom one intends to speak.'[38] For Ratzinger, 'faith is itself a hermeneutic, a space for understanding, which does not do dogmatic violence to the Bible, but allows the possibility for the Bible to be itself'.[39]

Here again Ratzinger's position is consistent with the treatment of Scripture in *Dei verbum*. He describes *Dei verbum* in this context as 'providing a synthesis between the lasting insights of patristic theology and the new methodological understanding of the moderns'.[40] While the document endorses the application of historical–critical methods it does so with several caveats: the Scriptures must be read and interpreted with its divine authorship in mind, and with reference to the unity of the whole of Scripture, taking into account the Tradition of the entire Church and the analogy of faith. Further, for a Christian, faith, reason, and Tradition do not work in a vacuum but are guided and in a sense guarded by the Holy Spirit, who is described in *Dei verbum* as the teacher of the 'spouse of the incarnate Word'. These themes have been reiterated by Benedict XVI in his *Jesus of Nazareth*, the Foreword to which contains a criticism of the alleged dichotomy between the Jesus of history and the Jesus of faith. Speaking of the reconstructions of the Jesus of history he writes that if one reads a number of these one after the other one sees at once that 'far from uncovering an icon that has become obscured over time, they are more like photographs of their authors and the ideals they hold'.[41]

In many of his works Ratzinger therefore emphasizes the cognitive importance of Christian practices, and the link between spiritual insight and membership of a specific community with its own culture. His general catechetical principle is that the way of knowledge that leads to God and to Christ is a way of living. In order to know Christ it is necessary to follow him. In this his position is very Augustinian (the practice of the faith leads to understanding) and here again it echoes much that has been written about the relationship between traditions and practices by MacIntyre. Where MacIntyre links virtue to practices and practices to knowledge of a Tradition, Ratzinger links the theological virtues to Christian practices and Christian practices to participation in the life of the Trinity. In practice this means that he is quite critical of approaches to evangelization which take the form of reducing the faith to the smallest possible number of theoretical propositions, or what he calls 'marketable short-formulas'. He says that anyone who would construct Christianity from formulas is on the wrong track. Nothing living comes into existence this way. So-called 'renewal programmes' in parishes and dioceses, which take the form of marketing fresh insights to small groups, often under the banner of buzzwords and posters reminiscent of the kind which promoted five-year plans in Communist countries, are typical examples of these 'wrong tracks'. Theoretically these find their impetus in an article published by Karl Rahner in 1967.[42] In *Principles of Catholic Theology* Ratzinger summarized the characteristics of the 'short formulas' recommended by Rahner:

1. They must be intelligible to their hearers.
2. They must be capable of being immediately assimilated by those for whom they are intended.
3. Given the pluralism of intellectual trends in contemporary society, there must be a large number of such formulas because of the many different mentalities to be addressed.
4. The need for brevity arises from the fact that the contemporary individual is a 'very busy' person.
5. Given the rapid fluctuation of intellectual outlooks that characterize the modern age, it must be expected that the short formulas will themselves be short lived; in other words, pluralism is to be understood as not only synchronous but also diachronous.

For purposes of classification:

1. the short formulas are compared to advertising slogans, or also to party programmes and manifestos;
2. their relationship to the classic *symbola* remains unclear, although there are many indications that they are intended to substitute for them. At times, however, they seem to be merely explanations of the ancient *symbola*, which continue to exist alongside them.[43]

Ratzinger is somewhat passionate in his critique of these principles. His analysis of how contrary they are to authentic catechesis runs for several pages in *Principles of Catholic Theology*. He notes that no one has ever used the formulas of the faith in the Old and New Testaments for purposes of 'advertising': 'the slogan, a borrowing from the *instrumentarium* of consumer economics, explains nothing where there is a question of transmitting the faith.'[44] The catechumenate is not merely a process of intellectual instruction, but a conversion requiring prayer.

He suggests that we can assume that a conversion to Christianity is 'not likely to consist in a request for a program but rather a favourable attitude fostered by personal relationships with Christians'.[45] According to his more classical understanding of Revelation, Revelation is fully present only when, in addition to the material statements which testify to it, its own inner reality is itself operative in the form of faith. Thus, 'it is only to one who has entered into the community of faith with all of its practices that the word of faith reveals itself'.[46] From these principles Ratzinger concludes that our urgent need is for a reconstruction of the existential context of catechumenal training in the faith.

In this work of catechesis and the reception of Revelation, all faculties of the soul have a role to play. Within the Augustinian–Bonaventurian tradition these faculties are listed as the memory, the intellect, and the will. In *De Trinitate* Augustine used the terms *memoria*, *intellectus*, and *voluntas* (memory, intellect, and will) and St Bonaventure tied these faculties to the processions of the Trinity: 'the generating Mind, the Word and Love are in the soul as memory, understanding and will, which are consubstantial, coequal and coeval and interpenetrate each other.'[47] Ratzinger is alert to the importance of each of these faculties in their work of receiving and handing on faith. Noting that St Augustine interpreted the Father as *memoria*, Ratzinger describes God as 'memory per se', and an 'all-embracing being, in whom, being is embraced as time'.[48] He thinks it important to study the biblical basis of a Christian doctrine of *memoria* and that St John's Gospel is a fruitful starting point: 'the fact that remembrance in the Spirit is the sit[e] of the growth and identity of the faith seems to me to be actually the basic formula of the Johannine interpretation of faith in contradistinction to *gnosis*.'[49] Christian faith, by its very nature, includes the act of remembering, and the seat of all faith is the *memoria Ecclesiae*, the memory of the Church, the Church as memory.[50] In *Principles of Catholic Theology* Ratzinger presents the relationship between memory, history, and tradition in the following passage:

Humanity and historicity, intellect and history, are inextricably related. The human spirit creates history; history conditions human existence ... it is as memory that intellect proves itself *qua* intellect; memory generates tradition; tradition realizes itself in history ... for without the necessarily trans-temporal relationship of person to person, humanity cannot be awakened to itself, cannot express itself ... The most distinctive characteristic of tradition is, in fact, the ability to recognise my now as significant also for the tomorrow of those who come after me, and therefore, to transmit to them for tomorrow what has been discovered today. On the other hand, a capacity for tradition means preserving today what was discovered yesterday, in that way forming the context of a way through time, shaping history. This means that tradition properly understood is, in effect, the transcendence of today in both directions... Tradition, as *constitutivum* of history, is constitutive of a humanity that is truly human, of the *humanitas hominis*.[51]

Ratzinger makes a further point that tradition requires a subject in whom to adhere, a bearer, whom it finds (not only, but basically) in a linguistic community. The matter of tradition therefore relates to both history and community and 'it is possible only because many subjects become, as it were *one* subject in the context of a common heritage'.[52] On the contrary, much of the above 'short-formulas' approach to catechesis is predicated on the belief that the subject of catechesis is the isolated and even alienated individual of modernity for whom the idioms and symbols of Christianity are no longer a part of her memory. Ratzinger's belief that a knowledge of the language and symbols of the Christian tradition is a necessary component of catechesis, and that this itself is best received by being immersed in a Christian community and sharing in its practices, is another position shared by philosophers of tradition such as MacIntyre, and also by linguistic philosophers who follow the 'expressivist' theory of language. According to this theory (also associated with the Sapir–Whorf hypothesis), concepts are never transmitted in a cultural vacuum but presuppose a particular communal and cultural context.[53] The alternative school of linguistic philosophy, known as the instrumentalist school, tends not to regard culture as a significant medium for the transmission of meaning. In this context it is significant that Cardinal George of Chicago believes that John XXIII's presumption about the easy transposition of doctrines into contemporary idioms was based on an instrumentalist view, regarding language as the means whereby a speaker gives expression to thoughts which exist independently of language.[54] Fergus Kerr also believes that Karl Rahner subscribed to the more instrumentalist position: 'Rahner's natural assumption—that communication comes after language, and language comes after having concepts—is precisely what the Cartesian tradition has reinforced.'[55] This is thus another case which illustrates the difference between the Rahnerian and *Ressourcement* trajectories. Not only does Rahner's account of nature and grace have a tendency to naturalize the supernatural but his approach to linguistics has a similar tendency to place little value on the medium of a Christian culture.

None the less, while Ratzinger regards an immersion in the ordinary life of a Christian community as a normal part of catechesis, he also believes that the faculty of the intellect is an important tool for making judgements about the merits of one's community, be it Christian or otherwise. Assuming that the memory has done its work in giving a person an understanding of the constituent elements of one's Tradition, the intellect, and in particular the intellect in the form of critical reason, can then be brought in to discern the value of this Tradition. Ratzinger frequently reminds academic audiences that the Church fathers found the 'seeds of the Word, not in the religions of the world, but rather in philosophy, that is, in the process of critical reason directed against the [pagan] religions'.[56] He notes that the habit of thinking about Christianity as a 'religion' among many religions, all of roughly the same intellectual merit, is a modern development. At its very origins Christianity sides with reason and considers this ally to be its principal forerunner.[57] Moreover:

Ultimately it [a decision to believe in God] is a decision in favor of reason and a decision about whether good and evil, truth and untruth, are merely subjective categories or reality. In this sense, in the beginning there is faith, but a faith that first acknowledges the dignity and scope of reason. The decision for God is simultaneously an intellectual and an existential decision—each determines the other reciprocally.[58]

Ratzinger therefore does not follow the trend of thinking of Athens and Jerusalem as short-hand terms for two fundamentally different ways of approaching religious matters: one fideistic and one philosophical. The great University of Chicago philosophy professor Leo Strauss (1889–1973) popularized this dichotomy to such a degree that now two generations later there are almost as many subcategories of Straussians as there are Thomists, according to which side of this apparently unbridgeable divide they find themselves most at home. However, Ratzinger's approach is to argue that there are quite amazing parallels in chronology and content between the philosopher's criticism of the myths in Greece and the prophets' criticism of the gods in Israel. While he concedes that the two movements start from completely different assumptions and have completely different aims, he none the less concludes:

the movement of the *logos* against the myth, as it evolved in the Greek mind in the philosophical enlightenment, so that in the end it necessarily led to the fall of the gods, has an inner parallelism with the enlightenment that the prophetic and Wisdom literature cultivated in its demythologization of the divine powers in favour of the one and only God.[59]

Ratzinger observes that, for all the differences between them, both movements coincide in their striving towards the *logos*.[60] In Christianity philosophical enlightenment has become part of religion and is no longer its opponent.[61] Christian existence means life in conformity to the *logos*; that is why Christians are the true philosophers and why Christianity is the true philosophy.[62] The paradox of ancient philosophy consists in the fact that intellectually it destroyed myth but simultaneously tried to legitimize it afresh as religion. It treated religion as a question of the regulation of life, not as a question of truth; however, Tertullian put the Christian position when he said that Christ called himself truth, not custom.[63]

Fundamentally, Ratzinger suggests that the question is whether reason, or rationality, stands at the beginning of all things and is grounded in the basis of all things or not? In response to this question he believes that the answer is Yes, the Christian faith does represent a choice in favour of the priority of reason and of rationality. He also argues that this ultimate question cannot be decided by arguments from natural science, and 'even philosophical thought reaches its limits here'.[64] In a statement which would upset some Neo-Scholastic sensitivities he says, 'in that sense [the sense of scientific rationality], there is no ultimate [empirical] demonstration that the basic choice involved in Christianity is correct'.[65] None the less, he also rhetorically asks whether reason can really renounce the claim that the *logos* is at the ultimate origin of things, without abolishing itself.[66]

Again, in a manner that is reminiscent of MacIntyre, the logic of Ratzinger's position is that the choice is between Christianity and nihilism. Both have their own internal logic. Both have their own God or gods and their own myths. The Christian God takes the form of absolute love, whereas the alternative gods are violent or selfish or both. What Ratzinger calls the 'evolutionary ethos' of those who would deny that the human person is made in the image and likeness of God is not only wrong but cruel. It has nothing to offer the weak and suffering. Contrary to the ethos of social Darwinism, Ratzinger holds that the ethos of Christianity must consist in love and reason converging with one another as the essential foundation pillars of reality: 'In the conception of early Christianity the primacy of the *Logos* and the primacy of love were revealed to be one and the same. The *Logos* was revealed to be not only the mathematical reasoning at the basis of all things, but as creative love to the point of becoming com-passion, co-suffering with creation.'[67] It is precisely here that the third faculty of the soul becomes effective, as it is for the will or, more biblically, the heart to make the choice for self-sacrificial love or against it. This is the Augustinian point about two cities being founded on two loves. The choice of myth is intimately connected to what and how a person loves.

Bringing all these strands together is a complex operation for they relate the territories of anthropology (the work of the memory, the intellect, and the will), ecclesiology (a view of the Church's magisterium as authoritative and a view of the Church as the community wherein the faith is first experienced and taught), scriptural exegesis (the critique of the 'historical–critical' method), Tradition (the criticisms of Trent and Vatican II and adoption of elements of the theology of the Tübingen school), and Revelation (the reversal of Suárez in favour of a more classically Thomist position). It is the last of these, the territory of Revelation, which has generated the greatest amount of criticism of Ratzinger from Catholic traditionalist quarters and there is a certain tragic irony in this, in that his treatment of Tradition when placed beside his account of Revelation actually gives some intellectual legitimacy to many post-conciliar traditionalist grievances. He does understand that a Catholic culture is an important medium for the transmission of the Catholic faith. He is not in favour of treating 1965 as a cultural year zero in the life of the Church. He effectively provides a defence of the reasonable traditionalist camp against the charge of its being in the eternal grip of old world nostalgia. However, all of this comes with his caveat that traditions do need constant purification and the space for an organic development. His is a position which favours an understanding of tradition as a medium for the transmission of Revelation while, paradoxically, though in some sense more liberal, Rahner's theology is much closer in effect to the propositional character of Suárez and to the whole post-Tridentine approach. Rahner's concern is really that the propositions need to be represented in accord with the demands of contemporary critical consciousness. The vulgarized end of this are trendy 'short formulas' which make laity who have been properly catechized cringe with embarrassment.

Perhaps because almost failing a *Habilitationsschrift* over an allegation of heresy is not something one would easily forget, Ratzinger has written somewhat apologetically:

It's not that Vatican II was endorsing a modernistic evolutionism, but the Vatican II orientation simply expresses our deeper knowledge of the problem of historical understanding, which is no longer adequately expressed by the simple ideas of a given fact and its explanation, because the explanation, as the process of understanding, cannot be clearly separated from what is being understood. This interdependence of the two . . . does not remove the ultimate basic difference between assimilation and what is assimilated, even if they can no longer be strictly isolated . . . [68]

In number 66 of the *Catechism of the Catholic Church* (1992), the *Dei verbum* theology is summarized in the statement that 'even if Revelation is already complete, it has not been made completely explicit; it remains for Christian faith gradually to grasp its full significance over the course of the centuries'. Newman, Daniélou, de Lubac, Ratzinger, and (coming from a different direction) Rahner ultimately won the day. As Gerard O'Shea has argued:

The merits of the Revelation as history approach is that it places the emphasis on the individual's relationship with God and picks up Biblical themes which tend to be understated in the [Suárezian] propositional model. Instead of claiming that the words of Scriptures contain direct doctrinal propositions, it places the focus on the total pattern of salvation history. In so doing, it opens up the Scriptures for personal reflection, and the possibility of personal encounter with the real source of Revelation, the Word of God himself— Jesus Christ.[69]

4

Beyond Moralism: God is Love

In a series of sermons preached at the Cathedral of Münster to members of the student chaplaincy in 1964 Ratzinger posed the question: 'What actually is the real substance of Christianity that goes beyond mere moralism?'[1] The term moralism generally refers to the Kantian rationalist tendency to reduce Christianity to the dimensions of an ethical framework, or to equate faith with obeying a law. Lorenzo Albacete has described it as a modern form of Pelagianism, a belief in salvation through good works and obedience which he suggests can only be overcome by a 'proper theology of grace in which grace is not presented as something added to and external to the natural law itself [as some Neo-Scholastics would have it], but rather as the possibility of a personal encounter with Jesus Christ'.[2] In such a theology of grace 'it is not life according to the natural law or to ethics that saves and fulfils us: more radically, it involves a relationship of Communion with the Person of Jesus Christ'.[3] This is essentially the response which the young Ratzinger gave to his own question in the third of his Münster sermons. Ratzinger proposed that the antidote to moralism is the theology of the First Letter of St John: God is love, and he who abides in love abides in God and God abides in him. A theology focused on divine love was his solution. Forty-two years later, as a newly elected pope, he published the encyclical *Deus Caritas Est*, the first paragraph of which announces that being Christian is not the result of an ethical choice or a lofty idea but the encounter with an event, a person, who gives life a new horizon and a decisive direction. The *Dei verbum* understanding of Revelation is reiterated here and added to it is a critique of moralism which builds on themes in von Balthasar's *Love Alone is Credible*.[4] It also resonates with the works of Luigi Giussani (1922–2005) who founded the Italian ecclesial movement *Communione e liberazione* in 1969 in the wake of the outbreak of enthusiasm for Marxism among Italian students and intellectuals. The movement has since produced many significant Italian politicians, journalists, and scholars, the most notable being Rocco Buttiglione (1948–), an Italian Christian Democrat politician and professor of political science. In his funeral eulogy for Giussani, Ratzinger praised him for understanding that 'Christianity is not an intellectual system, a collection of dogmas, or a moralism. Christianity is instead an encounter, a love story; it is an event.'[5] This, in a nutshell, is the message of *Deus Caritas Est*.

According to Ratzinger, von Balthasar, and others in the *Communio* school, the practice of the faith in the pre-conciliar era was hampered by moralism. They take the view that the problems which arose in the post-conciliar era were not simply the result of a spreading infection of the 1960s secular liberal virus but were more fundamentally the logical outgrowth of a centuries-long process separating the true and the beautiful from the good. Von Balthasar used the Greek word 'perichoresis' for a type of circular dance to describe the Trinitarian relationships which ideally should exist among these three properties (truth, beauty, and goodness), described in philosophical parlance as transcendentals. It was one of his key arguments that at least since the time of the Reformation the relationships among the three have been systematically severed. Differently defective accounts of human dignity, moral behaviour, and spiritualities have followed according to which transcendental is left standing when the others drop out. We can end up with immoral aesthetes at one end of the spectrum, and unattractive and iconoclastic puritans at the other, as well as people who get 'hooked' on dogma but who are none the less not very charitable to their neighbours, and people who are kind hearted but ignorant of the truth, together with numerous other permutations and combinations depending on which transcendental or combination of transcendentals is lacking. In any event, when this disjuncture occurs the transcendental of unity is lacking. In the absence of a Christian culture in which the relationship of the transcendentals to one another is clearly visible and culturally embodied, the temptation to moralism is strong.

In von Balthasar's account of the destruction of the *perichoresis* of the transcendentals particular emphasis is placed on the problems inherent within the Neo-Scholasticism of the Counter-Reformation, typified by the separation between theoretical and affective theology: 'While the theoretical theology of the baroque era proceeded from a fixed "teaching of the Church" as object [the Suárezan insistence on doctrinal propositions] and therefore missed the spiritual, existential dimension which runs through everything biblical; the affective theology of the baroque missed the biblical center and proceeded mystically instead of eschatologically.'⁶ According to this reading the problems faced by the Church in the 1960s and subsequent decades were caused as much by tendencies in post-Aquinas scholasticism as they were by the neo-Dionysian sex, drugs, and rock 'n' roll pop culture which arose in the 1960s. Catholic culture was unable to withstand the onslaught of the neo-Dionysians because of an insufficient integration of spirituality and dogma. Consistent with this reading is Peter Henrici's judgement that a specifically modern Catholic theology existed *between* Trent and Vatican II. It did not suddenly arise at Vatican II. In significant elements of post-Tridentine Catholic culture, the practice of Christian life consisted largely of duties that were performed because one was obliged to do so: 'moved by a kind of Christian Pharisaism, Christian existence had become viewed as a meritorious achievement that God commands and by virtue of which one is able to please him.'⁷ In short, the very Protestant Kant had become 'a secret father of the Church'.⁸

The Kantian emphasis upon duty and the notion of the moral as that which is done out of a sense of obligation rather than for the satisfaction of any affection, or even in accordance with any tradition, shares a logical affinity with Jansenism, a quasi-Calvinist heresy which infected the Church in France, Ireland, and countries of the New World where Irish missionaries (who had themselves been infected by the influx of Jansenist clergy from France in the eighteenth century) were deployed.⁹ The two movements (Jansenism and Kantianism) arose in different centuries and in different intellectual cultures, and although Kantian ethics is based on an exaltation of the faculty of reason, and it appears to be the dialectical opposite of Jansenism with its intensely pessimistic outlook for the capacities of fallen human nature, the two movements share the property of making obedience to a legislator (even if in Kant's case the legislator is reason itself) the driving force behind moral action. They also share the dialectical affinity for fostering a humanism without a religion (the project of Kant), and a religion without a humanism (the effect of Jansenius).¹⁰

In his various essays Ratzinger has shown that he both understands and is disturbed by the spiritual pathologies which Kantian and Jansenist tendencies have generated among the faithful. After the Council, when a majority of avant-garde theologians seemed to believe that there are no moral absolutes, the hitherto sharp focus on right moral conduct tended to blur. The point which Ratzinger and von Balthasar made was that there could not have been such an implosion of Catholic moral practices within such a short frame of time unless there was something deeply flawed about the motivations behind the pre-conciliar practices. They concluded that people in the pre-conciliar era had a tendency to live prescriptively, not because they believed that the moral injunctions were life-giving, not because they could see truth, goodness, and beauty in the practices themselves, but because of a fear of eternal damnation. Once the fear was eliminated the motivation holding up the practice dissipated. Referring to the parable of the workers in the vineyard (Matt. 20: 1–6), Ratzinger wrote: 'What a strange attitude it is that we no longer find Christian service worthwhile if the denarius of salvation may be obtained even without it!'[11] He added that 'becoming a Christian is not taking out an insurance policy, it is not the private booking of an entry ticket to heaven'.[12] Rather, 'in its simplest and innermost form, faith is nothing but reaching that point in love at which we recognize that we, too, need to be given something'.[13]

Ratzinger has also been acutely aware of the problems generated by Jansenism in the realm of sexuality. He has noted that towards the end of the nineteenth century French psychiatrists coined the phrase '*maladie catholique*' to describe a 'special neurosis that is the product of a warped pedagogy so exclusively concentrated on the Fourth and Sixth Commandments that the resultant complex with regard to authority and purity renders the individual incapable of free self-development'.[14] Such an experience of faith 'leads, not to freedom, but to rigidity and an absence of freedom'.[15] The *maladie* was not only fostered by prurient boarding school masters who traumatized teenagers with threats of eternal punishment for moments of impurity, but it was also fostered by the pre-conciliar marriage manuals which reduced the whole complex territory of sexuality to a calculus of marital dues and contractual obligations. Here Ratzinger has been strong in his criticism of the pre-conciliar manualist tradition for its 'decided rationalism' which marginalized sacred Scripture and Christology. It 'no longer allowed people to see the great message of liberation and freedom given to us in the encounter with Christ' but rather stressed above all the negative aspect of so many prohibitions, so many 'no's'.[16] While he acknowledges that these are present in Catholic ethics, he regrets that they were no longer presented for what they really are: the actualization of a great 'yes'.[17] Moreover, while biblical citations 'decorated' the discourse here and there the manuals placed an emphasis on natural-law-based casuistry whose appeal was limited to those with a positivist or legalistic mindset or those who were simply fearful of committing sin and looking for moral certitude.[18] The casuistry certainly provided guidelines and answers but not a deep understanding of the intrinsic beauty, truth, or goodness of the Christian moral life.

Notwithstanding the conciliar hope that 'a renewed moral theology would go beyond the natural law system in order to recover a deeper biblical inspiration', Ratzinger believes that it was precisely moral philosophy that ended by marginalizing sacred Scripture even more completely than the pre-conciliar manualist tradition. While Scripture was absent de facto in the manualist tradition, it was marginalized *de iure* in post-conciliar ethical traditions. It was claimed that Scripture offers only a horizon of intentions and motivations, but it does not enter into the moral contents of action. These contents are left properly to human rationality. Such a conception was then translated into the claim that 'ethics is purely rational, so that, in order to open itself to universal communicability and to enter into the common debate of humanity, ethics ought to be constructed solely on the basis of reason'.[19] Against these Kantian tendencies, Ratzinger holds that even the Ten Commandments are *not* to be interpreted first of all as law, but rather as a divine gift. They are not about precepts circumscribed within themselves. They are a dynamic that is open to an ever greater and deeper understanding. Moreover, Ratzinger stresses that Christians cannot prescind from the explicit theism of the first tablet of the Ten Commandments which begins: 'I am the Lord your God, you shall not have other gods before Me.' Christians 'cannot yield on this point: without God, all the rest would no longer have any logical coherence'.[20] As Ian Markham put it: 'You cannot assume a rationality and then argue that there is no foundation to that rationality. Either God and rationality go or God and rationality stay. Either Nietzsche or Aquinas, that is our choice.'[21] Ratzinger would no doubt quibble with equating the Christian option solely with Thomism, but he certainly shares the belief, so succinctly put by Markham, that natural law does not run, so to speak, without theological presuppositions. This point has been argued strongly by the Augustinian scholar Ernest Fortin

(1923–2002) and by classical Thomists like Russell Hittinger. In effect this means that a Catholic account of morality cannot ultimately be successfully defended at the Bar of eighteenth-century-style rationality, jurisdictional questions aside, because that tribunal is fundamentally flawed, as post-moderns agree. Positively, however, it does mean that in these post-modern times the battleground moves from the field of 'pure reason' and 'pure nature' to the theatre of the gods. It becomes your god against my God. Apollo and Dionysius face Christ. At least in many academies the rationalistic shadow-boxing is now passé, though it continues in courtrooms and government bureaucracies where the dominance of liberal political assumptions precludes any appeal to first principles.

The strongest assertion to be made from the side of Apollo and Dionysius is that they affirm life. They give their blessing to human creativity. They offer a vision of humanism which treats originality and individuality as goods. They take a liberal attitude to sexuality. In sharp contrast they claim that Christ opposed *eros* and fostered a religion in which the highest place goes to the celibate male priest who suppresses his sexuality and individuality and even sacrifices his own judgement and creativity to the orders of others in an ecclesial hierarchy with military standards of obedience and self-sacrifice.

It is to this charge that Benedict XVI addresses himself in the first part of *Deus Caritas Est*. Against Friedrich Nietzsche's claim that Christianity killed *eros* he declares that *eros* and *agape* are not two distinct realities: there is a symbiotic relationship between the two; one cannot function properly separated from the other.[22] In support of this reading Angelo Scola concludes that 'the fulfillment promised by amorous experience has nothing automatic or magic about it; it cannot be produced by ritual gestures or magic practices that avoid our having to commit our personal freedom', rather 'the erotic dimension of love, which does not ask my permission to happen, is fulfilled only in the agapic dimension of gratuitous self-giving'.[23] Unless *agape* fructifies *eros* it simply dies. Experiments with *eros* which deprive the person of his or her dignity, which commodify or otherwise dehumanize the person, which treat a person as a mere means to the achievement of some desire of another without any reciprocal self-giving, or which denigrate the body to the status of a mechanical object, cut short the ascent to the divine which is the work of *agape*. In these situations *eros* ultimately becomes sterile and boring.

Applying this theology one concludes that for Benedict XVI the sexual revolution of the 1960s should be opposed, not on the basis of archaic casuistry, not because sexuality is merely a means to the end of procreation, but rather because the underlying vision of the dignity and meaning of human sexuality offered by 1960s Freudians, Nietzscheans, and New Age sex therapists is really not truly erotic. It is not only destructive of human dignity and integrity but it takes the pathos out of the whole experience. It trivializes sex and undermines romance and courtly love because both romance and courtship presuppose spiritual chivalry. Being prepared for heroic self-sacrifice for the good of another is the very essence of chivalry and the very antithesis of the morality of Nietzsche's supermen or the feminist superwoman. Just as God and rationality either stay together or reason goes off on its own tangent and becomes violent, sexuality and romantic courtship either remain together or sexuality goes off on its own tangent and becomes banal and depressing. If, in the Nietzschean tradition, all experience is a good in itself, then Benedict XVI can respond that among other things the Nietzschean *sola erotica* stance operates so as to narrow the range of possible human experiences.

Benedict therefore tends to look on the post-sexual revolution generations with paternal pity, especially those who now belong to the second and even third generation for whom notions like romance, chivalry, courtship, and lifelong love and fidelity are often no longer a part of their memory and personal experience but are at best academic. Members of alphabetically described Generations X and Y often lack the sapiential experience of seeing *eros* and *agape* working together. For many the only advice they were given is that of how to avoid an unwanted pregnancy. Benedict believes that this situation is not only robbing youth of the chance of forming successful lifelong partnerships, but it is actually sapping the joy from this axiological moment of their life:

Thus today we often see in the faces of the young people a remarkable bitterness, a resignation that is far removed from the enthusiasm of youthful ventures into the unknown. The deepest root of this sorrow is the lack of any great hope and the unattainability of any great love: everything one can hope for is known, and all love becomes the disappointment of finiteness in a world whose monstrous surrogates are only a pitiful disguise for profound despair.[24]

In drawing together the roles of *eros* and *agape* into a symphonic harmony, and gutting the Catholic tradition of every last remnant of

Jansenism which no doubt made Nietzsche's claim that Christianity killed *eros* credible to a generation brought up on the idea that holy people become nuns and priests while the spiritually defective class get married, Benedict XVI has built on the theology of the body of John Paul II. In his *Love and Responsibility* and the series of Wednesday papal audiences which came to be labelled the theology of the body, John Paul II launched the first papal assault on the root causes of the *maladie catholique*. They were the first antidote to the Jansenist and Stoic treatment of sexuality and marital intimacy. They affirmed the intrinsic goodness of human sexuality and placed it within a whole Trinitarian framework encapsulated in the expression 'the nuptial mystery'. Jansenism was a self-inflicted wound in the life of the Church. Once it has been seen off the stage, the way lies open to commence a battle to reclaim *eros* which the Church, too beset with internal problems at the time, did not undertake in 1968.

While Paul VI at least anticipated many of the problems which would arise if the unitive and procreative dimensions of sexual intimacy were severed, and while Ratzinger agrees with him on this issue, Ratzinger none the less concedes that the theology behind *Humanae vitae* was 'relatively slim'.[25] Karol Wojtyla was also of the view that in the midst of the media furore which followed the promulgation of *Humanae vitae*, authors of various articles and publications spoke out on behalf of a misguided concept of natural law as biological regularity and they in turn 'imposed upon the Holy Father, and along with him upon the magisterium of the Catholic Church, an understanding of natural law that in no way corresponds to the Church's understanding of it'.[26] Wojtyla's 1969 essay 'The Teaching of the Encyclical *Humanae vitae* on Love' tried to undo some of the damage by placing the whole encyclical in a context of a theology of love which he later expanded during the early years of his pontificate.[27] Instead of using Stoic categories to analyse marriage and sexuality Wojtyla spoke of love as a gift of the self, of spousal love being the paradigmatic gift of the self, and of the Trinity as the archetype of such a gift.

Michael Waldstein, who has undertaken the definitive translation of John Paul II's theology of the body lectures, interprets them as an explicitly Trinitarian response to what he terms 'Kant's anti-trinitarian personalism'.[28] Whereas Kant's personalism glorifies the autonomy of the individual person as 'the only true value to which everything else must be subordinated', and whereas for Kant 'fatherhood is the worst despotism imaginable and sonship the worst slavery', within Wojtyla's personalism there is no glorification of autonomy and no opposition to the situation of dependency that exists in the normal father and son relationship. Instead human dignity is rooted in a Trinitarian paradigm. Persons can only be understood in a relationship of mutual self-giving. According to John Paul II, the ability to understand these things is undermined by the effects of Cartesian rationality. As Waldstein puts it, 'the claim is that the nature of sex has become invisible through our Cartesian glasses'.[29] John Paul II tried to remedy this blindness with his critique of Kantian autonomy and his insistence that the highest meaning of the human body and sexual intimacy is to be found in nothing less than the nuptial mystery of the Trinity. Here we find foreshadowed Benedict's argument that *eros* and *agape* belong together and that God's way of loving is the measure of human love.

In article 11 of *Deus Caritas Est* Benedict declares that 'marriage based on an exclusive and definitive love is the icon of the relationship between God and his people and vice versa' and that this close connection between *eros* and marriage in the Bible 'has practically no equivalent in extra-biblical literature'. It was not some hypothesis doing the rounds of all the tribes of the ancient Middle East but was something uniquely special about the revelation of the Old Testament, reaffirmed and elevated in the new dispensation.

Benedict's strategy is therefore not so much to prove that Christian ethics are more rational than the alternatives, but to exhort married Christians to demonstrate in culturally embodied practices that they are more true, good, and beautiful; as it were, more erotic:

[In classical times] Christians were able to demonstrate persuasively how empty and base were the entertainments of paganism, and how sublime the gift of faith in the God who suffers with us and leads us to the road of true greatness. Today it is a matter of the greatest urgency to show a Christian model of life that offers a liveable alternative to the increasingly vacuous entertainments of leisure-time society, a society forced to make increasing recourse to drugs because it is sated by the usual shabby pleasures.[30]

In short, Ratzinger thinks that Christians will be victorious here because 'the actual advance registered by the Christian idea of God over that of the ancient world lies in its recognition that God is love'.[31] No one else has a god who is so much for love. No other tradition begins with a baby in a stable whose birth is announced by a choir of angels and who receives gifts from kings and homage from shepherds while cattle keep Him warm with their breath. The example Ratzinger chooses to illustrate the principle is taken from the Council of Trent. At that time the Catholic practice of holding Corpus Christi processions was opposed by Protestants who had rejected the belief in the real presence of Christ in the Eucharist, preferring to regard the sacred host as a mere symbol. The response of the fathers at Trent was that processions 'must show forth the triumph of the truth in such a way that, in the face of such magnificence and such joy on the part of the whole Church, the enemies of the truth will either fade away or, stricken with shame, attain to insight'. Ratzinger suggests that if we remove the polemical element about enemies of the Church being stricken with shame, what we have left is this: 'the power in virtue of which truth carries the day can be none other *than its own joy*.' This is essentially his strategy for dealing with the sexual revolution of the 1960s. He wants it to be more obvious that there is actually nothing very romantic or liberating and ultimately really erotic about laissez-faire sex, while, conversely, those whose lives seek an integration of *eros* and *agape* paradoxically end up closer to achieving the Romantic ideal of a life narrative which is not only true and good but beautiful.

For this to happen, however, the Church has to get her own house in order and here Ratzinger observes that other strains of the Jansenist virus continue to weaken her constitution. In particular he speaks of the twin pathologies of bourgeois pelagianism and the pelagianism of the pious. He describes the *mentalité* of the bourgeois pelagian as follows: 'If God really does exist and if He does in fact bother about people He cannot be so fearfully demanding as He is described by the faith of the Church. Moreover, I am no worse than others: I do my duty, and the minor human weaknesses cannot really be as dangerous as all that.'[32] This attitude is a modern version of 'acedia'—a kind of anxious vertigo that overcomes people when they consider the heights to which their divine pedigree has called them. In Nietzschean terms it is the mentality of the herd, the attitude of someone who just cannot be bothered to be great. It is bourgeois because it is calculating and pragmatic and comfortable with what is common and ordinary, rather than aristocratic and erotic. Here Ratzinger is using the adjective 'bourgeois' to describe an attitude to life which sociologists like Werner Sombart (1863–1941) and Max Weber (1864–1920) have associated with the upwardly mobile entrepreneurial classes. It is a

technical sociological term and should not be construed as meaning
that to belong to any particular class is spiritually defective. Ratzinger
himself was from a lower middle-class family. Similarly, the use of
the word 'aristocratic' in this context means a personality type which
prefers the excellent over the serviceable. Here it does not mean 'born
with a title'. Both Sombart and Weber regarded Protestant cultures as
'bourgeois' and Catholic cultures as 'aristocratic' and 'erotic'. Weber
thought that this helped to explain why Protestant cultures were
wealthier. Catholics spent too much time either on their knees praying
or around a table feasting. Protestants were more sensible and pragmatic. Their rituals were less elaborate and time consuming, leaving
more time for work and making money.

Contrary to the bourgeois spirit Ratzinger argues that the Christian
is the person who does *not* calculate. A Christian with an authentic
spirituality does not ask 'How much farther can I go and still remain
within the realm of venial sin, stopping short of mortal sin?' Rather,
the Christian is the one who simply seeks what is good, without
any calculation.[33] In this one can hear an echo of the French writer
Georges Bernanos, well known as the author of *The Diary of a Country
Priest* and *The Dialogues of the Carmelites*. Bernanos remarked that
'the moment a person feels the need to consult the casuists in order
to know the amount starting from which stealing money may be
considered a mortal sin ... we may say that his social value is nil,
even if he abstains from stealing'.[34] In contrast one can find an example
of an erotic and aristocratic disposition in the prayer of St Ignatius of
Loyola:

> To give, and not to count the cost,
> to fight, and not to heed the wounds,
> to toil, and not to seek for rest,
> to labour, and not to ask for any reward
> save that of knowing that we do thy will.

The Pelagianism of the pious shares the property of not seeing any need
for repentance and forgiveness and it is also quite pragmatic, but it falls
into another Augustinian category of spiritual disorder, known as
presumption:

They [pious pelagians] want security, not hope. By means of a tough and
rigorous system of religious practices, by means of prayers and actions, they

want to create for themselves a right to blessedness. What they lack is the humility essential to any love—the humility to be able to receive what we are given over and above what we have deserved and achieved. The denial of hope in favor of security that we are faced with here rests on the inability to bear the tension of waiting for what is to come and to abandon oneself to God's goodness.[35]

The Pelagianism of the pious is also part of a broader cultural quest for self-sufficiency. Here Ratzinger speaks of a desire to get rid of all reliance on other people and their inner tension. Just as the Enlightenment sought to reduce religion to morality, he believes that a second reduction is taking place. Morality is being narrowed to the concept of human well-being.[36] The self-help, self-healing, and self-motivating strategies of the New Age Movement are but one prominent example of this reduction. Ratzinger believes that this is further evidence of a loss of belief in creation and without an understanding of human life as a divinely created gift the door is open for its commercialization. Here all Ratzinger can do is to reiterate the credal Christian position: 'We are not some casual and meaningless product of evolution. Each of us is the result of a thought of God. Each of us is willed; each of us is loved, each of us is necessary.'[37] His response to the whole raft of contemporary medical practices which treat the human person in some sense as a commodity is encapsulated in the following paragraph:

To fabricate man and make him a product of our chemical arts or any other technology is a fundamental attack on the dignity of man, who is no longer considered, no longer realized as an immediate creature of God and his immortal vocation . . . It is essential to respect the unique dignity of man, who is wanted and created immediately by God, through a new miracle of creation. [Through cloning] the human person becomes our product, a product of our art: thus his dignity as a human person is violated from the start.[38]

The loss of belief in creation and the related idea of there being an intelligent pattern in creation is also linked to the treatment of homosexuality within the Catholic tradition, which Ratzinger as prefect of the CDF upheld in a number of documents. Ratzinger believes that God inscribed 'instructions for use' objectively and indelibly in his creation and, consequently, 'nature, and with it precisely also man himself, so far as he is part of that created nature, contain that morality within themselves'.[39] For the Church 'the language of *nature* is also the language of *morality*'.[40] He regards homosexual practices as completely contrary to these 'instructions for use' inscribed by God indelibly in his creation:

The call for homosexual partnerships to receive a legal form that is more or less the equivalent of marriage ... departs from the entire moral history of mankind ... If this relationship [marriage] becomes increasingly detached from legal forms, while at the same time homosexual partnerships are increasingly viewed as equal in rank to marriage, we are on the verge of a dissolution of our concept of man, and the consequences can only be extremely grave.[41]

None the less, in this context he has always been careful to distinguish between the immorality of homosexual acts and the unjust discrimination against homosexual persons, between tolerance and affirmation, and between an unintended homosexual tendency and individual homosexual actions.[42] The most significant document here is entitled 'Some Considerations Concerning the Response to Legislative Proposals on the Non-discrimination of Homosexual Persons'. It includes the following propositions:

Although the particular inclination of the homosexual person is not a sin, it is a more or less strong tendency ordered toward an intrinsic moral evil; and thus the inclination itself must be seen as an objective disorder (n. 2) ... It is deplorable that homosexual persons have been and are the object of violent malice in speech and in action ... The intrinsic dignity of each person must always be respected in word, in action and law (n. 7) ... There are areas in which it is not unjust discrimination to take sexual orientation into account, for example, in the placement of children for adoption or foster care, in employment of teachers or athletic coaches, and in military recruitment (n. 11).

Apart from overseeing the promulgation of CDF documents Ratzinger has not devoted much attention to anthropological questions about the relationship between masculinity and femininity in the order of creation. This is more in the territory of the work of Angelo Scola, the leading Italian *Communio*-circle scholar who is now the patriarch of Venice. The following principles can be found in the works of Scola and have been brought together by David L. Schindler in an essay on Catholic theology and gender.[43] Given the general closeness of the thought of Scola to that of Benedict they may serve as guideposts to Benedict's likely general approach in this area:

1. The gender difference should be seen as a perfection.
2. While Aristotle anchored the meaning of feminine in 'matter' and in 'potency' rather than in 'act', and while Aquinas followed Aristotle on this point, Hans Urs von Balthasar and Adrienne von Speyr anchored the meaning already in 'act'.

3. This means that, for those who follow von Balthasar and von Speyer, femininity is a perfection, not a defect.

4. Men and women are both created in the image and likeness of the Trinitarian God, in and through Jesus Christ. What this means is that each images the whole of the Trinity but does so differently.

5. Men and women are not two halves destined to merge so as to regenerate a lost unity. The dual unity of the sexes does not signify the symmetrical reciprocity as Aristophanes supposed in Plato's *Symposium*.

6. Every form of chauvinism contradicts the creative design.[44]

The work of Scola seeks to link considerations of the nature of femininity and masculinity into the framework of Trinitarian theology. He has argued that a culture that does not accept the Revelation of the Trinitarian God ultimately renders itself incapable of understanding sexual difference in a positive sense. The Trinity is the model *par excellence* of a relationship of equality within difference. Scola believes that without a Trinitarian theism, or with a merely theistically coloured theism, the feminine sex usually ends up being perceived as defective. All of this is consistent with the general approach of *Deus Caritas Est*.

Ratzinger has also spoken of a kind of extreme denial of the importance and value of sexual difference at work within contemporary culture. He speaks of a technological rationalism that pushes the emotional side of human nature to the irrational periphery and allots a merely instrumental role to the body.[45] Against this he states that the body is not something external to the spirit, it is the latter's self-expression: its 'image'.[46] He notes that Plato would put men and women into barracks and place their children in a state-run nursery. He thinks this represents a mental condition of despising the body, a kind of spiritualism that refuses to recognize that the body itself is the person. He believes that this kind of egalitarianism actually diminishes the status of women; they are 'dragged down' to being 'undistinguished and ordinary'.[47] It 'horrifies' him that people want women to be soldiers and to work as refuse collectors or miners.[48]

In his series of essays published in 2005 under the title *On the Way to Jesus Christ* Ratzinger was critical of a prevalent image of Jesus as someone who 'demands nothing, never scolds, who accepts everyone and everything, who no longer does anything but affirm us'.[49] The fact

that God is love and that Benedict wishes to highlight this dimension
of the tradition should not therefore be construed as evidence that he is
a universal salvationist, that is, someone who believes that everyone
will be saved. He is firm in his statements that hell and purgatory do
exist and he expects that some people do occupy them:

> There is no quibbling: the idea of eternal damnation which had taken ever
> clearer shape in the Judaism of the century or two before Christ has a firm
> place in the teaching of Jesus, as well as in the apostolic writings. Dogma takes
> stand on solid ground when it speaks of the existence of Hell and of the
> eternity of its punishments.[50]

Ratzinger links this stance to God's unconditional respect for the
freedom of his creatures. None the less he also notes that for many of
the saints, including St John of the Cross and St Thérèse of Lisieux, hell is
not so much a threat to be hurled at other people as a challenge to oneself
to suffer the dark night of the soul that comes with Christian faith.
Ratzinger has also been influenced by Joachim Gnilka's theology of
purgatory for which he finds scriptural support in Corinthians 3: 10–15
and the support of the magisterium, most particularly at the Council of
Trent. According to Gnilka, 'the purification involved does not happen
through some thing, but through the transforming power of the Lord
himself, whose burning flame cuts free our closed-off heart, melting it,
and pouring it into a new mould to make it fit for the living organism of
the body'.[51] By this reading: 'Purgatory is not, as Tertullian thought,
some kind of supra-worldly concentration camp where man is forced to
undergo punishment in a more or less arbitrary fashion. Rather it is the
inwardly necessary process of transformation in which a person becomes
capable of Christ, capable of God and thus capable of unity with the
whole communion of saints.'[52]

Ratzinger further notes that the doctrine on the existence of an
inter-mediate state was never in dispute between the eastern and
western branches of Christianity. It was only called into question by
the Reformation in the face of what he calls 'objectionable and
deformed practices', such as the sale of indulgences.[53] Ratzinger
firmly believes that it is effectual to pray for those in purgatory because
'self-substituting love is a central Christian reality and the doctrine of
purgatory holds that for such love the limit of death does not exist'.[54]
As pope he has affirmed the practice of offering indulgences (though
not, of course, in return for money).

Ratzinger also believes that it is not wrong to speak of the immortality of the soul, even though some academics have argued for its scrapping and replacement with the concept 'resurrection in death'. He describes this project as a manifestation of an 'anti–Hellenic syndrome sceptical of ontology', and the phrase 'resurrection in death' as something of no pastoral value:

> Historically, it must be affirmed that the concept of soul found in Christian tradition is in no sense a simple borrowing from philosophical thought. In the form in which Christian tradition has understood it, it exists nowhere without that tradition. Christian tradition has seized upon pre-existing insights, elements of thought and language of diverse kinds, has purified and transformed these in the light of faith, and fused them into a new unity.[55]

Although Ratzinger clearly believes in heaven, hell, and purgatory, his works do not specifically make a list of the kind of behaviour that may land one in hell. Significantly, however, he does make it clear that he rejects the theory that those who with a clear conscience commit heinous crimes will probably be saved:

> It is indisputable that one must always follow a clear verdict of conscience, or at least that one may not act against such a verdict. But it is quite a different matter to assume that the verdict of conscience (or what one takes to be such a verdict) is always correct, i.e. infallible—for if that were so, it would mean there is no truth, at least in matters of morality and religion, which are the foundations of our very existence.[56]

The authority commonly presented for a liberal interpretation of the primacy of conscience is Newman's statement in his *Letter Addressed to his Grace the Duke of Norfolk* that he would toast conscience first, then the papacy. This is usually interpreted to mean that he put the authority of his own conscience above that of the pope's. None the less, Ratzinger offers a completely different interpretation. He says that Newman intended this to be a clear confession of his faith in the papacy, in response to the objections raised by British Liberal Party politician William Gladstone (1809–1898) to the dogma of infallibility. At the same time, against erroneous forms of ultramontanism (unhealthily bloated accounts of the ambit of papal infallibility), he meant it to be an interpretation of the papacy as an office which guarantees, rather than opposes, the primacy of conscience. In other words, Newman was making the point, which Ratzinger himself made prior to assuming the Office of Peter, that the pope cannot do whatever he likes, that the exercise of his prerogative powers are circumscribed by both Scripture and Tradition, that is, by the very data upon which a well-formed conscience relies. Ratzinger suggests that it is difficult today for people to grasp this point because they think on the basis of an antithesis between authority and subjectivity.[57]

In addition to offering a correction of the popular interpretation of Newman, Ratzinger has also sought to offer his own account of conscience which he thinks clarifies the medieval tradition. He agrees with the medieval tradition that there are two dimensions to conscience which must be clearly distinguished from each other but remain inseparable, and he believes that problems of interpretation have frequently arisen because scholars neglect either the distinction or the interrelatedness of the two dimensions.[58]

The main stream of medieval scholasticism described the two dimensions of conscience by means of the concepts *synderesis* and *conscientia*. The word *synderesis* is of Stoic provenance and Ratzinger prefers to replace it with the Platonic concept *anamnesis* (memory). He suggests that this is linguistically clearer, deeper, and purer in philosophical terms.[59] The word 'anamnesis' affirms St Paul's idea that God's laws have been written on the hearts of the gentiles (Rom. 2: 14–15) and St Basil's idea of there being a spark of the divine love innate in each person. St Basil wrote that 'the love of God is not based on some discipline imposed on us from outside, but as a capacity and indeed a necessity it is a constitutive element of our rational being'.[60] Consequently, on what Ratzinger calls the ontological level, 'conscience' means the primal remembrance of the good and the true.

The second dimension or level is *conscientia*. Here Ratzinger argues that St Thomas saw conscience, not as a *habitus*, but as an *actus*, an action that is performed. It is on this level that an erring conscience obligates. None the less, Ratzinger argues that the fact that one's conviction is naturally binding at the moment one acts does not mean that one is free of culpability, since 'guilt may very well consist in arriving at perverse convictions by trampling down the protest made by the memory (*amnesis*) of one's true being'.[61] The guilt would then lie on a deeper level, not in the act itself, not in the specific judgement pronounced by conscience, but in that neglect of my own being that has dulled me to the voice of truth and made me deaf to what it says within me.[62]

Thus an immoral act is still an immoral act, even if one's poorly formed conscience permits it. Ratzinger notes that if a person with an erring conscience could be saved then even the SS troops under Hitler could be justified and now would be in heaven.[63] He surely thinks that they are more likely not enjoying the beatific vision. Finally, in this context, as a matter of intellectual history, Ratzinger believes that problems have arisen over the meaning of conscience because of the publication of a work in 1942 by Antonin-D. Sertillanges OP in which he attributed to St Thomas the teaching of Peter Abelard (1079–1142), although St Thomas's goal was to refute Abelard. In Ratzinger's judgement, the modern theories of the autonomy of conscience vis-à-vis the magisterium can appeal to Abelard but not to Thomas.[64]

Ratzinger believes that the antidote to moralism and the narrowing of moral theology to mere casuistry is the revival of an understanding that God is love and that the human person is a composite of body and soul, heart and mind, created in God's own image. It is therefore consistent with his general orientation to the whole territory of ethics that Benedict has called on the Jesuits, the traditional foes of the Jansenists, to rekindle devotion to the Sacred Heart. He has described the 1956 encyclical *Haurietis aquas* of Pius XII as offering a theology of bodily existence. He believes that devotion to the Sacred Heart of Jesus explicitly invites entry into a spirituality involving the senses, corresponding to the bodily nature of the divine–human love of Jesus Christ. This, he says, is spirituality in the sense of Newman's motto: *Cor ad cor loquitur*: 'Over against the Stoic ideal of *apatheia*, over against the Aristotelian God, who is thought thinking itself, the heart is the epitome of the passions, without which there could have been no Passion on the part of the Son.'[65]

Finally, in a reflection on his early patron, Cardinal Frings, Ratzinger has written that Frings and Newman shared a spiritual vision which is encapsulated in the following paragraph from the late fourth-century Cappadocian Father, Gregory of Nyssa:

This is true perfection: not to avoid a wicked life because like slaves we servilely fear punishment; nor to do good because we hope for rewards...On the contrary, disregarding all those things for which we hope and which have been reserved by promise, we regard falling from God's friendship as the only thing dreadful and we consider becoming God's friend the only thing worthy of honour and desire.[66]

This spirituality would seem to be at the core of Ratzinger's moral theology.

5

The Structure of
the Communion

The conciliar document on the Church, *Lumen gentium*, was mainly
the work of Belgian theologians who belonged to the circle of
Leo Joseph Cardinal Suenens (1904–1996). They wanted to get away
from the emphasis on the Church's juridical nature and the clericalism
this had fostered. In theological language they wanted to emphasize
that the Church is determined by Pnuematological as well as Christological elements. As such it is 'neither a parliamentary nor monarchical
super-State, but rather a fabric of worshiping congregations whose
unity consists in the essential unity of divine worship and the faith
witnessed to in that worship'.[1] In Germany there had been a movement in this direction in the theology of Romano Guardini who was
similarly concerned that Catholics tended to think of the Church as
something external to themselves, like a club or college to which they
were affiliated. The fact that individual Catholics themselves are a part
of the mystical body of Christ was often overlooked. In Ratzinger's
words, 'the Church grows from within and moves outwards, not vice-
versa'.[2] Similarly, in France Henri de Lubac's ecclesiology centred on
the relationship between the Eucharist and the understanding of the
Church as the mystical body of Christ.[3] From this it came to be
emphasized that the Church exists in Eucharistic communities and
that she is a service for the transformation of the human person and the
entire world. Ratzinger has described de Lubac's *Corpus Mysticum* as a
work of imposing and comprehensive scholarship.[4] He has also said
that 'in all its comments about the Church, [Vatican II] was moving,
precisely in the direction of de Lubac's thought'.[5]

De Lubac's Eucharistic ecclesiology taken together with the work (on ecclesial missions or vocations) of his student von Balthasar set the foundations for what became in the 1970s and beyond the ecclesiology of the *Communio* school. *Communio* (communion) can be read as a shorthand form of the concept *communio hierarchica* (hierarchical communion) or simply taken on its own to mean a special type of sacred relationship or, literally, communion. In his 'Announcements and Prefatory Notes of Explanation on the Dogmatic Constitution on the Church' (*Lumen gentium*), published in 1966, Ratzinger wrote that the use of the term *communio hierarchica* by the Council fathers was intended to make it as clear as possible that communion as understood by the ancient Church is both juridically and ontically the fundamental structure of the Church for all time, and therefore in our day as well.[6] The *Communio* concept was also inherent in Ratzinger's *Das neue Volk Gottes: Entwürfe zur Ekklesiologie* (1969) and as early as 1962, in a publication with Rahner, he was already endorsing the concept of communion for an understanding of ecclesiology.[7] Ratzinger does acknowledge, however, that the concept did not have a central position in the Council and that it really only came to prominence in 1985 at the Synod to reflect on the reception of the Council. None the less, he argues that, if properly understood, it can serve as a key to a synthesis for the essential elements of conciliar ecclesiology. He summarizes its content in the following paragraph:

Ecclesial communion is at the same time both visible and invisible. As an invisible reality, it is the communion of each human being with the Father through Christ in the Holy Spirit, and with the others who are fellow sharers in the divine nature, in the passion of Christ, in the same faith and in the same spirit. In the Church on earth there is a relationship between the invisible communion and the visible communion in the teaching of the Apostles, in the sacraments and in the hierarchical order. By means of these divine gifts, which are very visible realities, Christ carries out in different ways his prophetical, priestly and kingly function for the salvation of mankind. This link between the invisible and visible elements of ecclesial communion constitutes the Church as the Universal Sacrament of Salvation.[8]

The general Conciliar orientation (begun in fact prior to the Council with Pius XII's *Mystici Corporis*) was to steer away from a bureaucratic and clericalist vision of the Church by broadening and deepening the understanding of the complex network of relationships in which the Church is embodied. Here the relations with the Trinity are of

primary importance, but also important are the typological relationships found in the Scriptures, the sacramental relationships, the historical relationships between the Old and New Testaments, and the social
relationships both within the Church and between members of the
Church and those outside her governance.

Immediately after the Council, however, it was not the *Communio*
ecclesiology of de Lubac which became fashionable but the idea of the
Church as the People of God.[9] While accepting that there is a legitimate
theological meaning behind this concept Ratzinger has none the less been
clear in his criticism of the nuances it implies. He believes it hides
influences of ecclesiologies which de facto revert to an exclusively Old
Testament vision and it misses the point that the New Testament character of the Church is more distinctively underlined by the concept of the
Body of Christ—'in reality, there is no truly New Testament, Catholic
concept of Church without a direct and vital relation not only with
sociology but first of all with Christology.'[10] The post-conciliar fashion
of speaking of the Church almost exclusively as the People of God:

> involves no small danger of sinking once more into a purely sociological and
> even ideological view of the Church through ignoring the essential insights of
> the Constitution on the Liturgy [*Sacrosanctum concilium*] and the Constitution
> on the Church [*Lumen gentium*] and by over-simplifying, externalising and
> making a catchword of a term which can only keep its meaning if it is used in a
> genuinely theological context.[11]

Here the concrete example of Ratzinger's criticism is the middle
European *Wir sind Kirche* (We are Church) movement which is
quite congregationalist in its ecclesial vision. Its emphasis is on a
democratization of the Church's offices and structures, the abolition
of celibacy for clergy, the ordination of women, and the promotion of
liberal attitudes towards the meaning and purpose of human sexuality.
As Prefect for the Congregation for the Doctrine of the Faith, Ratzinger stated that 'it is self-evident that such initiatives cannot be con-
doned by the Church in any manner'.[12] Moreover, such approaches
'suffer from a clearly inadequate awareness of the Church as a mystery
of communion, especially insofar as they have not sufficiently integrated the concept of communion with the concepts of People of God
and of the Body of Christ, and have not given due importance to the
relationship between the Church as communion and the Church as
sacrament'.[13]

With reference to the specific pro-ordination of women platform of *Wir sind Kirche*, Ratzinger's stance on this issue is strongly based on his observation that all religions of the ancient world had priestesses, *except* Judaism. The Jews stood alone in reserving the priesthood to men. He believes that this is theologically significant and that there is nothing in the New Testament to suggest that Christ desired for this to be changed. For Ratzinger the Old Testament is a valuable source of Revelation; it is not just a history book with some fine literature thrown in. He first encountered the topic of the relationship between the two testaments, and of their inner unity-in-diversity, in a course of lectures delivered by Gottlieb Söhngen in the Munich Faculty of Theology in the winter semester of 1947–1948. The question has stayed with him ever since and influenced his whole theological outlook.[14] In this context he has also been keenly interested in the contribution of the Old Testament to Mariology. He has said that Mariology is woven entirely out of the Old Testament faith. Mary is the true Zion, towards whom hopes have yearned throughout all the devastations of history. She is the true Israel in whom the Old and New Covenants, Israel and Church, are indivisibly one.[15] For Ratzinger, Mariology exercises an indispensable clarifying and deepening influence on the concept of the Church. Against the masculine, activist, and sociological approach of the 'People of God' there is the deeper reality that Church—*Ecclesia*—is feminine. The Church, he says, is 'more than structure and action: in her lives the mystery of motherhood and of that spousal love which makes motherhood possible'.[16]

Ratzinger also cites the judgement of feminist theologian Elisabeth Schüssler-Fiorenza that 'true feminists' should actually oppose the ordination of women and work to abolish the phenomenon of ordination itself. While of course in no way agreeing with her call for the abolition of the priesthood, Ratzinger none the less acknowledges that there is a certain internal logic in her position which is not present in the thought of those feminists who criticize the whole idea of hierarchy as something that could only develop out of a masculine epistemology, but then demand the right to be a part of this fundamentally masculine order. Her position, while errant, at least demonstrates the courage of her convictions and enjoys its own internal consistency. Thus, while he has no opposition to appointing women to senior administrative, academic, and advisory posts within the Church, he does not accept ordination for women because of his approach to

Scripture and Tradition, including the authority he gives to the Old Testament. Likewise for Ratzinger the hierarchical nature of the Church is not a historical accident which can only be ascribed to male reasoning, other than in the sense that he believes that the essential structure of the Church was laid down by Christ himself and no one else has the power to change it:

> If the Church, in fact, is our Church, if we alone are the Church, if her structures are not willed by Christ, then it is no longer possible to conceive of the existence of a hierarchy as a service to the baptized established by the Lord himself. It is a rejection of the concept of an authority willed by God, an authority therefore that has its legitimation in God and not—as happens in political structures—in the consensus of the majority of the members of an organization. But the Church of Christ is not a party, not an association, not a club. Her deep and permanent structure is not democratic but sacramental, consequently hierarchical.[17]

Ratzinger describes democracy as a 'daring experiment', and suggests that it would be *absurd* if it were extended to questions of truth, or of the good itself.[18] As a result he fundamentally disagrees with the ecclesiology of Hans Küng as presented in his book *Structures of the Church*, and many subsequent publications.[19] Küng argues that the concept of the Church is determined by the form of the Church in any given historical era. In other words, for each era there arises a new ecclesiology. For Ratzinger, however, what Christ did and said has permanent significance and he will not accept that truth could ever be subject to the majority principle:

> [A]uthority in the Church stands on faith. The Church cannot conceive for herself how she wants to be ordered. She can only try ever more clearly to understand the inner call of faith and to live from faith. She does not need the majority principle, which always has something atrocious about it . . . the sacramental order guarantees more freedom than could be given by those who would subject the Church to the majority principle.[20]

Ratzinger wishes, however, to distinguish between the teaching authority of the Church and the practice of enlightened despotism. The Church, he says, is *not* in the business of leading in the same sense of the enlightened ruler who knows that he is in possession of better reason, translates it into regulations, and counts on the obedience of his subjects who have to accept his reason and its articulation as their divinely willed standard. Rather, it is a case of there being certain teachings which have been withdrawn from any possibility of majority judgement, by the bishops or by anyone else, because they are things which of themselves human reason has not discovered. They are the gifts of Revelation.[21]

Similarly, while the sacred hierarchy is charged with the responsibility of keeping the sacred teachings undefiled, and therefore has power and authority with respect to matters of faith and morals, Ratzinger does not view the Church in sociological terms as a network of power structures. He is completely hostile to this mentality. He does not see the Church as one large multinational corporation with franchise operations across the globe, the bishops as the executive staff, the pope as the CEO, and the laity as the shareholders. He thinks it is precisely this kind of narrowly sociological thinking that is fostered by the People of God concept. Rather than analysing the Church from the vantage point of corporate models he prefers the perspective of the *Communio* ecclesiology which acknowledges the existence of a unified symphonic network of different spiritual missions. This is where the contribution of von Balthasar comes in.

In his treatment of typology von Balthasar referred to a 'Christological constellation' of characters or types to be found in the life of Christ as presented in the scriptures. Each was taken to represent a different spiritual mission in the life of the Church. For example, the mission represented by the type of St John is the contemplative vocation of self-sacrificial love, prayer, and study; the mission represented by the type of St James is one of preserving the tradition pure and unmutated; the mission of St Peter is one of governance; the mission of St Paul is one of prophetic movement and utterance; and the Marian mission that of absolute fidelity and receptivity to the will of God. Each mission is dependent on the others and operates in a symphonic harmony. These charisms are not mutually exclusive. Since there is more than one spiritual mission there is not one particular blueprint or formula for holiness. Rather, the constellation of persons surrounding Christ in Scripture presents an array of spiritual types with which Catholics may identify their own unique personal vocations. They are all responding to the same score, but their modes of participation are different. Taking up von Balthasar's theme, Ratzinger describes the faith as:

A polyphonic melody composed of the many apparently quite discordant strains in the contrapunctual interplay of law, prophets, gospels and apostles.

The omission of one of the thematic elements of this symphony simplifies the performance but is rejected by the fathers as heresy, that is, as a reductive selection, because the truth lies only in the whole and in its tensions.[22]

Within this Balthasarian framework a spiritual mission is not really chosen by the individual. It is received as a gift from God and responded to and discerned through prayer. The individual has the freedom to reject the gift, but true individuality and the affirmation of one's personal uniqueness comes by correctly discerning the vocation which God has chosen to offer. It is in accepting the vocation or mission chosen by God that the individual finds itself and is at peace with his or her identity:

For each Christian, God has an Idea which fixes his place within the membership of the Church: this Idea is unique and personal, embodying for each his appropriate sanctity . . . The Christian's supreme aim is to transform his life into this Idea of himself secreted in God, this 'individual law' freely promulgated for him by the pure grace of God.[23]

There is thus a complex network of ecclesial missions at work within the Church. Within this network there is a sacerdotal hierarchy but this is only one dimension of the whole. Here Ratzinger writes:

The universality of the Church involves, on the one hand, a most solid unity, and on the other, a plurality and a diversification, which do not obstruct unity, but rather confer upon it the character of 'communion'. This plurality refers both to the diversity of ministries, charisms and forms of life and apostolate within each particular Church and to the diversity of traditions in liturgy and culture among the various particular Churches.[24]

Ratzinger no doubt accepts the idea that grace works on one's natural endowments, and thus that God does not offer people vocations to which they are by nature, or more specifically, personality, unsuited. He is not like the often parodied sadistic mother superior in a preconciliar convent who would allot jobs deliberately designed to 'go against the grain' in order to test the obedience of a novice. A person's spiritual mission will relate to the other gifts which providence has provided. In this vision what determines one's place in the heavenly hierarchy is the degree to which one is open to responding to divine grace. On several occasions Ratzinger has referred to Christ's comment to his disciples that those who want to be first must first be the servants of everyone else. One of the problems with the sociological model of Catholic Inc. is that it analyses participation in political rather than spiritual terms. Thérèse of Lisieux did much to promote the work of the missions, and through her teaching on the spirituality of holy childhood she helped to undercut Jansenist elements in French Catholicism, but she never sat on one single episcopal subcommittee. She could still end up a Doctor of the Church like her Carmelite confrère Teresa of Avila, without going anywhere near a board meeting of a Catholic agency.

An interest in the theology of spiritual missions and their symphonic harmony has been fostered by the rise of numerous new ecclesial movements in the life of the post-conciliar Church. These movements are still quite young and, without mentioning any one group in particular, Ratzinger has stated that they have had their share of childhood diseases. In particular, there have been tendencies to exclusivity from the over-accentuation of one charism that has made them unable to insert themselves into the life of the local churches without friction.[25] Often when meeting members of new ecclesial movements one gets the impression that they believe that nothing worthwhile happened in the life of the Church between the death of the last apostle and the birth of the founder of their particular movement, and that merely being a common garden variety Catholic is no longer sufficient for salvation. Ratzinger has therefore suggested that the many new ecclesial movements operative within the post-conciliar Church need to 'suppress [their] individual peculiarities'.[26]

Notwithstanding the above criticisms, Ratzinger is not opposed to these new movements and in fact welcomed their social arrival in the 1970s when people were speaking of a wintry season in the life of the Church. They have provided much hope on the horizon. He believes that such 'charismatic irruptions' occur periodically as part of the normal life of the Church. However, he offers several caveats both to bishops who have to contend with the new movements in their dioceses and to the leaders of the new movements themselves. First, he says it is important that the priesthood should itself be lived charismatically. This means in practice that there needs to be some strong quality control mechanisms operative in the selection of candidates for the priesthood: 'the Church must not put numbers in the foreground and lower spiritual standards out of zeal for the development of its organizational structures.'[27] Secondly, where the priestly office is lived charismatically, the priest will develop a 'sort of nose' for the Holy Spirit and his action, so that ways of fruitful collaboration with leaders of the new ecclesial movements in the discernment of spirits can be found. Third, the Church must keep the number of self-created administrative structures as small as possible. She must not over-institutionalize herself. While 'emergency stopgap' measures are sometimes licit, the Church must never stop praying for vocations to the priesthood. If the Church began to use the emergency of the shortage of priests to make herself independent of God's gift of religious vocations, by setting up a whole new raft of structures and offices with members of the laity, this would be acting like the Old Testament character Saul. Saul waited for Samuel to perform the sacred rites, but when Samuel failed to appear and the people were breaking rank, he lost his patience and offered the holocaust himself. Ratzinger observes that Saul thought he was doing the right thing given the urgency of the situation, that there was no other option. However, Saul was told that by doing just that he had thrown everything away: I want obedience, not sacrifice (cf. 1 Sam. 13: 8–14; 15: 22).[28] A constant refrain in Benedict's reflections is that the priestly office cannot be understood ultimately in purely functional and bureaucratic terms: there must always be a charismatic dimension. For Benedict the priest's role cannot be adequately fulfilled by a lay administrator who assumes some of his functions.

While the leaders of the new ecclesial movements are warned against playing down the importance of the priesthood, Ratzinger pleads with bishops to avoid making an ideal of uniformity in pastoral organization and planning: 'they must not make their own pastoral plans the criterion of what the Holy Spirit is allowed to do.'[29] Moreover, 'an obsession with planning could render the churches impermeable to the Spirit of God' and, 'above all, *communio* must not be conceived as if the avoidance of conflict were the highest pastoral value'.[30] He notes that faith is always a sword, too, and it can demand conflict precisely for the sake of truth and love.[31] In other words, he is concerned that a kind of mania for bureaucratic uniformity and centralization of decision-making can take such a grip over the life of a diocese that the work of the Holy Spirit is thwarted. Those bishops whose highest priority is the efficiency of administration or who spend their best energies duplicating in the Church the procedures and processes of the corporate world run the risk of 'losing their nose' for the Holy Spirit and the sense of the Church as the means of salvation. As far as we know, the apostles never produced a single mission statement or business management plan. Ratzinger believes that 'if the Church can only be recognized in her human organization' (her agencies and administrative structures) then, in fact, 'all that is left is desolation': 'Paul was effective, not because of brilliant rhetoric and sophisticated strategies, but rather because he exerted himself and left himself vulnerable in the service of the gospel. The Church even today can convince people only insofar as her ambassadors are ready to let themselves be wounded.'[32]

When one moves from the macro-level vision of the Church as a hierarchical communion to more micro-level questions about the various relationships within the communion, Ratzinger's *Theological Highlights*, published in 1966, and his *The Episcopate and the Primacy*, published in 1962, are foundational sources of material on his understanding of the relationship between episcopal and papal authority.

Of the Petrine Office he has written that its powers are circumscribed by the tradition itself. The unity of the Church, he argues, is rooted in the unity of the Episcopate, and the unity of the Episcopate requires the existence of a Bishop who is Head of the Body or College of Bishops. He sees this head as the Roman pontiff, who as the successor of Peter is a perpetual and visible source and foundation of unity. He believes that there can be no number of bishops large enough to counterbalance the decisive weight of the See of St Peter: 'anything else would mean substituting some sort of profane arithmetic for the holy bond of tradition.'[33] To this extent a council is never an independent subject of infallibility, distinct from, or even against, the pope. The primacy of the Bishop of Rome and the Episcopal College are proper elements of the universal Church that are 'not derived from the particularity of the Churches', but are nevertheless interior to each particular Church. Consequently, Catholics must see the ministry of the Successor of Peter not only as a 'global' service, reaching each particular Church from 'outside', as it were, but as belonging already to the essence of each particular Church from 'within'.[34] The following list of principles summarizes what Ratzinger believes are the doctrinal principles to be discerned in *Lumen gentium* in the context of the relationship between the episcopacy and the papacy:

1. The college of bishops includes the pope as its head. It cannot therefore be seen as a separate body apart from him, but can only be understood in unity with him;

2. The pope has in the Petrine succession full, supreme, and general power over the Church, which he is free to exercise at any time;

3. The community of bishops is the form in which the apostolic community continues throughout the time of the Church. Therefore, this community of bishops (including the bishop of Rome) also has full and supreme power over the Church, the same power of binding and loosing that the pope has;

4. In its variety and fullness the college of bishops represents the variety and universality of the People of God. However, inasmuch as it has a common head, it also gives expression to the unity of Christ's flock;

5. The full power which this college or community of bishops possesses is exercised in a solemn way in the Council. Therefore, in order to be ecumenical, a Council must be at least 'accepted' by the bishop of Rome.[35]

In his early commentaries on the documents of Vatican II Ratzinger noted that national bishops' conferences now had the authority to make decisions in relation to the liturgy which were regarded as matters for the local Church not in need of centralized supervision. He enthusiastically concluded that this authority recognized that bishops' conferences had a certain theological significance in their own right. None the less, the later Ratzinger was to hold that bishops' conferences are more like meetings held by professional laity—a pooling of expertise in a given area and the provision of opportunities for exchanging ideas—but certainly not a structure of any deep theological significance. In *The Ratzinger Report*, published in 1985, he stated that episcopal conferences have 'no theological basis, they do not belong to the structure of the Church as willed by Christ . . . no Episcopal conference, as such, has a teaching mission; its documents have no weight of their own save that of the consent given to them by the individual bishops'.[36] In the same series of interviews he also noted that the really powerful documents against National Socialism were those that came from individual courageous bishops, not from the German bishops as a national bloc, and that the search for agreement between different tendencies and the effort at mediation which takes place to reach agreements, often yield flattened documents in which decisive positions (where they might be necessary) are weakened.[37] On this point there has been a definite change in the direction of Ratzinger's thought which might be explained again by the change in ecclesiastical climate. In a time of widespread dissent from magisterial teaching the danger of individual conferences spinning out of the orbit of communion with the papacy may have been perceived by Ratzinger to be simply too grave a danger. Another possibility is that his earlier stance was limited to the recognition of real theological authority in a very narrow field never intended to encompass the territories of doctrine and morals. Deciding, for example, that the Solemnity of the Ascension is to be transferred to the nearest Sunday is somewhat different from a decision about the morality of nuclear war. In 1998, with Ratzinger's support, John Paul II released the Apostolic Letter *Apostolos suos* in which it was declared that bishop's conferences cannot issue statements on doctrine or morality without either unanimity among its members or prior approval of the Holy See.

While the People of God concept was distorted by being narrowed to a sociological vision of the people as shareholders in a corporate enterprise, by the early 1990s Ratzinger had become concerned that the *Communio* ecclesiology was also being distorted. The ecclesiology of communion began to be reduced to the theme of the relationship between the local Church and the universal Church, which in turn degenerated into the problem of the division of the areas of competence between them. The egalitarian cause, which claimed that there could only be complete equality in communion, was again disseminated.[38] To confront this distortion the Congregation for the Doctrine of the Faith under Ratzinger's leadership produced a 'Letter to the Bishops of the Catholic Church on Some Aspects of the Church Understood as Communion', which was published on 28 May 1992. In this document it was stated that the universal Church is a reality that in its essential mystery is logically and ontologically prior to the particular Churches. This was to counter the theory that the universal Church is merely a composite of numerous local churches throughout the world. As Prefect of the CDF, Ratzinger wrote:

Baptism does not derive from the local community. It is a Trinitarian event, totally theological, not sociological. Whoever is baptized in Berlin, is as much at home in the Church in Rome or New York or Kinshasa or Bangalore or in any other place, as he is in the Church were he was baptized. The Eucharist is not born from the local church and does not end in her. She [the Church] is not a local community that grows gradually, but the leaven that is always destined to permeate the whole, and consequently, embodies universality from the first instant.[39]

These issues had already been anticipated by de Lubac. In *The Mother-hood of the Church* de Lubac argued that the 'particular Church is always universalist and centripetal'.[40] The particular or local Church is not merely an administrative division of the total Church, in the way of the French provinces vis-à-vis the French state, for example.[41] Rather, 'at the heart of each particular Church all the universal Church is present in principle' and between the two there is a mutual interiority. Ratzinger agrees with de Lubac and adds the weight of patristic authority to his stance. He notes that according to both St Clement of Rome and the Shepherd of Hermas the universal Church ontologically precedes the local churches in the order of creation and gives birth to the particular/local Churches as her daughters. She is the mother and not the product of particular Churches. Ratzinger claims that the merely geographical and quantitative element can never adequately account for what it means to be Catholic, because the Church was Catholic even when she consisted merely of small minorities of people around the Mediterranean basin, as was the case at the time of St Ignatius of Antioch. The decisive element must be qualitative cathol-icity.[42] He further argues that the popular opinion is wrong that on Pentecost a local Church of Jerusalem was founded at first, 'the original Christian community in Jerusalem', which was then extended little by little into a universal Church: 'the Twelve are not simply a component of a local Church in Jerusalem; instead, in them is virtually present the Church of all peoples, to which they are sent and whose fathers they are destined to become.'[43] Many of these principles have been reiterated by Ratzinger in a series of exchanges with Cardinal Kasper, who takes a different view of the *Communio* concept, giving greater emphasis to the local Church.[44]

The 'Letter to the Bishops on Some Aspects of the Church Under-stood as Communion' was followed in 2000 by another significant document of the CDF, the 'Declaration on the Unicity and Salvific Universality of Jesus Christ and the Church', otherwise known by its Latin title *Dominus Iesus*. This declaration began with the observation that the Church's constant missionary proclamation is endangered by relativistic theories which seek to justify religious pluralism, not only de facto but also *de iure*. The popularist version of this is the 'God is like an elephant' fable (Catholics have got hold of the elephant's trunk, Protestants his ears, Buddhists his tail, Muslims his back foot, and so on: no one religious tradition has a picture of the whole elephant).

Contrary to these relativist perspectives, the document declares that the Catholic faithful are required to profess that there is a historical continuity—rooted in the apostolic succession—between the Church founded by Christ and the Catholic Church:

> This is the single Church of Christ ... which our Saviour, after his resurrection, entrusted to Peter's pastoral care (cf. John 21: 17), commissioning him and the other Apostles to extend and rule her (cf. Matt. 28: 18 ff.), erected for all ages as 'the pillar and mainstay of the truth' (1 Tim. 3: 15). This Church, constituted and organized as a society in the present world, subsists in the Catholic Church, governed by the successor of Peter and by the Bishops in communion with him.[45]

The words 'subsists in' come from the Conciliar document *Lumen gentium*. In this general area of ecumenism its interpretation is something of a theological keystone. In *Dominus Iesus* it is stated that with this expression ('subsists in') the Second Vatican Council sought to harmonize two doctrinal statements: on the one hand, that the Church of Christ, despite the divisions that exist among Christians, continues to exist fully only in the Catholic Church, and, on the other hand, that outside of her structure, many elements can be found of sanctification and truth, that is, in those Churches and ecclesial communities which are not yet in full communion with the Catholic Church.[46] In case there be any lingering ambiguity, footnote 56 of the document declares: 'The interpretation of those who would derive from the formula *subsist in* the thesis that the one Church of Christ could subsist also in non-Catholic churches is contrary to the authentic meaning of *Lumen gentium*.' Moreover, according to *Dominus Iesus*, the Catholic faithful are not permitted to imagine that the Church of Christ is nothing more than a collection of Churches and ecclesial communities (as members of a congregationalist community might believe), nor are they free to hold that the Church of Christ nowhere really exists, and must be considered only as a goal which all ecclesial communities must strive to reach (as is commonly believed in many Protestant communities).[47] In his *Theological Highlights*, published during his so-called radical theological teenager period, Ratzinger wrote what would now be regarded by many as a quite conservative statement: 'The Catholic is convinced that the visible existence of the Church is not merely an organizational cover for a real Church hidden behind it, but on the contrary that, for all its humanity and insufficiency, the visible Church is the actual dwelling place of God among men, that it is *the* Church itself.'[48]

Accordingly, the dialogue which has been fostered by the conciliar decree on ecumenism is just one of the actions of the Church in her mission to the world; it is not an exercise in working out what bits of other religious traditions are insights hitherto unavailable to Catholics which should be incorporated into the Catholic tradition. The equality to which *Dominus Iesus* refers is therefore the equal personal dignity of the participants in ecumenical and inter-religious dialogue and not any equal status of doctrinal content and much less an equal position of the founders of the other religions with that of Jesus Christ. Ratzinger is emphatic that Christians cannot accept such a liberal model of dialogue.[49] Catholics have sight of the whole elephant, not just its trunk or ears.

Ratzinger acknowledges that many received *Dominus Jesus* as 'an ecumenical train wreck'. None the less, he states that the unity of the Church cannot be relegated to a Utopia or to eschatological times; it must be present corporeally, so to speak, in a bodily manner in history itself. Moreover, 'if it is true that all salvation has to do with Christ (in whatever way) and that the Church is inseparable from Christ, then it is clear that this Church participates in his universal mediation and that every relation to Christ somehow includes the Church as well'.[50] Thus, he is not prepared to compromise on the Church's claim to be the universal sacrament of salvation, as it was described in *Lumen gentium*, but within this doctrinal boundary he does work to understand the various doctrinal and cultural differences which the Protestant traditions have with the Catholic faith, and to clear away misunderstandings wherever possible. When the 'Joint Declaration on the Doctrine of Justification' was signed in 1999 with leaders of the Lutheran community, Bishop George Anderson (then head of the Evangelical Lutheran Church of America) said, 'it was Ratzinger who untied the knots. Without him we might not have had an agreement.'[51] Ratzinger summarizes his understanding of ecumenism by saying that it does not mean concealing truth so as not to displease others; full truth is part of full love; rather it must mean that Catholics cease to see other Christians as mere adversaries against whom they must defend themselves, they must recognize fellow Christians as brothers.[52]

When it comes to the more practical questions about the way of moving forward toward Christian unity, Ratzinger has stated that Catholics cannot demand that all the other Churches be disbanded and their members individually incorporated into the Catholic Church. However, Catholics can hope that the hour will come when 'the churches' that exist outside 'the Church' will enter into its unity. They must remain in existence as *churches*, with only those modifications which such a unity necessarily requires.[53] In the meantime the Catholic Church has no right to absorb the other churches. The Church has not yet prepared for them a place of their own to which they are legitimately entitled.[54] Here his position appears to be that the various contemporary Protestant denominations may ultimately be received back into full Communion as Uniate rites, retaining something of their own cultural patrimony in the process. For example, the Traditional Anglican Communion (TAC), which is currently seeking Uniate status within the Catholic Church, would, if accepted, be permitted to keep its Anglican liturgy with its particular English cultural accoutrements. Members of this communion may, if accepted, be entitled to receive the sacraments in any Catholic Church in the world, but provision may be made for them to retain certain distinctive cultural elements of their Anglican heritage which are perfectly consistent with the Catholic faith. The 40,000 or so members of TAC would not be expected to be individually absorbed within existing Catholic parish structures as such.[55] They would have their own parishes, their own clergy, and their own liturgy.

With reference to ecumenism with the Church of England and its derivatives throughout the British Commonwealth more generally Ratzinger has written the following with a certain tone of frustration:

Jesus did not found a Catholic party in a cosmopolitan debating society, but a Catholic Church to which he promised the fullness of truth . . . A body which reduces its Catholics to a party within a religious parliament can hardly deserve to be called a branch of the Catholic Church, but a national religion, dominated by and structured on the principles of liberal tolerance, in which the authority of revelation is subordinate to democracy and private opinion.[56]

The problem for Anglican–Catholic ecumenism in the present era is not so much that of the theology of the Petrine office but more significantly the problem of the decision of the Anglican communion to ordain women and to take fuzzy positions on questions of sexual morality. It may be, however, that some of the strong evangelical elements within the Church of England and its affiliates worldwide will come to find themselves more comfortable within the Catholic Church precisely because Catholic moral teaching is more clearly recognizable as consistent with Scripture than practices which are tolerated by the more high Church branches of their own communion. This is especially so as it becomes clearer to evangelical Protestants that post-conciliar Catholics are certainly not neglectful of Scripture, and nor do they generally regard themselves as ignorant people for whom their parish priest does their thinking, as has been a common, and perhaps once accurate, Protestant caricature of Catholic life. The support of the Loyal Orange Lodge of Scotland for Cardinal Murphy O'Connor's stance against the Blair government's legislation on homosexual adoption 'rights' is but one example of this kind of realignment of social forces. Just as American Catholics and evangelicals have grown closer through their political battles with secular liberals, a similar social movement of future ecumenical significance may emerge in countries of the British Commonwealth.

Closer to the heart and mind of Ratzinger, however, especially with his interest in the early Church Fathers, is the relationship between the Catholic Church and the Eastern Orthodox churches which followed Constantinople after the schism of 1054. From a theological perspective, Ratzinger believes that the union of the Churches of East and West is fundamentally possible, but he also believes that the spiritual preparation is not yet sufficiently far advanced and, therefore, not yet ready in practice.[57] When the spiritual preparations have been made, however, he believes that the following principles should govern the process of reunion:

Rome must not require more from the East with respect to the doctrine of primacy than had been formulated and was lived in the first millennium ... Rome need not ask for more. Reunion could take place in this context if, on the one hand, the East would cease to oppose as heretical the developments that took place in the West in the second millennium and would accept the Catholic Church as legitimate and orthodox in the form she had acquired in the course of that development, while, on the other hand, the West would recognize the Church of the East as orthodox and legitimate in the form she has always had.[58]

Beyond the work of ecumenism, there is also the territory of interfaith dialogue. Ratzinger argues that the whole panorama of the history of religions sets before us a basic choice between two types of religion: religion as mysticism and religion as monotheism. The first leads to a mysticism of self-identity, the second to a personal understanding of God. He believes that ultimately it is a question of whether the divine 'God' stands over against us, so that religion, being human, is in the last resort a relationship that does not do away with the opposition of I and Thou; or, whether the divine lies beyond personality, and the final aim of man is to become one with, and dissolve in, the All-One.[59] Mystical religion with its rigorously apophatic theology makes no claim to know the divine. It is not defined in terms of positive content and in terms of sacred institutions. For such religions what is important is mystical experience and this rules out a priori any clash with scientific reason. The New Age movement is the best contemporary example of a mystical religion. In this context Ratzinger refers to Albert Görres' concept of the 'Hinduization of the faith'. This occurs when doctrinal propositions no longer matter because the important thing is contact with a spiritual atmosphere which leads beyond everything that can be said. Against this kind of approach to religion Ratzinger has quipped that 'Jesus had no intention of producing some contentless state of exaltation'. While acknowledging that adoration is always linked to interiority and that interiority is always linked to self-transcendence, Benedict rejects the idea that the two approaches (mystical religion and monotheism) can meet as one, for a reduction to the mystical way means that the world of the senses, particularly the work of the intellectual faculty, drops out of our relation to the divine. Religion loses its power to form a communion of mind and will and becomes a mere therapy.

More recently a third alternative has appeared on the scene with the rise in popularity of what is commonly called a pluralist approach to theology. One of the leading proponents of the pluralist position is John Hick. He believes that God is present to and immanent in all the world religions, though this presence of God is manifest differently through the various scriptures, prophets, and sages of the different religions.[60] For proponents of pluralist theology the religions can retain all their formulas, forms, and rites (these do not really matter), but they need to be ordered to a common right praxis.[61] Ratzinger calls this a pragmatic approach. He first addressed these kinds of ideas in a series of articles in L'Osservatore Romano in the 1970s in response to the World Council of Church's project to view Christianity in terms of ortho-praxy, that is, to focus on practices, not beliefs. This project was also shared with the proponents of liberation theology and was fostered by Hans Küng in his work On Being a Christian. According to Küng, the distinguishing feature of the Old Testament ethos did not consist in the individual precepts or prohibitions, but in the faith in Yahweh. All that is specifically Israelite is the fact that their ethical requirements, which he claimed they shared with other tribes of the Middle East, are subordinated to the authority of Yahweh.

Ratzinger has consistently opposed all projects giving priority to orthopraxy, and in so doing follows the lead of Romano Guardini, who as early as the 1920s spoke of the primacy of *logos* over *ethos*. He argues that 'important as the apophatic element may be, faith in God cannot do without truth, which must have a specifiable content'.[62] He also observes that, paradoxically, those who wanted to reduce Christianity to mere orthopraxy also had a tendency to affirm that there is no such thing as a specifically Christian morality, and thus that Christianity ought to take its norms of conduct from the anthropological insights of the day. This is the inverse of moralism. Instead of regarding Christianity as useful for the provision of a moral framework, Christianity is taken as having nothing to say in the territory of ethics which a good Kantian could not conclude for himself without any reference to Christ or the Scriptures. Ratzinger flatly rejects this outlook:

The fact that the Bible's moral pronouncements can be traced to other cultures or to philosophical thought in no way implies that morality is a function of mere reason—this is a premature conclusion we should not allow to pass unchallenged any longer. What is important is not that such utterances can be found elsewhere, but the particular position they have or do not have in the spiritual edifice of Christianity.[63]

Ratzinger further argues, especially against Küng, that historically speaking it is not correct to say that biblical faith simply adopted the morals of the surrounding culture. Often dramatic battles took place between elements which were deemed not to be capable of assimilation and those that were so assimilated. Ratzinger cites several examples of prophets holding Israel to higher standards than those commonly accepted.

At the level of *praxis* Ratzinger has also warned the faithful not to get mixed up in interfaith situations which require them implicitly to deny their belief in the Trinitarian God. In response to confusion caused among the faithful after the interfaith events at Assisi in 1986 and 2002 he has offered the following principles for multi-religious prayer:

1. Multi-religious prayer cannot be the normal form of religious life but can only exist as a sign in an unusual situation.
2. What is happening must be so clear in itself, and to the world, that it does not become a demonstration of that relativism through which it would nullify its own significance.

3. One must distinguish between multi-religious prayer and inter-religious prayer. Multi-religious is several people praying in the same location to different gods; inter-religious is the one prayer. He doubts whether this is ever possible. It can only happen if there is agreement about the addressee, about who or what God is. It must be clear that God is a person. Any confusion of a personal and an impersonal understanding of God and the gods, must be excluded.
4. There must also be agreement about what is worth praying about and the content of prayer. The Lord's prayer is the measure of what we might ask of God.
5. Multi-religious prayer must not put into question the belief in Christ as the only saviour.[64]

Of all the interfaith groups, it is the Jewish people to whom Christians are obviously the closest. In this context Ratzinger has strongly endorsed the principles of *Nostrae aetate*, the Vatican II 'Declaration on the Relationship of the Church to Non-Christian Religions', in which it is emphasized that salvation comes from the Jews. He reminds people that the *shema*, the 'Hear, O Israel' from Deuteronomy 6: 4–9, was and still is the real core of the believer's identity, not only for Israel, but also for Christianity:

The believing Jew dies reciting this profession; the Jewish martyrs breathed their last declaring it and gave their lives for it ... the fact that this God now shows us his face in Jesus Christ (John 14: 9)—a face that Moses was not allowed to see (Exod. 33: 20)—does not alter this profession in the least and changes nothing essential in this identity.[65]

In summary, Ratzinger's ecclesiology must be read as a synthesis of a number of currents. There are strong resonances of Guardini, de Lubac, and von Balthasar, there are theological presuppositions about the importance of Scripture and the relationship of the Old to the New Testaments, there is the place of Mariology, Pneumatology, and Christology, there is the critique of the People of God concept and the Catholic Inc. model which it fostered, and there is a strong endorsement of *Lumen gentium*, especially the notion of the Church as a hierarchical communion. Underneath all of this there is a basic belief that the Church is an institution of Divine origin and that her sacred offices are not a mere human construction. There is also a genuine openness to finding ways of welcoming back ecclesial communities that bailed out in the sixteenth century, but not in such a way that doctrine is treated as irrelevant. As a scholar Ratzinger knows that heresies usually occur when some element of the tradition is distorted or completely neglected, and he is open to finding legitimate concerns in other traditions, and to acknowledging that the trouble arose in the first instance because of some reality in the life of the Church in previous times which was not as it should have been. With those of non-Christian faith traditions he does not see that there is much common ground at all between Christians and the proponents of 'mystical religions', since for him religion is about a relationship between the human person and God, it is not about achieving a certain psychological state or feeling. There are, however, fields of common ground with members of other monotheistic religions since they all start from the same baseline of believing that the world and all that is within it was created by God and therefore that human beings exist in a relationship with God who demands things of them. The monotheistic traditions thus end up sharing common concerns about contemporary liberal attitudes to the foundations of human dignity and to the sacrality of marriage and family life. He is, finally, opposed to the relativism of the 'God is like an elephant' fable, and recommends to those who have only got hold of a tail or trunk that they use their intellect to broaden their vision. The closing words of his Regensburg Address were the following:

The courage to engage the whole breadth of reason, and not the denial of its grandeur—this is the programme with which a theology grounded in biblical faith enters into the debates of our time ... It is to this great *logos*, to this breadth of reason, that we invite our partners in the dialogue of cultures.[66]

6

Modernity and the Politics of the West

In his homily at the Mass prior to his election Ratzinger rhetorically asked: 'how many winds of doctrine have we known in recent decades, how many ideological currents, how many ways of thinking?' He suggested that the western world was currently in the throws of a dictatorship of relativism that did not recognize anything as definitive and whose goal consists solely of the satisfaction of the desires of one's own ego. However, while post-modern relativism is replacing the Ten Commandments in the area of private morality, in the area of public morality eighteenth-century 'Enlightenment' conceptions of freedom and truth continue to provide the foundation of the dominant political cultures of the West. Paradoxically, these theories are now being used to promote nineteenth-century romantic-movement visions of human dignity, which, at least implicitly, and sometimes quite explicitly, reject the eighteenth-century accounts of reason and morality. For this reason contemporary public life in the western world has been described as a three-cornered 'civil war' of hostile traditions.[1] The pattern of alliances in this war is constantly changing from issue to issue, country to country, and political forum to political forum. This is the political environment in which the Catholic Church finds herself at the beginning of the twenty-first century. Benedict has to navigate between the Charybdis of eighteenth-century-style attacks on the rationality of Christianity and the Scylla of nineteenth-century 'post-modern' attacks on Christian conceptions of human dignity and the meaning and purpose of sexuality. Depending on the context, Benedict's statements can sound more or less hostile, more or less favourable to the Enlightenment(s). When dealing with conceptions of the meaning and value of human life which have a nineteenth-century neo-pagan Romantic pedigree he tends to implore recourse to reason. When dealing with political philosophies which flow from eighteenth-century thought he reminds his interlocutors that philosophy has always been nourished by religious traditions. He is almost on a weekly basis contending with the theological presuppositions of hostile traditions. He believes that the Church cannot simply retreat into her own ghetto: the Church 'cannot enclose men and cultures in a kind of spiritual nature reserve'.[2]

So what is the framework from within which Benedict operates when judging aspects of contemporary culture? The point is often made that where a person stands on the issue of the culture of modernity depends upon how she or he views the evolution or, in academic parlance, genealogy of this culture. In other words, what is its pedigree, where did it come from? How did we get to this state of civil war among hostile traditions? There are several schools of interpretation, but most can be slotted into one of three academic stables: (i) modernity represents the severance of the classical–theistic synthesis: what we have now are free-floating concepts which have lost their meaning once separated from the whole; (ii) modernity represents a mutation of the classical–theistic synthesis since the key concepts once severed from their Christian roots are given new meanings; and (iii) modernity is an entirely new culture based on concepts and values which were specifically developed to take the place of the defunct Greek and Christian concepts.

The above categories are not necessarily closed or always exclusive. For example, one can accept Alasdair MacIntyre's 'first stable' account of the severance of faith from reason, and the severance of politics and economics from ethics, at the same time as accepting von Balthasar's 'first stable' account of the severance of the true, the beautiful, and the good from one another, as well as agreeing with William T. Cavanaugh, Catherine Pickstock, and John Milbank's 'second stable' account of the emergence of the liberal state as an entity which comes with its own heretical soteriology. They each hold pieces of a puzzle which can be fitted together. Those who study the cultures of modernity and post-modernity are rather like art curators who each work on understanding one or two pieces of a great mosaic in order to discern where they once fitted into the picture. The insights of many scholars can be brought together to get a clearer and larger picture. Some focus on the processes of severance and disintegration, others on the form of the mutation. So the question arises: where does Ratzinger fit into these categories? Is there a stable in which he might feel at home?

Ratzinger has not written one all-encompassing comprehensive exposition of his own genealogy but he has offered pieces of the puzzle in various books and articles. The first general point to be made is that he has no sympathy at all for the third category which views modernity as something completely new, nor does he have any patience for the doctrine of social evolution and the Hegelian belief in constant progress to which it is closely allied. Ratzinger rejects all materialistic and deterministic theories of history.[3] The English historian Christopher Dawson (1889–1970) once made the observation that the Christian view of history is not a secondary element derived by philosophical reflection from the study of history. It lies at the very heart of Christianity and forms an integral part of the Christian faith. As a consequence there is no Christian 'philosophy of history' in the strict sense of the word. There is, instead, a Christian history and Christian theology of history.[4] This is essentially the position that Ratzinger has taken since at least the time of his *Habilitationsshrift* on the theology of history in the thought of St Bonaventure. It echoes the position of the German philosopher Josef Pieper who has been one of the seminal influences on the thought of Ratzinger and it resonates with the whole Christocentric trajectory of von Balthasar. Pieper argued that 'there is no philosophical question, which, if it really wants to strike the ground intended by itself and in itself, does not come upon the primeval rock of theological pronouncements' and as a consequence 'the beginning and end of human history are conceivable only on acceptance of a pre-philosophically traditional interpretation of reality; they are either "revealed" or they are inconceivable'.[5] While this is cold comfort for those who want a philosophy of history, its positive side is that it means that 'the Incarnation is not the nth performance of a tragedy already lying in the archives of eternity'.[6] It is an event of total originality. In accord with Dawson, Pieper, and von Balthasar, Ratzinger holds that Christian Revelation is the foundation of a new history which, paradoxically, is experienced as the end of all history:

The beginning and end of this new history is the Person of Jesus of Nazereth, who is recognized as the last man (the second Adam), that is as the long-awaited manifestation of what is truly human and the definitive revelation to man of his hidden nature; for this very reason, it is oriented toward the whole human race and presumes the abrogation of all partial histories, whose partial salvation is looked upon as essentially an absence of salvation.[7]

Ratzinger thus rejects all philosophies of history which would find in the historical process some dynamic outside the theo-drama of God's offer of grace and the human response to this offer. He describes secular theories of historical progress, especially the Marxist and liberal accounts, as examples of ideological optimism and a secularization of Christian hope.[8] His genealogy of modernity does not follow the school of thinking which reads modernity as an entirely new culture, completely severed from all Christian roots. He believes that it is entangled with the Christian heritage however much secular liberal political elites may want to deny this.

What Ratzinger offers by way of his own contribution to the critique of the culture of modernity is a kind of 'double helix' genealogy with reference to two sets of three intellectual moments in which the Hellenic component of the culture was severed from the Christian and in which the Christian component was fundamentally undermined by the mutation of the doctrine of creation. Indeed in both cases the severances are accompanied by mutations. When faith in creation is lost, Christian faith is transformed into *gnosis*, and when faith in reason is lost, wisdom is reduced to the empirically verifiable which cannot sustain a moral framework.[9]

With reference to the Christian side of the 'double helix', Ratzinger identifies the first moment of severance with the philosophy of Giordano Bruno (1545–1600). He acknowledges that, at first sight, 'it may seem strange to accuse him of suppressing faith in creation, since he was responsible for an emphatic rediscovery of the cosmos in its divinity', but he argues that it is precisely this reversion to a divine cosmos that brings about the recession of faith in creation: 'Here "renaissance" means relinquishing the Christian so that the Greek can be restored in its pagan purity. In the Greek conception, the world appears as a divine fullness at peace within itself. While for the Christian account of creation, the world is dependent on something other than itself.'[10] Ratzinger concludes that this is the aesthetic prelude to an increasingly prominent idea in the modern mind: the idea that the human dependency implied by faith in creation is unacceptable.[11]

The second significant moment arrives with the thought of Galileo (1564–1642) in which there is also a return to the Greeks, not to their aesthetic insights, but to the mathematical side of Platonic thought. Here Ratzinger writes:

'God does geometry' is the way [Galileo] expresses his concepts of God and nature as well as his scientific ideal. God wrote the book of nature with mathematical letters. Studying geometry enables us to touch the traces of God. But this means that the knowledge of God is turned into the knowledge of the mathematical structures of nature; the concept of nature in the sense of the object of science, takes the place of the concept of creation . . . Determined by this axiom ['God does geometry'], God has to become Platonic. He dwindles away to be little more than the formal mathematical structures perceived by science in nature.[12]

Ratzinger concludes:

A mere 'first cause' which is effective only in nature and never reveals itself to humans, which abandons humans to a realm completely beyond its own sphere of influence, such a first cause is no longer God but a scientific hypothesis. On the other hand, a God who has nothing to do with the rationality of creation, but is effective only in the inner world of piety, is also no longer God; he becomes devoid of reality and is ultimately meaningless. Only when creation and covenant come together can either creation or covenant be realistically discussed—the one presupposes the other.[13]

The third form of deviation from the classical–theistic idea of creation came with Martin Luther (1483–1546). While Bruno and Galileo represent a return to a pre-Christian, Greek, and pagan world, Luther went in the extreme opposite direction. He wanted to purge Christian thought of its Greek heritage, and the Greek element he found most objectionable was the concept of the cosmos in the question of being, and therefore in the area of the doctrine of creation. For Luther, redemption sets humans free from the curse of the existing creation and thus grace exists in radical opposition to creation. Developing an argument taken from Angelo Scola and Rocco Buttiglione, Ratzinger concluded that 'without the mystery of redemptive love, which is also creative love, the world inevitably becomes dualistic: by nature, it becomes geometry: as history, it becomes the drama of evil'.[14]

After these three moments in which the doctrine of creation was mutated, the German philosopher Georg Wilhelm Friedrich Hegel (1770–1831) tried to resolve the dualism by positing God not as the eternal self-existent Almighty, who stands facing the evil of the world, but rather God who exists in the process of reasoning.[15] He reinterprets the whole of human history as the unfolding of reason. With Karl Marx, the greatest of the left-wing Hegelians, redemption was then construed as something which humanity must achieve through its own efforts by an intellectual and political process. In the Marxist schema, the place of creation is reoccupied by the category of self-creation, which is accomplished through work. Against the Marxist idea that the human person is someone defined by the capacity to work and produce things, Ratzinger believes that the human person is first of all a being created for worship. Against Marx's idea that redemption should take a political form, Ratzinger argues that 'the only goal of the Exodus [the liberation of the Jews from slavery to Pharaoh], was worship, which can only occur according to God's measure'.[16] He suggests that this orientation of creation to the rest of the Sabbath is not a peculiarly Christian idea, but that all the great pre-Christian civilizations point to the fact that the universe exists for worship and for the glorification of God. From this premiss he concludes that 'the danger that confronts us today in our technological civilisation is that we have cut ourselves off from this primordial knowledge which serves as a guidepost and which links the great cultures, and that an increasing scientific know-how is preventing us from being aware of the fact of creation'.[17] As a consequence, 'those who reject God's rest, its leisure, its worship, its peace and its freedom, fall into the slavery of activity'.[18]

On this reading the Christian component of the classical–theistic synthesis was mutated in the above three moments represented by the figures of Bruno, Galileo, and Luther, whose dualist consequences Hegel sought to overcome by a completely new idea of God and history.

Ratzinger then further identifies three moments in the subversion of the Greek strand of the helix. This subversion was actually the central theme of his famous Regensburg address. This time Luther remains in the trilogy but as the representative of the first rather than third moment. As stated above, the Reformation he fostered sought to sever all the Greek components of the synthesis from the Christian. For Luther, reason was the bastard child of Aristotle brought up by the pimp Thomas Aquinas. Two centuries later the Lutheran Immanuel Kant carried through the programme of severance. Although Ratzinger seems to include Kant as an heir to the Lutheran 'first moment' he does say that in his anchoring of faith 'exclusively in practical reason, denying it access to reality as a whole' he carried through Luther's programme with a radicalism that the Reformers could never have foreseen.[19]

The second moment in the programme of de-Hellenization arrived in the nineteenth century with Adolf von Harnack (1851–1930) as its leading representative. Von Harnack sought to distinguish between the God of the philosophers and the God of Abraham, Isaac, and Jacob. The God of the philosophers was said to have put an end to worship in favour of morality. He was presented as the father of a humanitarian message. Harnack's goal was to liberate Christianity from philosophy altogether as well as to purge it of doctrinal elements such as faith in Christ's divinity and the belief in the Trinity. Ratzinger concludes that the end result of this second moment is that the radius of both science and reason has been severely narrowed and the question of God is made to appear either unscientific or pre-scientific. In this situation any attempt to maintain theology's claim to be 'scientific' would end up reducing Christianity to a mere fragment of its former self.

The third moment is contemporary and is associated with the anti-European attitude which surfaced in the aftermath of two world wars started in Europe and the rise of Asian and African nationalism in the 1960s. It holds that the synthesis of Greek and Christian thought in the first centuries after Christ was an important project for those times but has no relevance to contemporary non-European cultures. To put the position somewhat crudely, the Greek component may be of some interest to Europeans but it is irrelevant in outback Australia, the highlands of New Guinea, or the safari parks of Kenya. Ratzinger says that there is some element of truth in this position. It is true that a knowledge of classical letters is not necessary for salvation. None the less, Ratzinger believes that the relationship of faith to human reason arose providentially from the junction of the Greek and Hebraic cultures. For him an understanding of this relationship is indispensable. This is the universal cultural patrimony of Catholics across the globe and its importance was also recognized in paragraph 72 of John Paul II's encyclical *Fides et Ratio*: 'In engaging great cultures for the first time the Church cannot abandon what she has gained from her inculturation in the world of Greco–Latin thought. To reject this heritage would be to deny the providential plan of God who guides His Church down the paths of time and history.'[20] It is something of a paradox that Luther was hostile to the Greek interest in rationality and yet it was a philosopher deeply influenced by Lutheran pietism who did more than anyone else to drive a wedge between faith and reason and in effect exalt the faculty of reason. The cumulative effect of

Luther and Kant was to force a choice between scripture alone and so-called 'pure' reason alone. Those who took the path of reason alone tended to instrumentalize Christianity by turning it into a moralism. Thus reduced, the task of evangelizing the peoples of Asia, Africa, and the Pacific came to be seen, at least in the 1960s and 70s, as a project of transmitting a Christian moral vision along with helping these peoples to improve their material standards of living, particularly their access to medical treatment. While Ratzinger is not opposed to either the transmission of a moral vision or improving material standards of living, he does believe that to reduce Christianity to these goods is severely to truncate it, and to drain it of its most dynamic, most life-giving elements.

Ratzinger's genealogy of modernity thus takes the form of both severance and mutation (first and second stable accounts) wherein the classical–theistic synthesis is unravelled through three successive attacks on the doctrine of creation on the one side, and at least three successive attacks on the relationship of faith to reason on the other. Linked to the mutation of the Christian doctrine of creation is the emergence of a notion of human freedom as the ability to pursue any vision of the good which might appeal. Once the relationship between nature and creation has been severed, then the way lies open for the severance of nature and morality and the arrival of the Nietzschean project of the transvaluation of the Judeo–Christian heritage.

Politically the end result is that the Church has to contend with the argument that only Enlightenment culture can be constitutive for the identity of Europe, and the countries of the western world generally. Within the culture of modernity different religious cultures can coexist with their respective rights only on the condition and to the degree in which they respect the criteria of this culture, and are subordinated to it. Ratzinger, however, believes that the Church cannot accept this kind of marginalization. In the collection of essays published in 1988 under the title *The Church, Ecumenism and Politics* he noted with approval that the early Christians would not allow Christ to be included in the pantheon alongside the pagan gods.[21] They would not pay their dues to the pagan gods and nor would they accept that the life of the *polis* was the highest good there is.

In this context Ratzinger has been influenced by the work of the German philosopher Robert Spaemann who has warned against a 'fatal tendency' to understand Christianity as just one of an ensemble of social forces. According to Spaemann, the Church must understand herself as 'the place of an absolute public validity surpassing the state under the legitimizing claim of God'.[22] Ratzinger agrees with this but says that this claim to public validity should not be construed as an opposition to a genuine religious tolerance. He agrees with the basic principle of the Conciliar document *Dignitatis humanae* that religious observance can never be coerced. None the less, he argues that the state must recognize that a basic framework of values within a Christian foundation is the precondition for its own existence and it must learn that there is a truth which is not subject to consensus but which precedes it and makes it possible.[23]

Included in this judgement is Ratzinger's assessment that there is no such thing as a theologically neutral state which is the good which the liberal tradition claims to offer. It is logical nonsense. He quotes Rudolf Bultmann's line that 'an unchristian state is possible on principle, but not an atheistic state'.[24] It is at this point that Ratzinger's thought resonates with much contemporary scholarship from the Radical Orthodoxy and evangelical Protestant stables and also with the Thomist political philosophy of James V. Schall SJ and Alasdair MacIntyre. The evangelical scholar Oliver O'Donovan has written that 'the appearance of a social secularity could only be created by understanding society as a quasi-mechanical system, incapable of moral and spiritual acts', and, thus, 'the false consciousness of the would-be contemporary secular society [*or theologically neutral liberal state*] lies in its determination to conceal the religious judgements that it has made'.[25] The Anglican John Milbank, and the Catholic William T. Cavanagh, have both traced the mutation in the meaning of the concept of the secular realm. Prior to modern times it referred to this temporal world before Christ's second coming; it has only recently come to mean a separate social space which is impermeable to grace and the intrusion of theological principles. They argue that within the traditional meaning of the term *saeculum* society as a whole could never be secular.

The fact that the concept is one of those which has undergone a process of mutation was also recognized by Ratzinger in an interview with the Italian newspaper *La Repubblica* in 2003. Here he stated: 'Secularism is no longer that element of neutrality which opens up areas of freedom for everyone. It is beginning to turn into an ideology that imposes itself through politics and leaves no public space for the Catholic and Christian vision, which thus risks becoming something purely private and essentially mutilated.'[26] Similarly, in 2000 he wrote:

'the problem with the liberal privatization of religion is that, in the name of tolerance, it favours what is in fact an intolerant suppression of the (ultimately religious) question of this fidelity.'[27] In *The Yes of Jesus Christ: Spiritual Exercises in Faith, Hope and Love*, he concluded: 'A society that turns what is specifically human into something purely private and defines itself in terms of a complete secularity (which moreover inevitably becomes a pseudo-religion and a new all-embracing system that enslaves people)—this kind of society will of its nature be sorrowful, a place of despair: it rests on a diminution of human dignity.'[28]

In part this diminution of human dignity stems from the fact that the criterion of rationality by which this Enlightenment culture runs is increasingly taken from an experience of technological production based on science. At its most extreme this leads to a scientific domination and manipulation of nature that is problematic in view of the dramatic environmental problems the world now faces and in view of its effects on the very conception of what it means to be human. Conception no longer needs to be the result of an act of love but can be the result of a laboratory technique; parents are encouraged to abort genetically imperfect babies; the sick and elderly in some countries can now choose to end their lives rather than being a burden on their families. In each of these cases human life is no longer accepted as sacred and inviolable. It has its market value. Ratzinger writes that according to the values of this culture imperfect individuals must be weeded out and the path of planning and production must aim at the perfect man. Suffering must disappear, and life is to consist of pleasure alone. This leads to new forms of coercion and the emergence of a new ruling class.[29]

Ratzinger believes that members of this new ruling class are fostering a 'new political moralism' whose key words are justice, peace, and the conservation of creation. He includes Hans Küng's *Weltethos* (world ethos) project in this category and he strongly endorses the criticisms of this project by Robert Spaemann.[30] Küng's project is to try and boil down the values of all the great religious traditions to a short list of moral principles upon which they might all agree. In some ways it is a variation on the Kantian political philosophical project of John Rawls with its concept of 'reflective equilibrium'. Neither Spaemann nor Benedict has any opposition to justice, peace, and the conservation of creation per se, but they make the point that the content which is commonly given to these terms by members of the new ruling class is different from what a credal Christian would give them, and they also believe that the project simply will not work.

Spaemann argues that Küng's *Weltethos* reduces religion to being merely 'a booth in the fairground of post-modernism, adding an ambiguous offer of "sense and meaning beyond death" to the somewhat plausible "be nice to each other" '.[31] This is the very claim of religion's 'educated', 'benign', and 'enlightened' detractors. For Spaemann any political philosophy which tries to ignore the reality of original sin becomes just another utopian ideology. He asks, why would a chap who is otherwise going to commit adultery refrain from doing so because it might offend the world ethos? If it is not enough for a Christian that Jesus Christ tells him the same thing, why should this person suddenly change his judgement because Muhammad or some other religious figure has joined the chorus? Spaemann concludes that Hans Küng is firmly rooted in the tradition of modernity's instrumentalization of religion in the service of morals and morals in the service of national preservation. In other words, Küng's *Weltethos* is a kind of warmed-up version of Adolf von Harnack's nineteenth-century project. Benedict adds to this his judgement that there is no rational or ethical or religious universal formula about which everyone could agree and which could then support everyone, and it is for this reason that the so-called world ethos remains an abstraction.[32] He also cites the judgement of the German historian and anti-Nazi hero Joachim Fest (1926–2006) that 'the farther the agreements—which cannot be reached without concessions—are pushed, the more elastic and consequently the more impotent the ethical norms become, to the point that the project finally amounts to a mere corroboration of that unbinding morality which is not the goal, but the problem'.[33] Ratzinger concludes:

The political moralism that we have lived through, and are living through still, not only does not open the way to regeneration, it actually blocks it. The same also holds therefore for a Christianity and a theology that reduce the core of Jesus message, the 'kingdom of God' to the 'values of the kingdom' while identifying these values with the main watchwords of political moralism, and proclaiming them, at the same time, to be the synthesis of all religions—all the while forgetting about God, despite the fact that it is precisely He who is the subject and the cause of the kingdom of God.[34]

None the less, as was stated in Chapter 2, Benedict is not calling for a return to some particular pre-Enlightenment political order. He says we do not need to bid adieu to the heritage of the Enlightenment in so far as this is construed as a quest for freedom as such, but he suggests that the West does need to correct its course in three essential points. First, it needs to appreciate that law is not the opposite of freedom but is its necessary condition; second, against all utopian projects, there needs to be an understanding that within human history no absolutely ideal situation will ever exist and a perfected ordering of freedom will never be able to be achieved because it is impossible to eradicate original sin, and all its consequences; and thirdly, the leaders of the western world need to bid farewell to the dream of the absolute autonomy of reason [from theology] and of its self-sufficiency.[35] As an aspect of this third course correction there needs to be a recognition that the first service that Christian Revelation delivered to the political order was to liberate it from the burden of being the highest good for humanity. It destroyed the myth of the divine state, and in its place it put the objectivity of reason. However, Ratzinger warns that this does not mean that it has produced a value-free objectivity, such as is sometimes claimed for sociology: 'to genuine human reason belongs the morality that is fed by God's commandments. This morality is not some private affair; it has public significance.'[36] He reiterates the advice that Jeremiah gave to the Jews exiled in Babylon to seek the welfare of the city where God has placed them. He believes that the morality of the exile contains fundamental elements of a positive political ethos. As a general statement of principle, he concludes:

Although politics does not bring about the kingdom of God, it must be concerned for the right kingdom of human beings, that is, it must create the preconditions for peace at home and abroad and for a rule of law that will permit everyone to 'lead a quiet and peaceable life, godly and respectful in every way' (1 Tim. 2: 2).[37]

In *Values in a Time of Upheaval* Benedict stated that he did not wish to offer a new theory about the relationship between the state and moral truth, he merely wanted to summarize a number of insights that could form a kind of platform that permits a conversation:

1. The state is not itself the source of truth and morality;
2. The goal of the state cannot consist in a freedom without defined contents;
3. Accordingly, the state must receive from outside itself the essential measure of knowledge and truth with regard to that which is good;
4. This outside cannot be 'pure reason' however desirable in theory, because, in practice, such a pure rational evidential quality

independent of history does not exist. Metaphysical and moral reason come into action only in a historical context;

5. Christian faith has proved to be the most universal and rational religious culture;

6. The Church may not exalt itself to become the state, nor may it seek to work as an organ of power in the state or beyond the state boundaries;

7. The Church remains outside the state . . . [but] must exert herself with all her vigour so that in it there may shine forth the moral truth that it offers to the state and that ought to become evident to the citizens of the state.[38]

In the more specific context of the Church's teaching on economic ethics, Ratzinger, like his papal predecessors going all the way back to Leo XIII, has been strongly critical of both utopian socialist and laissez-faire, liberal capitalist theory. He observes that they share common philosophical presuppositions about the relationship of ethics to economics, and a common deterministic core. In his essay 'The Church and Economics' he argued that the lives of many people are completely controlled by the laws of the market, while at the same time liberal theorists argue that the market is morally neutral and associated with the promotion of human freedom. He described as 'astounding' the presupposition that the laws of the market are in essence good.[39] With reference to the work by P. Scholl-Latour, *Afrikanische Totenklage: Der Ausverkauf des Schwarzen Kontinents* (Munich, 2001), he has written of the 'tragic legacy' and 'cruelty of the liberal capitalist system':

Behind the superficial solidarity of the developing-nations model has some-times been hidden the desire to expand the reach of one's own power, one's own ideology, one's own market share. In the process, old social structures have been destroyed, and spiritual and moral forces have been wasted, with consequences that should ring in our ears as an unprecedented indictment.[40]

Ratzinger thinks it is wrong to rely solely upon putatively 'value-neutral' marketplace mechanisms since 'pre-existing values are always determin-ants in making market decisions'.[41] He believes that contemporary world economic affairs are driven by a form of liberalism which 'specifically excludes the heart' and the 'possibility of seeing God, of introducing the light of moral responsibility, love and justice into the worlds of work, of commerce and of politics'.[42] He argues that 'if globalization in technol-ogy and economy is not accompanied by a new openness to an awareness of the God to whom we will all render an account, then it will end in catastrophe'.[43] Indeed, he asserts that 'any kind of social or political unity that is created without God, or even in opposition to him, ends like the experiment of Babylon: in total confusion and destruction, in the hatred and violence of universal conflict'.[44]

In some contemporary schools of Thomism the analogue for the idea of a theologically neutral secular social space is the project of discovering common ground between Liberals and Christians on the plain of natural law. The viability of this project is currently under question by a number of scholars, including those who identify their work with the Thomist tradition. This project received its greatest impetus in the twentieth century with the scholarship and diplomatic work of the French Thomist Jacques Maritain (1882–1973). In *Faithful Reason* John Haldane concluded that anyone reviewing the degree of ideological and moral diversity and conflict exhibited today, half a century after Jacques Maritain's attempt in *The Person and the Common Good*, must wonder how feasible is the project of finding common ground between the Thomist and other traditions with reference to natural law.[45] James V. Schall has also noted that 'reading Maritain on rights and values requires a constant internal correction to recognize that what he means by these terms is something very different from what is generally meant by them in the [contemporary] culture'.[46] To the same end, Ernest Fortin has argued that 'natural law becomes intelligible only within the framework of a providential order in which the words and deeds of individual human beings are known to God and duly rewarded and punished by him'.[47] In societies where there is no longer a belief in any rational order within creation, or indeed any belief in creation itself, the project of using the language of the natural law tradition to negotiate with non-Christians becomes extremely difficult. This is Benedict's conclusion also. In *Values in a Time of Upheaval* he wrote:

Natural law has remained—especially in the Catholic Church—one element in the arsenal of arguments in conversations with secular society and with other communities of faith, appealing to shared reason in the attempt to discern the basis of a consensus about ethical principles of law in a pluralistic, secular society. Unfortunately, this instrument has become blunt, and that is why I do not wish to employ it to support my arguments in this discussion [about the moral foundations of a free state]. The idea of the natural law presupposed a concept of 'nature' in which nature and reason interlock;

nature itself is rational. The victory of the theory of evolution has meant the end of this view of nature.[48]

Benedict is not saying that he does not believe in natural law. He believes in it because he believes in a divinely created order and he referred to it in *Deus Caritas Est*. He simply thinks it is a 'blunt instrument' for dealing with those who no longer accept a Genesis account of the creation. He recognizes that human rights have remained the last element of the natural law tradition operative within contemporary liberal political cultures, and he suggests that the doctrine of human rights ought today to be complemented by a doctrine of human obligations and human limits.[49] He has not, however, made any pronouncements about the rhetorical effectiveness of the human rights discourse in the promotion of the Church's teaching on the sanctity of human life and the foundation of human dignity.

In his essay 'Prepolitical Moral Foundations of a Free Republic' he wrote of a need for a polyphonic correlation in which the different religious traditions would open themselves up to the essential complementarity of reason and faith.[50] He stated that there is a necessary correlativity of reason and religion which are appointed mutually to cleanse and heal one another, which mutually need one another, and mutually must recognize this need.[51] He is not, therefore, a fideist; he does want people to use their intellectual faculty to make judgements about the merits of different social practices. This theme was reiterated in *Deus Caritas Est* at article 28:

From God's standpoint, faith liberates reason from its blind spots and therefore helps it to be ever more fully itself. Faith enables reason to do its work more effectively and to see its proper object more clearly. This is where Catholic social doctrine has its place: it has no intention of giving the Church power over the State. Even less is it an attempt to impose on those who do not share the faith ways of thinking and modes of conduct proper to faith. Its aim is simply to purify reason and to contribute, here and now, to the acknowledgment and attainment of what is just.

In the following article Benedict endorses the notion of an autonomous use of reason in the world of politics at the same time as noting that the Church has an indirect duty to contribute to the purification of reason and to the reawakening of those moral forces without which just structures are neither established nor prove effective in the long run. In this context, the expression 'the autonomous use of reason' would appear to mean 'reason' in the sense of a prudential or practical judgement made without recourse to any ecclesial authority. In another sense, however, the Church remains involved in the whole process, albeit indirectly, through the judgements of lay Catholics and other Christians and persons of good will who operate with purified reason. A purified reason is the 'Magna Carta of all ecclesial service'.[52] For Benedict such 'purified reason' is something vastly different from Kantian 'pure reason'. One might say that for Benedict so-called 'pure reason' is impure reason. In *Deus Caritas Est* he concludes that the figures of saints such as Francis of Assisi, Ignatius of Loyola, John of God, Camillus of Lellis, Vincent de Paul, Louise de Marillac, Giuseppe B. Cottolengo, John Bosco, Luigi Orione, and Mother Teresa of Calcutta stand out as lasting models of social charity for all people of good will.[53] They are the true bearers of light within history, for they are men and women of faith, hope, and love.[54] In other words, the saints, rather than the rationality of the Enlightenment, are the true bearers of light in human history and the best models of how to engage the world.

The notion of the importance of a reasoned or reasonable faith most often arises in contemporary discussions about Islam. Significantly, and contrary to popular attitudes, Ratzinger does not believe that the solution to the problem of Islam in the western world is for it to undergo its own eighteenth-century style Enlightenment. Generally, he believes that Muslims do not feel threatened by the Christian moral foundations of the West but by 'the cynicism of a secularized culture that denies its own bases'.[55] He suggests that it is not the mention of God that offends the adherents of other religions but the attempt to build the human community without any reference to God whatsoever.[56] He believes that Islam comes alive as faith precisely when its adherents experience cultures, and, in particular, legal systems, that are God-less.[57] None the less he is concerned that Islam has never really come to grips with the importance of the relationship between faith and reason. In 1988 he wrote:

Already in its emergence Islam is to a certain extent a reversion to a monotheism which does not accept the Christian transition to God made man and which likewise shuts itself off from Greek rationality and its civilization which became a component of Christian monotheism via the idea of God becoming man. It can of course be objected to this that in the course of history there were continually approaches in Islam to the intellectual world of Greece; but they never lasted. What this is saying above all is that the separation of faith and law, of religion and tribal law, was not completed in Islam and cannot be completed without affecting its very core. To put it another way, faith presents itself in the form of a more or less archaic system of forms of life governed by civil and penal law. It may not be defined nationally, but it is defined in a legal system which fixes it ethnically and culturally and at the same time sets limits to rationality at the point where the Christian synthesis sees the existence of the sphere of reason.[58]

In his Regensburg address he was clearly trying to encourage the development of Islamic thought in the direction of a consideration of Greek ideas about reason. In his commentary on the address, James V. Schall made the point that, at their philosophic roots, the two cultures—modern secularism and Islam—are not that much different. He suggests that this is what Benedict implies in his citation from Ibn Hazn concerning voluntarism. Islam and modern secularism share the same voluntarist tendency. They both eschew the possibility that there is an obligatory order of reason. In the case of modernity and post-modernity reality is itself a product of human artifice, of mere human will. In the case of Islam, what is good is defined by reference to the will of Allah.[59] In neither case is there a recognition of a *logos* inherent in the order of being itself. This is what Ratzinger was driving at, so to speak, in the Regensburg address. He was pleading at least as much with contemporary militant secularists as with contemporary militant Muslims to recognize that they share a common philosophical starting point.

This is not to say that Benedict believes that all Muslims are irrational voluntarists. He acknowledges that Islam is not a uniform thing. There is no single authority for all Muslims, and for this reason dialogue with Islam is always dialogue with certain groups. There is no commonly regulated orthodoxy; no one speaks for Islam as a whole.[60] He does, however, believe that as a tradition Islam needs to engage with the intellectual heritage of Greece. He also believes that the attempt to graft on to Islamic societies what are termed western standards cut loose from their Christian foundations misunderstands the internal logic of Islam as well as the historical logic to which these western standards belong.[61] All such attempts are doomed to failure. He has consistently opposed the American-led western intervention in Iraq. There is no 'stem' on which to graft western liberalism and the attempt to do so just fuels the resentment which is one explosive element of the original problem. It plays into the hands of the Islamic terrorists. Benedict believes that for democracy to work it needs a Greco–Christian cultural foundation.

Underlying this position is an implicit belief that the rule of law so central to democracy is the key to the stability of the whole western system. More than anything else Ratzinger's interventions in the area of political theory have taken the form of exhorting liberal elites to recognize that the rule of law must itself be based on solid foundations, not on the will of the people—whatever that happens to be, which is no more secure a foundation than the will of Allah—but on the *logos* inherent in creation. Discerning this inherent rationality, this natural order of being itself, requires a synthesis of the gifts of the Greek and Hebraic cultures. If any component of the double helix is severed and mutated then western culture finds itself in crisis, and when the whole framework is broken and mutated then there is an institutional civil war involving theists, moderns, and post-moderns.

Benedict does not believe that this conflict can be resolved by removing Christ and Christianity from western culture. Any attempt to do so will not only be a kind of cultural suicide (which is already far advanced) it will also require a change in social perceptions of the nature and dignity of the human person. Since Christianity and ortho- dox Judaism are the only theologies on the market, so to speak, which uphold the sanctity of human life from conception to natural death, regardless of its social utility, destroying the Judeo–Christian cultural roots of the West will lead to the emergence of a new ruling class with 'Social Darwinist' social practices not all that different from those which prevailed in Nazi Germany. From Benedict's perspective the suicide of the West began when people stopped believing in the Christian account of creation and started to sever the intrinsic rela- tionship of faith and reason. With the political arrival of Islam within western countries, including the heartland of what was once Chris- tendom, a new four-cornered battle is emerging between Christians, Muslims, and different varieties of secularists and Nietzscheans. In this context Benedict's approach is best summarized as: charity to all under the unambiguous standard of the cross, and, if need be, martyrdom and persecution before accommodation. The 265th successor to St Peter will not allow Christ to be placed in any contemporary pantheon. Not on his watch will Christianity be reduced to a mere 'booth in the fairground of post-modernity'.

7

Liturgy since Vatican II

On the same day as the assassination of President John F. Kennedy in Dallas, Texas (22 November 1963) the Council fathers adopted the Constitution on the Liturgy, *Sacrosanctum concilium*. It was formally promulgated on 4 December 1963. This document was not attempting to break new ground theologically. This had already been done in the encyclical of Pius XII, *Mediator Dei*, of 1947, which was occasioned by the early twentieth-century movement for liturgical renewal. This movement was particularly strong among the Benedictines in western Europe and is associated with the names of Prosper Guéranger of Solesmes (1805–1875), Odo Casel (1886–1948) of the Maria Laach monastery in Germany, the Munich-based theologian Romano Guardini (1885–1968), and the Austrian Augustinian Pius Parsch (1884–1954).[1] The young Ratzinger was strongly influenced by this movement. One of the first books he read after starting his theological studies in 1946 was Guardini's *The Spirit of the Liturgy*, published Easter 1918. In 2000 Ratzinger published his own work under the same title in which he reiterated Guardini's central liturgical principles, but in the light of the liturgical problems of the present era. One of the chief concerns of the movement was to overcome the tendency of laity to regard Mass attendance as a form of duty parade. There was a concern that laity were not properly participating in the liturgical action which was taking place but had accepted the standing of spectators. *Sacrosanctum concilium* reiterated that the liturgy is the embodiment of the Paschal Mystery, which is a mystery of worship, and consequently that the liturgy is intimately related to the mystery of the Church herself, that is, to her nuptial union with Christ. It also emphasized that the earthly liturgy is an anticipation of the heavenly one, so that at the same time as it renews the Paschal mystery it anticipates the consummation of the work of redemption and the renewal of the cosmos at the end of time. It has both cosmic and eschatological dimensions. The participation in the Sacred Liturgy should have an effect on a person's subjective response to God's gift of grace, which is difficult to achieve if his or her spiritual disposition is that of the merely passive spectator.[2]

Sacrosanctum concilium also provided for the formation of a post-conciliar liturgical commission which would oversee a complete revision of the Church's liturgical life. Most of the document is taken up with the enunciation of principles and guidelines for doing this. The fundamental principle for ritual reform was enunciated in article 23:

That sound tradition may be retained, and yet the way remain open to legitimate progress, careful investigation is always to be made into each part of the liturgy which is to be revised. This investigation should be theological, historical and pastoral. Also the general laws governing the structure and meaning of the liturgy must be studied in conjunction with the experience derived from recent liturgical reforms and from the indults [privileges] conceded to various places. Finally there must be no innovations unless the good of the Church genuinely and certainly requires them; and care must be taken that any new forms adopted should in some way grow organically from forms already existing.

The rather conservative stance of this article was followed in article 36 which stated that the use of Latin was to be preserved in the Latin rites, though 'the limits of the employment of the vernacular may be extended'. It was suggested that this would be most appropriate for the scripture readings. Article 38 also provided that 'provisions shall be made when revising the liturgical books, for legitimate variations and adaptations to different groups, regions, and peoples, especially in mission lands'.

All of this sounds quite innocuous, but anyone reading the document critically would realize immediately that its effect is to place wide-ranging powers in the hands of liturgical experts. In *A Tale of Two Documents*, which is a commentary on the relationship between *Mediator Dei* and *Sacrosanctum concilium*, Aidan Nichols concluded that 'with the benefit of hindsight one could regret that the predominantly practical character of their proposals, made as these were in a culturally pragmatic age, were not balanced in advance by a fuller theology of worship'.[3] He further quipped that '*Sacrosanctum concilium's* licence to national liturgical commissions to propose pastoral adaptations turned out to be a blank cheque of the kind known to no bank, for this one can be perpetually re-presented'.[4] As early as 1966, in his *Theological Highlights of Vatican II*, Ratzinger predicted that 'the value of the reform will of course substantially depend on the post-Conciliar commission of Cardinal Lercaro and what it is able to achieve'.[5] In particular, he queried whether it would be possible to minimize excessive centralism without losing unity?

The choice of Lercaro as the Liturgical Commission's President was significant. In 1955 he had given a paper, 'The Christian Church', in which he expressed the view that liturgical tradition should adapt itself to and express itself in the cultural forms of its present age. This was followed up at the Council with an influential speech during the debate on *Gaudium et spes* in which he recommended a complete makeover of the Church's cultural practices.[6] Lercaro was firmly of the view that the Church's 'glorious cultural patrimony' (his words) had passed its 'use-by date' and that a new generation of 'modern men' wanted something less formal, more down to earth, and in the vernacular. As a matter of liturgical theory he believed that liturgy should be subject to perennial reconstruction in order to achieve pastoral ends. He used amusing and often colourful language to describe those Cardinals who opposed this judgement. Cardinal Bacci was a 'useless caryatid sustaining Cicero's language' and Cardinal Staffa was a 'concentrate of moldy tradition'.[7] Lercaro was assisted by Archbishop Annibale Bugnini (1912–1982), who as Secretary of the *Consilium* was the person who directed the developments on a daily basis. Much has been written about Bugnini, especially about the reasons behind the decision of Paul VI to 'exile' him to a diplomatic post in Iran in 1976. However, since the reasons of Paul VI remain in the territory of speculation, one can only say with certainty that he was someone who shared Lercaro's liturgical outlook and who was known for an ability to get things done.

Implicit within Lercaro's attitude was a certain Neo-Scholastic approach to liturgy according to which it is possible to boil down sacramental theology to considerations of form and matter. Ratzinger explains the mentality when he says that people think of the bread and wine as the material of the sacrament, and the words of institution as its form, and then go on to believe that only these two things are really necessary, that everything else is freely disposable. If one takes this as one's major theological premiss, then there is no problem with constantly trying to update the liturgy which reference to contemporary cultural movements, providing one retains the words of institution and the bread and wine. With reference to this attitude, in his Preface to Alcuin Reid's *The Organic Development of the Liturgy*, Ratzinger wrote:

At this point Modernists and Traditionalists are in agreement. As long as the material gifts are there, and the words of institution are spoken, then everything else is freely disposable. Many priests today, unfortunately, act in accordance with this motto; and the theories of many liturgists are unfortunately moving in the same direction. They want to overcome the limits of the rite, as being something fixed and immovable, and construct the products of their fantasy, which are supposedly 'pastoral', around this remnant, this core which has been spared, and which is thus either relegated to the realm of magic, or loses any meaning whatever. The Liturgical Movement had in fact been attempting to overcome this reductionism, the product of an abstract sacramental theology, and to teach us to understand the Liturgy as a living network of tradition which had taken concrete form, which cannot be torn apart into little pieces, but has to be seen and experienced as a living whole. Anyone like myself, who was moved by this perception in the time of the Liturgical Movement on the eve of the Second Vatican Council, can only stand, deeply sorrowing, before the ruins of the very things they were concerned for.[8]

The Neo-Scholastic obsession with conceptual definitions and formulae was always somewhat ahistorical and acultural. As discussed in Chapter 2, it lacked a proper account of the relationships between tradition, memory, and the transmission of the faith.

In this context it is significant that John XXIII, who was otherwise open to suggestions about how the doctrines of the faith might be given a more contemporary gloss, was staunchly opposed to any jettisoning of the use of Latin, either in a liturgical context or in the education of seminarians and the administration of the Church. In February 1962 he promulgated the Apostolic Constitution *Veterum sapientia*, on the Promotion of the Study of Latin. In this document he described Latin as a 'venerable language which, of its very nature, is most suitable for promoting every form of culture among peoples'.[9] It does not favour any one nation, but presents itself with equal impartiality to all and is equally acceptable to all. It gives rise to 'no jealousies'.[10] Knowledge of this language is said to be intimately bound up with the Church's life. It is important not so much on cultural or literary grounds (although these are acknowledged) as for *religious* reasons. Quoting Pius XI, John XXIII wrote that precisely because the Church 'embraces all nations and is destined to endure to the end of time' it of its very nature 'requires a language which is universal, immutable and non-vernacular'.[11]

This was the stance of John XXIII in 1962. However, seven years later, at a general audience address on 26 November 1969, Paul VI delivered what is best described as his eulogy for the Latin Mass. With genuine pathos he acknowledged that the introduction of the vernacular Mass will 'certainly be a great sacrifice for those who know the beauty, the power and the expressive sacrality of Latin' and that 'we have reason indeed for regret, reason almost for bewilderment' at its loss.[12] His grief is palpable when he states that 'we are giving up something of priceless worth' and that 'the change is something that affects our hereditary religious patrimony, which seemed to bring the prayer of our forefathers and our saints to our lips and to give us the comfort of feeling faithful to our spiritual past, which we kept alive to pass onto the generations ahead'.[13] He describes Latin as 'the language of the angels' and accepted that by abandoning it he was 'parting with the speech of Christian centuries [and Catholics were] becoming like profane intruders in the literary precincts of sacred utterance'.[14] Notwithstanding his frank articulation of the inherent dangers, he used an instrumentalist sound bite to defend the introduction of the new rite of the Mass with its preference for the vernacular. Participation, he believed, was worth more than the speech of Christian centuries, 'particularly by modern people, so fond of plain language which is easily understood and converted into everyday speech'.[15] He concluded that the 'understanding of prayer is worth more than the silken garments in which it is royally dressed'.[16]

Leaving aside the fact that linguistic philosophers now agree that it is not so easy to convert a liturgical language into everyday speech, and that many people, if not most, did not find the silken garments a barrier to understanding, the important point is that Paul VI was persuaded to make the change not for any theological reason but in an attempt to satisfy the perceived pastoral needs of 'modern man'. In his 'eulogy' one gets the impression that in his mind there were only two competing goods at stake: the good of the aesthetic beauty of the tradition on the one side and the good of the participation of the laity in the sacramental life of the Church on the other. No doubt historians will one day write books examining the question of the data Paul VI used to make this prudential judgement. Was there actually any hard sociological evidence that Mass attendance rates were falling because of dissatisfaction with the current rite? Was he simply persuaded by courtiers that this is what a majority of the faithful wanted? Anyone reading the speech would be inclined to put the question to Paul VI: what are you going to do about the pastoral needs of those for whom you concede this decision will be received with regret and even bewilderment? Why is it only the 'modern men' whose pastoral needs must be satisfied? What about the millions of Catholics who studied Latin at school and who knew perfectly well what the words meant, especially when they heard the same ones over and over every week and had no trouble following a missal? Is not the suggestion that non-Europeans lack the ability to understand a hieratic liturgical language patronizing when the use of hieratic languages was known in many cultures? While the reasons behind the decisions of Paul VI are still a subject for historians to sort out, what is historical fact is that the decision caused massive pastoral unrest and even contributed to a schism in the following decade. The English philosopher Roger Scruton succinctly summed up the dangers inherent in liturgical experiments in the following paragraph:

Changes in the liturgy take on a momentous significance for the believer, for they are changes in his experience of God—changes, if you wish to be Feuerbachian, in God himself. The question whether to make the sign of the cross with two fingers or with three split a Church. So can the question whether or not to use the Book of Common Prayer or the Tridentine Mass.[17]

Ratzinger has stopped short of saying that his predecessor made a gross pastoral error in his attempted suppression of what is popularly called the Tridentine Mass, but he has come rather close to this mark. In his Reid Preface he remarked that a 'pope is not an absolute monarch whose will is law, but is the guardian of the authentic Tradition'.[18] A pope cannot do as he likes. With respect to the liturgy 'he has the task of a gardener, not that of a technician who builds new machines and throws the old ones on the junk-pile'.[19] He also refers to the following paragraph 1125 of the Catechism of the Catholic Church as 'golden words': 'For this reason no sacramental rite may be modified or manipulated at the will of the minister or the community. Even the supreme authority in the Church may not change the liturgy arbitrarily, but only in the obedience of faith and with religious respect for the mystery of the liturgy.'[20]

His general assessment is that the reform of the liturgy in parts of the Church has been 'culturally impoverishing' and that the 'great cosmic dynamism of the liturgy has grown short of breath, and thus its scope in many respects has been dangerously diminished'.[21] Some contemporary liturgies he believes are even forms of apostasy, analogous to the Hebrews' worship of the golden calf. He argues that the point about the golden calf was not that people thought the calf was God, they knew it was just a statue, but they wanted something brought down to their level to which they could easily relate.[22] He believes that the whole idea of worship is to be transformed in Christ and raised up towards His level. Transcendence only works in a vertical dimension.

While being critical of the kind of ghetto culture which pervades some communities of those who prefer to attend Masses said according to the traditional rite, Ratzinger asks whether 'all their reproaches [against the Rite of Paul VI] are unfounded?' He acknowledges that there is something 'incongruous about bishops allowing every kind of liturgical experimental while cracking down hard on those who simply want to use a rite which had been in use since the time of Pius V'.[23] He observes that 'anyone who nowadays advocates the continuing existence of this liturgy or takes part in it is treated like a leper' and that 'there has never been anything like this in history'.[24] Notwithstanding the deterrent of being treated like a leper, he has not been shy in accepting invitations to celebrate the traditional rite, and has publicly done so at the Seminary of the Fraternity of Saint Peter in Witgratzbad, Germany, in April 1990; at the Benedictine Abbey of St Madeleine, Le Barroux, France, in September 1995; in Weimar, Germany in April 1999; and at the Benedictine Abbey of Fontgombault, France, in July 2001.[25] His general attitude is that the 'real contrast is not between old and new books but between a liturgy of the whole church and homemade liturgies'.[26]

The various rites which have existed throughout the Church's history grew out of the apostolic sees, the central places of the apostolic Tradition, and Ratzinger believes that this connection with apostolic origins is essential to what defines them. From this it follows that there can be no question of creating totally new rites. However, there can be variations within ritual families and Ratzinger is quite in favour of this plurality.[27] In one address he noted that up until the Second Vatican Council there existed, alongside the Roman Rite, the Ambrosian Rite, the Mozarabic Rite of Toledo, the Rite of Braga, the Rite of Chartres, the Rite of the Carmelites, and the best known of all was the Rite of the Dominicans. He added that no one was ever scandalized that the Dominicans, who were often present in parishes, said Mass differently from the diocesan clergy: 'we had no doubt that their rite was as Catholic as the Roman Rite, [and] we were proud of this richness in having many different traditions.'[28]

With respect to the specific issue of the use of Latin, Ratzinger's stance is governed by two principles: first, a liturgical language must always be comprehensible to the congregation, and second, when liturgies develop organically it is the case that they carry within them older linguistic usages which are perfectly legitimate and should not fall victim to what he calls 'iconoclastic revelry'.[29] In this context he cites as examples the adoption of the Semitic words *amen, alleluia, hosanna,* and *marana-tha* and the Greek expression *Kyrie eleison.* He believes that while the liturgy of the Word should be in the mother tongue there ought to be a basic stock of Latin elements that bind all Catholics linguistically together.[30] In these times of globalization it is useful to have a liturgical language which is transcultural and transnational. He has therefore expressly recommended the use of Latin for large-scale liturgies such as those associated with papal events. The clearest example would be the World Youth Day Masses attended by millions of pilgrims from all over the world. While the readings and prayers of the faithful and homily would be in the vernacular language of the country hosting the event, the use of Latin for the parts of the Mass is recommended as a way of transcending all the linguistic divisions with the one universal liturgical language.[31] This was precisely John XXIII's point about Latin giving rise to no jealousies. It is a universal language for a universal church. In taking this stance Benedict has the support of Cardinal Arinze, the Prefect for the Congregation of Divine Worship. Arinze has recommended that large city parishes could have a weekly Latin Mass, while smaller rural parishes could have one a month. Like Benedict XVI, he has specifically recommended the use of Latin at large Masses.[32] He can probably do so without fear of being accused of Eurocentrism since he is a Cardinal from Nigeria who converted to Catholicism from a tribal religion. In other words he is precisely the sort of person for whom Paul VI thought Mass in Latin was not pastorally appropriate.

Ratzinger acknowledges that both the *Constitution on the Liturgy* and the *Decree on the Church's Missionary Activity* explicitly allow for the possibility of far-reaching adaptations to the customs and cultic traditions of peoples. None the less, it seems to him 'very dangerous that missionary liturgies could be created overnight, so to speak, by decisions of bishop's conferences, which would themselves be dependent on memo-randa drawn up by academics'.[33] He suggests that it is 'not until a strong Christian identity has grown up in the mission countries can one begin to move, with great caution and on the basis of this identity, toward christening the indigenous forms by adopting them into the liturgy and allowing Christian realities to merge with the forms of everyday life'.[34]

There is also another significant difference between the stance of Ratzinger and that of Paul VI in that he does not see the category of beauty as something that stands outside theology. When reading Paul VI it is easy to get the impression that he had imbibed the Kantian attitude that aesthetics is a mere matter of taste, at least in the liturgical context. However, in Benedict's first Apostolic Exhortation, *Sacramentum caritatis*, he states that 'everything related to the Eucharist should be marked by beauty'.[35] He reminds his priests and faithful that 'like the rest of Christian Revelation, the liturgy is inherently linked to beauty: it is *veritatis splendor* (the splendor of the truth)'.[36] Citing St Bonaventure, he says: 'in Jesus we contemplate beauty and splendor at their source' and this is 'no mere aestheticism, but the concrete way in which the truth of God's love in Christ encounters us, attracts us and delights us, enabling us to emerge from ourselves and drawing us towards our true vocation, which is love'.[37] He reiterates Bonaventure's theme that God allows himself to be glimpsed first in creation, in the beauty and harmony of the cosmos. With reference to the experience of Peter, James, and John of the Transfiguration, he argues that beauty is 'not mere decoration' but an essential element of liturgical action.[38]

This stance has profound repercussions for liturgical music. In this context Ratzinger has been critical of a commentary on *Sacrosanctum concilium* by Karl Rahner and Herbert Vorgrimler in which they drew a contrast between utility music and what they called 'esoteric church music' and in which they promoted the use of utility music. The concept of utility music means music which is promoted because of its popularity and pedagogical usefulness, not because of any intrinsic aesthetic quality of the music itself. Ratzinger suggests that it would probably be a 'mistake to look for some deep philosophical factor behind this attitude; largely it is the average pastoral reaction, recalling the perennial dispute between the pragmatic, practical man and the specialist'.[39] He notes that St Thomas Aquinas came down on the side of utility music as well. This was in the context of his analysis of the concept of '*religio*', by which he did not mean 'religion' in the modern sense but the whole context of the cult, of the worship of God. In question 91, article 2 of the *Summa Theologica* Aquinas states that the use of music within the liturgy is justified by the fact that the 'minds of the weak are more effectively summoned to piety'. Ratzinger construes this response of St Thomas to mean, in effect, that church music is put at the level of what is pedagogically useful and, in practice, therefore, it is subject to the criterion of utility.[40] Against this mentality he offers the following defence of what Rahner and Vorgrimler dismissed as esoteric church music:

The movement of spiritualization in creation is understood properly as bringing creation into the mode of being of the Holy Spirit and its consequent transformation, exemplified in the crucified and resurrected Christ. In this sense, the taking up of music into the liturgy must be its taking up into the Spirit, a transformation which implies both death and resurrection. That is why the Church has had to be critical of all ethnic music; it could not be allowed untransformed into the sanctuary. The cultic music of pagan religions has a different status in human existence from the music which glorifies God in creation. Through rhythm and melody themselves, pagan music often endeavours to elicit an ecstasy of the senses, but without elevating the sense into the spirit; on the contrary, it attempts to swallow up the spirit in the senses as a means of release. This imbalance toward the senses recurs in modern popular music: the 'God' found here, the salvation of man identified here, is quite different from the God of the Christian faith.[41]

Ratzinger concludes none the less that it is difficult to lay down a priori musical criteria for this process of spiritualization—'it is easier to say what ought to be excluded than included'.[42] He is, however, quite sure that all rock music should be excluded, 'not for aesthetic reasons, not out of reactionary stubbornness, not because of historical rigidity but because of its very nature', which is neo-Dionysian.[43] With regard to instruments, 'the process of purification, of elevation to the spirit, must be considered with special care'.[44] While 'cuddle me Jesus' sort of songs may make some people feel warm inside, Ratzinger's argument is that liturgy is about worship of the Triune God: it is neither pedagogy nor psychotherapy. These have their place, but somewhere outside the Mass. Those who see the Mass as a teaching tool or a way of bonding people or making people feel affirmed and accepted have adopted what Nichols calls, a 'sub-theological ideology'. Ratzinger is emphatic that utility music which may have the effect of generating these emotions has *no place* in the Church's liturgy:

A Church which only makes use of 'utility' music has fallen for what is, in fact, useless. She too becomes ineffectual. For her mission is a far higher one . . . The Church must not settle down with what is merely comfortable and serviceable at the parish level; she must arouse the voice of the cosmos and, by glorifying the Creator, elicit the glory of the cosmos itself, making it also glorious, beautiful, habitable and beloved. Next to the saints, the art which the Church has produced is the only real 'apologia' for her history . . . The Church is to transform, improve, 'humanize' the world—but how can she do that if at the same time she turns her back on beauty, which is so closely allied to love? For together, beauty and love form the true consolation in this world, bringing it as near as possible to the world of the resurrection. The Church must maintain high standards; she must be a place where beauty can be at home; she must lead the struggle for that 'spiritualisation' without which the world becomes the 'first circle of hell'.[45]

It is perhaps on this point more than any other that Ratzinger is at the greatest distance from the Protestant traditions and also from those in his own Church who have accepted the Protestant belief that beauty is the concern of the Pharisee or the liberation theologian's belief that a love of beauty is somehow tied up with a bourgeois indifference to the plight of the poor. Ratzinger empathizes with the Protestant reverence for the Scriptures and the focus on Christology, but he has no empathy with the Protestant hostility to beauty. As von Balthasar wrote: 'anyone enamored of beauty will shiver in the barn of the Reformation, and feel the pull of Rome'. One of the problems of the moment, however, is that the average poor soul shivering in the barn of the Reformation will find it just as cold in the barn of many Catholic parishes. From Ratzinger's perspective this is not a problem which arose only after the Council. He has drawn attention to the fact that the Enlightenment had its own liturgical movement, the aim of which was to simplify the liturgy and restore it to its original basic structure. Excesses in the cult of relics and of saints were to be removed, and, above all, the vernacular, with congregational singing and participation, was to be introduced. Many of these aims were enshrined in the proceedings of the Synod of Pistoia of 1786, which was an attempt to export Jansenist ideas from France to Italy. Against puritanism in the liturgy, which might also be called the liturgical wing of Jansenism, Ratzinger argues that the Church 'must not forget that the celebration of the Lord's Last Supper means, by its very nature, the celebration of a feast, and that festive embellishments are an integral part of any feast'. Moreover:

The expression *praedarus calyx* (illustrious chalice) dates from the very hour of the Last Supper, and when the whole liturgy strives to be a *praedarus calyx*, a precious and illustrious chalice in which we are able to see and hear the glow of eternity, it must not allow itself to be deterred therefrom by any purism or archaism.[46]

[Further], as 'feast', liturgy goes beyond the realm of what can be made and manipulated; it introduces us to the realm of the given, living reality, which communicates itself to us. That is why, at all times, and in all religions, the fundamental law of liturgy has been the law of organic growth within the universality of the common tradition. Even in the huge transition from the Old to the New Testament, this rule was not breached, the continuity of liturgical development was not interrupted: Jesus introduced his words at the Last Supper organically into the Jewish liturgy at the point where it was open to them, as it were, waiting for them.[47]

Ratzinger believes that showing respect for faithfully transmitting the Liturgy to the next generation has the effect of guaranteeing the true freedom of the faithful. It makes sure that the members of the laity are not victims of something fabricated by an individual or group, it guarantees that laity are sharing in the same liturgy that binds the priest, the bishop, and the pope.[48] On the contrary, he observes that the 'freedom' of liturgical innovators can become 'dominion' for the rest.[49] In a statement that would seem incomprehensible to many parish liturgists, Ratzinger asserts that 'creativity cannot be an authentic category for matters liturgical'.[50] In the liturgy, 'we are all given the freedom to appropriate, in our own personal way, the mystery which addresses us' but that is where the ambit of personal freedom ends.[51] It is God's descent upon the world which is the source of real liberation. He alone can open the door to freedom.[52]

Another way to put these ideas is to say that the Catholic liturgy is a cosmic drama. When celebrated as Ratzinger envisions there is a dramatic tension in the Mass which builds to the consecration. The festive joy that is subsequently experienced is also related to the release of this tension. Protestant liturgy, by contrast, lacks the dramatic tension because there is no sacrifice, there is only the reading of scripture and fellowship. When the Catholic liturgy begins to take on the form of Protestant liturgy, and the sacrificial dimension is played down, it becomes banal and, at best, pedagogy, not liturgy. There is nothing cosmic about it. In contrast, in the following passage what is evident is that Ratzinger's experience of good liturgy is deeply sensual, communal, incarnational, and cosmic. Speaking of the Corpus Christi processions of his childhood, he writes:

I can still smell the carpets of flowers and the freshness of the birch trees; I can recall the decorations on all the houses, the banners, the singing; I can still hear the village band...I hear the firing of guns by which the local youth cele-brated their own *joie de vivre* while, at the same time, saluting Christ as a head of state, as *the* Head of State, the Lord of the world, and welcoming him to their streets and into their village. The perpetual presence of Christ was celebrated on this day as though it were a state visit in which not even the smallest village was forgotten.[53]

This was not an experience confined to Bavaria or the Tyrol. A similarly elegiac paragraph can be found in Paul Johnson's 'And Another Thing' column in the *Spectator*. Referring to the Corpus Christi celebrations at Stonyhurst, Johnson wrote:

In the early summer, on the feast of Corpus Christi, that supreme celebration of the Eucharist, the [school cadet] Corps provided a Sovereign's Guard of Honour at High Mass, to underline the doctrine of transubstantiation and mark the real presence of the King of Kings in our church. We lined the aisle with fixed bayonets and, as the moment of consecration approached, we marched up in front of the high altar and greeted the Host held on high with the Present Arms, the lamps and candles on display reflected in our naked steel. In the evening, at Benediction, there were 2,000 candles on the altar, all unlit but lined by a thin thread of gun-cotton. At a signal from the stately master of ceremonies...the outermost candle on each side was lit—and the flames leapt from one to another until the entire vast altar, was literally, incandescent. I have never forgotten those scenes, now vanished forever...[54]

Those in high-profile positions who speak in these terms of other times when liturgy was splendid and passionate and deeply solemn, but also, in the same breath, associate the memory with joy, youthful exuberance, and rollicking good fun, are often dismissed as bourgeois, or elitist, or people who live in the past, old-world romantics, aes-thetes, and snobs. Ratzinger's theological reading, however, is that they simply have a Catholic sensibility which is not the privilege of any particular social class, rank, or socio-economic group:

In the solemnity of the worship, the Church expressed the glory of God, the joy of faith, the victory of truth and light over error and darkness. The richness of the liturgy is not the richness of some priestly caste: it is the wealth of all, including the poor, who in fact long for it and do not at all find it a stumbling block.[55]

The reasons for the demise of such processions and liturgies are sociologically and theologically complex. They cannot be understood apart from the general trend in western cultures from the late 1960s onwards toward informality and a de-ritualization of public life. This may have been caused by the fact that fascism, communism, and various nationalisms all used secular forms of ritual to give their claims a veneer of respectability, pomp, and self-importance. However, the theological fashion of playing down the sacrificial nature of the Mass in an effort not to scandalize Protestants has been a significant factor which seems unrelated to the broader social movements. Rather, it seems to be related to interpretations of the meaning of the Second Vatican Council within the Church herself. To contemporary theologians who wish to emphasize that Christ instituted the sacrament of the Eucharist within the context of the Passover meal, and thus to highlight the whole communal meal dimension of the Mass, Ratzinger replies that Christ did *not* order his disciples to repeat the Passover meal.[56] The Passover meal constituted the framework of the first Holy Thursday but it was not his sacrament, not his new gift: 'the all-encompassing form of worship could not be derived simply from the meal but had to be defined through the interconnection of temple and synagogue, word and sacrament, cosmos and history.'[57] While Martin Luther said that to speak of sacrifice in the context of the Mass was 'the greatest and most appalling horror' and a 'damnable impiety', Ratzinger has quipped, 'I certainly do not need to say that I am not one of those who consider it the most appalling horror and a damnable impiety to speak of the sacrifice of the Mass'.[58]

The notion of the Mass as a community meal has also been fostered by the practice of priests saying Mass facing against the people (*versus populum*) rather than, as had been the custom for centuries, facing east (*ad orientem*), in the same direction as the people. In the words of Cardinal Heenan of Westminster to Evelyn Waugh: 'The Mass is no longer the Holy Sacrifice but the meal at which the priest is the waiter. The bishop, I suppose, is the Head Waiter and the Pope the Patron.'[59] Making the same point, Ratzinger quotes the humorous remark of Eugène Ionesco, one of the founders of the so-called theatre of the absurd, that 'before long they will be setting up a bar in church for the communion of bread and wine and offering sandwiches and Beaujolais'.[60] Ratzinger believes that the change in the direction faced by the priest has fostered a false (Protestant) understanding of what is happening in the Mass and he has therefore written of his preference for a return to the practice of saying Mass facing east. Positively, the *ad orientem* position situates the particular Eucharistic celebration in its true cosmic context as an anticipation of the return of Christ at the end of time. When the priest faces east he effects entry into the procession of history toward the future, the New Heaven and the New Earth.[61] Moreover, even if one takes a Protestant interpretation of the Eucharist as merely a memorial of the Last Supper without any sacrificial elements, Ratzinger quotes Louis Bouyer's argument that there is no historical basis for the *versus populum* position in the practices of the early Church. According to Bouyer, nowhere in Christian antiquity could there have arisen the idea of having to 'face the people' to preside at a meal. In no meal of the early Christian era did the president of the banqueting assembly face the other participants. They were all sitting, or reclining, on the convex side of a C-shaped table, or of a table having approximately the shape of a horse shoe. The other side was always left empty for service.[62]

There are a number of other controversial questions at the micro-level of liturgical practice on which Ratzinger has written an opinion. One of the most divisive has been the question of whether in the canon of the Mass the priest should say that Christ's sacrifice was 'for all' or 'for many'. Traditionalists insist on 'for many', regarding 'for all' as a declaration of belief in universal salvation and conversely an implicit denial of the possibility of eternal damnation, which is a position which has never been held by the Church. Here Ratzinger observes that the German translation says 'for all' but the Latin and Greek texts say 'for many'. He believes that both formulations are found in scripture and tradition and simply emphasize different aspects of the truth that Christ died for all, but that not all wish to accept his offer of redemption.[63] None the less, as Pope, and in consultation with Cardinal Arinze, the Prefect for the Congregation for Divine Worship and the Discipline of the Sacraments, he has taken a decision to insist on the use of *'pro multis'* (for many), which will appear in the next translation of the Roman missal. In the statement from Cardinal Arinze to this effect emphasis was given to the facts that the Synoptic Gospels make specific reference to 'many', the Roman Rite has always said *pro multis* and never *pro omnibus* in the consecration of the chalice, and the anaphoras of the various Oriental Rites, whether in Greek, Syriac, Armenian, or Slavic, all contain the equivalent of the Latin *pro multis* in their respective languages.

A second point of contention has been the practice in many countries of receiving communion in the hand rather than on the tongue.

With reference to this dispute Ratzinger notes that communion was taken in the hand until the ninth century and he exhorts priests to be tolerant of both approaches. He quotes from a catechetical homily of Cyril of Jerusalem from the fourth century in which Cyril advises those about to receive communion to make a throne of their hands, laying the right upon the left to form a throne for the King, forming at the same time a cross.[64]

Whereas with the above disputes he can appreciate the arguments on both sides, when it comes to the question of whether or not the practice of kneeling should be abolished, he has no time at all for the ideas of the anti-kneeling campaigners. He asserts that a 'faith or a liturgy no longer familiar with kneeling would be sick at the core'.[65] He argues that the practice of kneeling is not a common Middle Eastern religious custom into which Christians became inculturated but rather that it is a practice which comes directly from the Bible. The word for kneeling is unknown in classical Greek. It is, he says, 'a specifically Christian word'. Moreover, the word *proskynein* occurs fifty-nine times in the New Testament and twenty-four times in the Apocalypse, the book of the heavenly liturgy.[66] Jesus Christ prayed on his knees in the Mount of Olives (Luke 22: 41); Stephen fell on his knees just before his martyrdom and saw Christ in the heavens (Acts 7: 60); Peter knelt when praying for Tabitha (Acts 9: 20); Paul knelt and prayed with the elders at Ephesus (Acts 20: 36). In Paul's Letter to the Philippians (Phil. 2: 6–11) he says: Jesus Christ is the name before which every knee should bow in heaven and on earth and under the earth.[67] For Ratzinger this means that Christians should kneel, and parish and diocesan liturgical 'experts' who say anything to the contrary seem to have overlooked the scriptural basis for this practice.

While he strongly approves of kneeling, 'dancing is not a form of expression for the Christian liturgy'.[68] He describes as 'absurd' the practice of introducing dance pantomimes which frequently end with applause and he suggests that 'wherever applause breaks out in the liturgy because of some human achievement, it is a sure sign that the essence of the liturgy has totally disappeared and been replaced by a kind of religious entertainment'.[69] The common example here is of priests and particularly bishops after large solemn masses thanking the choir for its services before the end of Mass. Ratzinger's point is that this suggests that the congregation is being sung to, whereas the choir itself is supposed to have been praising God, not putting on a concert, and this is its *raison d'être*. It disrupts the solemnity of the liturgy, and if a bishop or priest is particularly happy with the quality of his choir then there are other more appropriate venues where he can praise its skill and dedication.

Another common disruption of the solemnity of the Mass is the sign of peace before Communion. At the time when this custom was introduced in its current form concern was expressed at very high levels about how it would operate in practice. It was suggested that in the case of a closed and educated community, such as in a seminary or convent, there would be no problem, but if several hundred or several thousand people are attending a Mass, and not arranged in an orderly manner, then it had the potential to become ridiculous.[70] Ratzinger has suggested that the sign of peace would be better placed before the presentation of the gifts if it is to be retained at all, so as not to disrupt the contemplative preparation for the reception of Communion.[71] In *Sacramentum caritatis*, as Pope Benedict XVI, he pleaded for 'greater restraint in this gesture which can become exaggerated and cause a certain distraction in the assembly before the reception of Communion'.[72]

The more general need to restore some contemplative space to the Mass is another of Ratzinger's liturgical concerns. *Sacrosanctum concilium* strongly encouraged the active participation of the faithful in the Mass. This was at a time when it was common for laity to immerse themselves in their own private devotional practices while the priest otherwise got on with the job of saying Mass. After the introduction of the Rite of Paul VI it became common for priests to delegate jobs to lay people as a way of meeting the criteria of increased participation. Here Ratzinger explains that active participation is primarily an inner process—contemplative participation in the liturgical act is primary. To this end Ratzinger has indicated his preference for a silent recitation of the canon of the Mass, as had been immemorially part of the Roman Rite. He believes that the entire Eucharistic prayer need not be recited aloud, especially if the congregation has undergone the requisite process of liturgical formation. The continual recitation of the canon aloud results in the demand for a variety of Eucharistic prayers, and the demand becomes insatiable. In *Sacramentum caritatis* he stated that 'participation does not refer to mere external activity during the celebration but to a greater awareness of the mystery being celebrated' and 'active participation is not equivalent to the exercise of a specific ministry'.[73]

Finally, in the context of contentious liturgical beliefs and practices, Ratzinger is strong in his opposition to the idea of open Communion for all, that is, to the idea that any person of any faith or none may receive Communion in a Catholic Church. Here he argues that the Eucharist is not itself the sacrament of reconciliation, but presupposes that sacrament. It is 'the sacrament of the reconciled to which the Lord invites all those who have become one with Him; who certainly still remain weak sinners, but yet have given their hand to him and have become part of his family'.[74] It is therefore a privilege open only to those who are members of the Church and who are in a state of grace. Ratzinger makes the point that the Last Supper was not held with publicans and sinners. To permit open Communion would be to permit a farce. It would mean allowing a severance of meaning from action. It would mean feigning a communion of life and of faith which simply does not exist. This applies to those conscious of unconfessed grave sin as well as to non-Catholics.

At a macro-sociological level, Ratzinger believes that calls for open Communion are indicative of the prevalence of an unconscious deism—'that a human deed could offend God has become a completely unthinkable thought for many'.[75] As a consequence, there has developed a tendency to change the primary object of the liturgy as divine worship to the 'we' of the ones celebrating it:

The concern for atonement, sacrifice and the forgiveness of sin is replaced by the goal of securing community and escaping the isolation of modern existence— the point is to communicate experiences of liberation, joy, reconciliation, denounce what is harmful and provide impulses for action. For this reason the community has to create its own liturgy and not just receive it from conditions that have become unintelligible; it portrays itself and celebrates itself.[76]

According to Ratzinger, not only are these self-centric liturgies idol-atrous and sinful, but as a community-building exercise he believes they are ineffectual:

Whoever elevates the community to the level of an end in itself is precisely the one who dissolves its foundations. What seems to be so pious and reasonable at the beginning is actually a radical inversion of the important concerns and categories in which we eventually achieve the opposite of what was intended. Only when the sacrament retains its unconditional character and its absolute priority over all communal purposes and all spiritually edifying intentions does it build community and edify humans.[77]

When one condenses much of the above the essence is that Benedict believes that the Mass is a Holy Sacrifice, offered ritually as worship, not a fellowship meal, that those who attend do so for the purpose of

Divine Worship, that music which is based on most contemporary popular musical forms is completely unworthy, and that everything that is related to the Mass and other liturgies of the Church should be marked by beauty. Beauty is not an optional extra or something contrary to a preferential option for the poor. It is not a scandal to clothe sacred words in silken garments. Catholics are not tone deaf philistines who will be intellectually challenged by the use of a liturgical language or put off by changeless ritual forms. However, banality can act as a repellent.

The Lercaro–Bugnini inspired liturgical experiments of the last three decades have been based on an overemphasis on baroque sacramental theology and eighteenth-century philosophy, and an obsession with pedagogy.[78] This in turn can be boiled down to a cocktail of scholasticism (the reduction of sacramental theology to considerations of matter and form), the Kantian obsession with pedagogical rationalism (the predominance of ethical values over strictly religious ones), moralism (a notion of Mass attendance as duty parade), and a Jansenist attitude to beauty (it is irrelevant: the only thing that matters is that the words are doctrinally sound and in the vernacular). In other words, one has a cocktail of theological and philosophical ingredients which Ratzinger has spent his entire ecclesial life trying to throw out of the pantry. Anyone wanting to escape the culture of modernity with its lowest-common-denominator mass culture will find it difficult to do so at many contemporary Catholic liturgies based on the Lercaro–Bugnini principles. As Catherine Pickstock has argued, 'a genuine liturgical reform would either have to overthrow our anti-ritual modernity, or, that being impossible, devise [or perhaps, develop] a liturgy that *refused* to be enculturated in our modern habits of thought and speech'.[79]

It is not surprising therefore that Ratzinger has spoken in an affirming manner of the *Oxford Declaration* of 1996 in which a number of prominent liturgical scholars declared that the 'manifest intentions of *Sacrosanctum concilium* have in large part been frustrated by powerful contrary forces, which could be described as bureaucratic, philistine and secularist'.[80] At a Wednesday audience address in 2003 even John Paul II (for whom beauty was probably not a primary transcendental) exhorted people to pray to God 'not only with theologically precise formulas, but also in a beautiful and dignified way', and he concluded: 'The Christian community must make an examination of conscience so that the beauty of music and song will return to the liturgy. It is necessary to purify worship of deformations, of careless forms of expression, of ill-prepared music and texts, which are not suited to the grandeur of the act being celebrated.'[81]

Benedict is sensitive to the harm caused by too dramatic a rupture or by proscribing a whole Rite overnight. It is likely that he will lead by example and that he will try to remove the stigma associated with the use of Latin and the preference for the traditional Rite at the same time as reminding bishops and the faithful (as he did in *Sacramentum caritatis*) that liturgy is meant to be cosmic and eschatological. In an interview given to *Le Figaro*, in Lent 2007, the Secretary of State, Cardinal Bertone, indicated that Pope Benedict intended to issue a decree (technically called a *motu proprio*) confirming a universal right upon all priests to say the Mass of Pius V. In other words, it was expected that Benedict would simultaneously affirm the rights of those who prefer the unreformed Roman Rite at the same time as fostering a reform of the reform based on what he regards as an authentic reading of *Sacrosanctum concilium*. The expression, 'the reform of the reform' is commonly used by laity who have no objection whatsoever to the principles enunciated in *Sacrosanctum concilium* but who simply regard what happens at many parish Masses to be inconsistent with the conciliar vision. Cardinal Bertone told *Le Figaro* that 'the sovereign pontiff will personally explain his vision for the use of the ancient Missal to the Christian people, and particularly to the bishops'.[82] He added that 'the pope is trying to make peace with the Church's own tradition'. Here Bertone seemed to be referring to the principle in article 23 of *Sacrosanctum concilium* that all liturgical change needs to take the form of an organic development. Ratzinger has in the past used strong language about the failure of the Lercaro–Bugnini reform to observe this principle. In an essay in tribute to Klaus Gamber, Ratzinger wrote that after the Council in the place of liturgy as the fruit of development came fabricated liturgy: '[w]e abandoned the organic, living process of growth and development over centuries, and replaced it, as in a manufacturing process, with a fabrication, a banal on-the-spot product.'[83] Conversely, as an example of a positive organic development, it has been suggested that Benedict might enhance the traditional Rite with the addition of some newly canonized saints to the calendar and additional prefaces and prayers, in order to prevent the ossification of the 1962 missal as a sort of relic.[84]

In line with his many statements on the problems of post-conciliar liturgical practices, on 7 July 2007 Pope Benedict issued the *Motu*

Proprio, Summorum Pontificum, which contains the ruling that the Roman Missal promulgated by Paul VI is to remain the ordinary expression of the 'Lex orandi' (Law of Prayer) of the Latin Rite of Catholic Church, but, none the less, the Roman Missal, promulgated by St Pius V and reissued by Blessed John XXIII, is to be considered as an extraordinary expression of that same 'Lex orandi', and must be given due honour for its venerable and ancient usage.

Rather than being ecclesial lepers, in the pontificate of Benedict XVI Catholics who have for several decades suffered behind an iron curtain of parish tea party liturgies and banal 'cuddle me Jesus' pop songs, liturgy as psychotherapy and a group bonding exercise, are more likely to be welcomed in from the cold and treated like ecclesial treasures. At an enormous personal cost they have contributed to a genuine reform whose beginning can be seen in *Sacramentum caritatis* and to the preservation of what even Paul VI called 'a thing of priceless worth' during a period of intense puritanism, reminiscent of Cromwellian England.

Conclusion

The university of Chicago theologian David Tracy has made the interesting sociological observation that those who spent their early years trying to rethink Aquinas' thought in modern terms—Chenu, Congar, Rahner, Lonergan, Schillebeeckx—remained, after Vatican II, open to further fundamental changes in Catholic thought and institutional and religious life. However, many of this generation who had spent their early years striving either to retrieve patristic thought, or among the medieval classics, Bonaventure rather than Aquinas, began after Vatican II to pull back from continuing intellectual and institutional change or, Tracy would argue, intellectual and institutional 'reform'. With scholars like Lieven Boeve, he observes that in their judgement 'the alliance, even the *entente cordiale*' established at Vatican II between modernity and Catholicism, had failed.[1] Tracy, Boeve, and others have suggested that Ratzinger fits into the category of those for whom any such *entente cordiale* has passed into history, though in Ratzinger's case it must be noted that he was always concerned about Pelagian interpretations of *Gaudium et spes*. He was never a party to the *entente cordiale* in so far as this was interpreted as an embrace of a secularist culture. For Ratzinger an engagement with Modernity was one thing, an accommodation to it something else. While he never followed the 'head in the sand' approach of the preconciliar Roman Schools, his interest in an engagement was simply that it was an important problem in the life of the Church which needed to be addressed. His interest was fostered by pastoral concerns not by any Catholic intellectual inferiority complex vis-à-vis fashionable currents of thought in the 1960s. Kenneth L. Schmitz, who is sympathetic to Ratzinger's position, has commented that, at the time of the Council, had Catholic scholars been more perceptive they might have discerned that the foundations of modernity were beginning to crack under an increasingly incisive attack. However, he noted that in the early 1960s they were not working with a cultural concept like 'Modernity'. All they had was the historical category of modern philosophy.[2]

These two sociological observations (those of Boeve and Tracy as one, and that of Schmitz as a second) point to a third, which is that those who tended to think of the relationship between Modernity and Catholicism as purely a matter of effecting a new synthesis or *rapprochement* between the Catholic faith and modern philosophy have tended to examine the whole subject wearing philosophical glasses, missing the culturally embodied aspects of the problem. As Schmitz acknowledged, it is not just modern philosophy, or, more narrowly, modern epistemology, which is at issue. 'Modernity' is an entire cultural package with a complex array of philosophical and theological foundations affecting every aspect of life, including music, literature, architecture, agriculture, medicine, politics, courtship, and marriage. Its complexity is further deepened by the fact that it is not an internally coherent package. Part of its character is the phenomenon of internal contradictions. As Charles Taylor has put it: 'It is not that we have sloughed off a whole lot of unjustified beliefs, leaving an implicit self-understanding that had always been there, to operate at last untrammeled. Rather one constellation of implicit understandings of our relation to God, the cosmos, other humans, and time, was replaced by another in a multifaceted mutation.'[3]

Western culture is fractured since each of its institutions, from the family up to parliaments, universities, and courts, are operating on concepts and values which are unstable and at varying stages in the process of 'multifaceted mutation'. There is not even one single *telos* to which these mutations are heading. In such circumstances Catholic philosophers can perform all manner of brilliant intellectual gymnastics to find points of agreement with non-Catholic philosophers, and in some situations this work can be valuable, especially in the context of government committees, where Catholic philosophers find themselves in a situation of being the token theist. However, at a broader and deeper social level the challenge faced by the Church at the beginning of the twenty-first century is to heal this fractured culture and to heal the fractures within the Church herself. This is much more extensive a problem then finding points of convergence and correlativity with contemporary philosophical trends. In this context, Ratzinger's position is that the 'accommodation to modernity' pastoral strategies of the 1960s were myopic and facile:

That all-too-guileless progressivism of the first post-conciliar years, which happily proclaimed its solidarity with everything modern, with everything that promised progress, and strove with the self-conscious zeal of a model schoolboy to prove the compatibility of what is Christian with all that is modern, to demonstrate the loyalty of Christians to the trends of contemporary life—that progressivism has today come under suspicion of being merely the apotheosis of the late-capitalistic bourgeoisie, on which, instead of attacking it critically, it sheds a kind of religious glow.[4]

Ratzinger is emphatic that 'evangelisation is not simply adaptation to the culture, nor is it dressing up the gospel with elements of the culture, along the lines of a superficial notion of inculturation that supposes that, with modified figures of speech and a few new elements in the liturgy, the job is done'.[5] Rather, 'the gospel is a slit, a purification that becomes maturation and healing' and the cut must occur 'in the right place, at the right time, and in the right way'.[6] Using St Basil the Great's metaphor of pagan culture being like a sycamore tree, Ratzinger argues that the necessary transformation cannot come from the tree itself and its fruit—an intervention of the dresser, an intervention from outside (that is, from the Church) is necessary. For as long as the culture of modernity remains hostile to the very notion of a 'non-democratic educative sphere' and to a Christocentric theology of history and anthropology there are unlikely to be many *pierres d'attente* (toothing stones), as Chenu called them, jutting out from this culture to which the Church might be able to attach herself and her teaching.[7]

In a letter written to Paul VI in 1965, Romano Guardini, who was one of the seminal influences on Ratzinger's intellectual formation, counselled the pontiff that, in his judgement, 'what can convince modern people is not an historical or a psychological or a continually ever modernizing Christianity but only the unrestricted and uninterrupted message of Revelation'.[8] This is a good, succinct summary of Ratzinger's position. In *Co-Workers of the Truth*, published in 1992, Ratzinger wrote: 'Christianity is not a philosophical speculation; it is not a construction of the intellect. Christianity is not "our" work, it is a Revelation, a message that has been given us, and we have no right to reconstruct it as we wish.'[9] This point was reiterated in the very first paragraphs of *Deus Caritas Est* where Benedict argued that Christianity is not a moral system, it is an encounter with the Person of Christ, indeed with the whole Trinity. He concludes that 'what is needed, therefore, is an intellectual affirmation by which one understands the beauty and the organic structure of the faith'.[10] The organic structure is important, because if one considers principles in isolation from the architectonic framework in which they are embedded it is possible for there to appear to be convergences which in fact are illusory. It is only when one considers where they sit in relation to other aspects of a tradition that one reaches a different judgement. As Nigel Biggar has put in, it is not that the content of theistic and atheistic moralities is always entirely different, but rather that 'the particular moral beliefs that they share are differently located in larger wholes that qualify—sometimes slightly, sometimes radically—the significance of each of their parts'.[11]

The emphasis given by Benedict to 'an intellectual affirmation by which one understands the beauty and the organic structure of the faith' means that the primary task of the Church in this era is one of catechesis and healing rather than accommodation and assimilation. His mode for both is non polemical. It is not a matter of proving that the alternatives are stupid. For example, he acknowledges that the positive thing about *Gaudium et spes* is that it deals with atheism not simply as a metaphysical failure or a breakdown of epistemology but as an authentic desire for a true humanism.[12] Atheism must therefore be answered on an anthropological plane. He believes that the foundation of the crisis in which western culture finds itself lies in its inability to answer the question: Is God merely a projection of man or is it God who makes it possible for man to be human? Whereas many of the early twentieth-century Neo-Scholastic enterprises aimed at proving that atheism was just plain stupid, Ratzinger tends to read the current crisis as more of a failure of loving than a failure of thinking. Many of the secular humanisms have a certain internal coherence once one accepts their atheistic presuppositions. In the interview with Peter Seewald, published as *Salt of the Earth*, Ratzinger described history as a whole as the struggle between love and the inability to love, between love and the refusal to love.[13] He often makes the point that the refusal to accept the gift of Christianity has tragic consequences for the prospects of love: 'When God is not there, the world becomes deso-late, and everything becomes boring, and everything is completely unsatisfactory... The great joy comes from the fact that there is this great love, and that is the essential message of faith. You are unswervingly loved.'[14] For Ratzinger, this love of God for his creatures is constant, and His Revelation, once given, is for ever. Christianity is therefore not a project to be updated throughout history. The challenges faced by Christians will differ from generation to generation but the general 'plot' or 'script' does not change. The principles within which this theo-drama unfolds are not determined by human beings. The Scriptures are authoritative, and cannot be deconstructed into a pile of theologically irrelevant historical facts. History in general, but especially the history of Israel and the early Church, is a rich treasury of theological truths.

Ironically, it has been Ratzinger's stance on the theological significance of history and Scripture that has led him to take what is popularly regarded as a conservative stance on questions in ecclesiology, such as his belief in the impossibility of ordaining women, while the post-Tridentine Neo-Scholastic emphasis on reason or rationality without recourse to history has been less effective in its defence of the traditional ecclesial forms and offices, although it is from this perspective that Ratzinger has been most consistently criticized for modernist or otherwise liberal tendencies. It has been von Balthasar's work on the Petrine mission, rather than the work of any of the contemporary scholastics, which has been the most effective defence of the power of the papacy in the post-1968 ecclesial context; and this may be judged by observing the number of theses devoted to criticizing the treatment of gender and ecclesiology in the works of von Balthasar. If one wants to promote the ordination of women, or democratize the whole Church in the manner of evangelical Protestants, then it is von Balthasar's works which are the most significant intellectual roadblock, apart from the authority of the whole ecclesial tradition itself.

One might therefore conclude that what happened to the Catholic Church in the twentieth century is that it was forced to confront the question of the relationship between history and dogma, and, in doing so, it had to rethink the whole territory of Revelation. The response of Pius X in *Pascendi Dominici Gregis* (his 1907 encyclical against Modernism) was to try and avoid the iceberg of history. At Vatican II the majority decided that the iceberg, so to speak, could not be avoided: it had to be engaged. The names of Rahner, Schillebeeckx, and Küng (notwithstanding their internal variations) are now shorthand terms for one form of engagement, the names of Ratzinger, de Lubac, Wojtyla, and von Balthasar, shorthand terms for another.

In the previous chapters an attempt has been made to outline key themes in the works of Ratzinger and to explain where he stands on some of the more contentious contemporary theological fault lines. Every attempt has been made faithfully to present Ratzinger as Ratzinger. Other works will no doubt be written examining aspects of these themes in greater detail. For example, a book could very well be written about where Ratzinger agrees with Rahner and where he agrees with Aquinas. This book has not been written to annoy Rahnerians or other species of Thomists. The author is actually very much in favour of academic enterprises like the Pinckaers' school of Biblical Thomism, Alasdair MacIntyre's Thomist critique of liberalism, and Rudi te Velde's work on the doctrine of participation within the thought of St Thomas, to name but a few of the contemporary Thomist projects. However, at a time when everyone is saying that the key to Ratzinger is to understand his Augustinian preferences, some effort has been made in this book to explain in greater detail what this means. In particular, some effort has been made to explain that Ratzinger's Augustinianism is very different from Martin Luther's and others in the Protestant traditions. There is nothing neo-Manichean about Ratzinger. The idea that the world can be divided into 'grace-sniffers' and 'heresy-sniffers' and that Ratzinger was born with a personality disposition (as the son of a policeman) to be a 'heresy-sniffer' is just a bit too simplistic. One of the strongest Augustinian things about him is his concern for the transcendental of beauty. A person who writes that the greatness of western music from Gregorian chant, to polyphony, to the Baroque age, to Bruckner, and beyond is, 'the most immediate and the most evident verification that history has to offer of the Christian image of mankind and of the Christian dogma of redemption' is not primarily a 'heresy sniffer'.[15] As Prefect for the Congregation of the Doctrine of the Faith he was given the job of being the Church's doctrinal watchdog, the guardian of the treasury of the deposit of the faith, so 'heresy sniffing' was something of an occupational necessity. However, his sympathy for Augustine and Bonaventure lies not in any Manichean propensities but primarily in the place they give to love, the way that they envisage the relationship between love and truth, and their common concern for the transcendental of beauty. Another way to put this is to say that even though he is probably one of the most intellectual popes in history, for him Christianity is above all a matter of the heart. However, it is not thereby something soapy and saccharine. In *Faith and the Future* he wrote: 'The very toughness of the adventure [of Christianity] is what makes it beautiful.'[16]

Significantly, while acknowledging the importance of Augustine for Ratzinger in his understanding of the Church, his epistemology, his interest in the relationship between love and truth, and his concern for the transcendental of beauty, the reading of Ratzinger on the predicament of contemporary western culture and his hostility to liberal readings of *Gaudium et spes* as presented in Chapters 2 and 6 of this work does not rely on the strong Augustinian currents in his work. This is contrary to the stance taken by a number of commentators who argue that his judgements on the liberal and post-modern traditions are derivative of his Augustinian and Bonaventurian pedigree. Foremost here are the articles by Lieven Boeve and Joseph Komonchak. Similarly, in a review of John L. Allen's biography, *Cardinal Ratzinger: The Vatican's Enforcer*, John Thornhill took the view that Ratzinger's reservations about some aspects of *Gaudium et spes* are 'associated with his choice of Augustine as his principal theological guide' and further that 'the divergence of views between John Paul II (a follower of Aquinas) and Joseph Ratzinger (a follower of Augustine) is profound'.[17]

The reading offered in the previous chapters, however, is that it is not so much a choice between Augustine and Aquinas (this is too general a proposition) as a choice between different versions of Thomism. Most precisely, it is a choice between the Transcendental Thomism of Karl Rahner and the 'Augustinian Thomism' of Henri de Lubac, coupled with von Balthasar's theology of history. Of course, some would argue that one cannot speak of either de Lubac or von Balthasar as 'Thomists'. This is certainly true in the sense that their work was not focused on the study of the thought of St Thomas. It is also a fact that the pre-conciliar Thomists were hostile to de Lubac and the contemporary ones often think of von Balthasar as an unsystematic Swiss eccentric who spent too much time listening to Mozart and taking seriously the spiritual visions of Adrienne von Speyr. There are, of course, notable exceptions of scholars who are equally at home in the world of St Thomas and von Balthasar, such as Aidan Nichols. However, the point is that when it comes to debates about how *Gaudium et spes* is to be interpreted it is not a macro-level choice between reading it with

Augustinian spectacles and reading it with Thomist spectacles. It is more of a micro-level choice between reading it with the mindset of de Lubac or Rahner in relation to the specific issue of the nature and grace relationship, and here it is significant that de Lubac claimed that his position was classically Thomist, notwithstanding the judgements of Garrigou-Lagrange and Labourdette. It is also a fact that contemporary non-partisan scholarship favours de Lubac's historical claim that what the pre-conciliar Thomists regarded as a classical Thomist account of the grace and nature relationship was not classically Thomist at all, but a baroque revision.

Rather than setting up a dichotomy of open-to-the-world Thomists against closed-to-the-world Augustinians it would seem to be a more profitable exercise to examine more closely what Ratzinger calls the 'mediation of history in the realm of ontology' as it is dealt with in de Lubac and Rahner, and also to look at von Balthasar's criticisms of Rahner in his monograph *Das Ganze im Fragment*, of which Ratzinger has spoken with approval. Such an approach to identifying the underlying theological fault line which divides Ratzinger from those who continue to favour the pastoral strategies of the immediate post-conciliar era also has the merit of being consistent with the latest Augustinian scholarship. The idea that Augustine was hostile to the world and all the achievements of pagan culture is now coming to be regarded as a discredited stereotype that owes much to Protestant and Jansenist spin.

Whether one is an Augustinian or almost any species of Thomist the same theology of history will be operative. For both Augustine and Aquinas the world is essentially good. It is an epiphany of God's love in which there appears vestiges of God's trinitarian form. It is the theatre in which the drama of human salvation is played and within this drama the nobility of the human person is manifest in man's spiritual and cultural achievements, in accord with the movement of grace. Thus the more or less Thomist John Paul II wrote that the world was created within the dimension of time within which the history of salvation unfolds, finding its culmination in the fullness of time of the Incarnation and its goal in the glorious return of the Son of God at the end of time.[18] Similarly, the more or less Augustinian Benedict has written that the necessary condition for life in community lies in steadfast adherence to the law of God which orders human affairs rightly by organizing them as realities that come from God and are intended to return to God.[19]

There is no fundamental difference between John Paul II and Benedict XVI on the question of the place of the world in the economy of salvation and the place of Christ in the theology of history, nor is there anything in the writings of John Paul II which would suggest he might demur from elements of Ratzinger's genealogy of the culture of modernity. It was the more Thomistically inclined John Paul, not the Augustinian Benedict, who first described the predicament of contemporary western culture as a choice between a civilization of love and a culture of death. On all the major issues dividing liberals from non-liberals, John Paul II and his Prefect for the Congregation of the Doctrine of the Faith stood shoulder to shoulder.

Rather, differences between the two pontiffs only appear when it comes to the narrower question of strategies for evangelizing contemporary culture. Here the difference would seem to lie, not in their understanding of the world, nor their preferred interpretation of *Gaudium et spes*, nor the preference of one for Aquinas, and of the other for Augustine, but in their readiness to use some of the language and idioms of the liberal tradition, of 'the modern Egyptians', so to speak, in order to present the teaching of the Church to that part of the world remaining unconverted to Christ. While John Paul II 'plundered' such concepts as rights, modernity, feminism, liberty, equality, and fraternity, his usual approach was to adopt the concept, gut it of those elements he deemed hostile to the faith, then repack it with Christian material. For example, he wrote: 'if by modernity we mean a convergence of conditions that permit a human being to express better his or her own maturity, spiritual, moral, and cultural, then the Church of the Council saw itself as the "soul" of modernity.'[20] No other author has ever thus defined modernity. In this example he did not take over the substance of what almost all cultural theorists would identify as essential components of the culture of modernity, instead he adopted the concept, but then attempted to redefine its meaning. Similarly, at a Mass outside Rheims to celebrate the 1,500th anniversary of the conversion of King Clovis to the Catholic faith, he endorsed the slogans of Republican France, 'liberty, equality, and fraternity', but then redefined them with a Christian content. With feminism he kept the concept, gave it a new anthropology, and relabelled it a 'new feminism'. With human rights, he again kept the concept, but tried to root it in the idea of the human person having been made in the image and likeness of God.

Where Wojtyla did undertake substantial synthetic work infusing the Thomist tradition with elements borrowed from mid-twentieth-century personalism, phenomenology, and existentialism, especially during his Lublin period, he was not doing anything with which Ratzinger would disagree. As was stated in the Introduction, this development of classical Thomism in a personalist direction dovetailed with Ratzinger's interests in the personalist dimensions of Augustine. This cannot be presented as the source of any tension between them. From Ratzinger's perspective, Wojtyla's work on the Thomist tradition was simply opening it to a consideration of relationality, something which he thinks was long overdue. Wojtyla's 'Lublin Thomism' was notable for being an exception to the more general Thomist trend of ignoring the importance of individuality. Moreover, the very bits of *Gaudium et spes* of which Ratzinger strongly approved were those most closely associated with the collaboration of Wojtyla, and throughout his pontificate John Paul II frequently made reference to the theological anthropology of *Gaudium et spes* 22, so much so that it is argued that he quoted this paragraph of the documents of Vatican II more often than any other. Thus the differences between them are more at the level of pedagogy and philology than the level of their favourite theologians or their judgements about what is good and bad in contemporary western culture.

Philosophically, the problem is that liberal idioms which may in some sense have had Christian or Aristotelian or even Stoic memories were over several centuries taken over and mutated in what von Balthasar has called a *spoliatio Christianorum* (a plundering of the Christian intellectual framework). Often, by the time they emerged within the liberal tradition, they were hardly recognizable and conveyed very different meanings from their original classical–Christian 'shadows'. The question which John Paul II faced and Benedict XVI now faces is whether to pursue a strategy of trying to reclaim the language which has been plundered, despoiled, and mutated, or to find other language with which to address the world. John Paul II's strategy of philological taxidermy is problematic in that some words and concepts obstinately retain their liberal meaning in a culture so deeply imbued with liberal principles. Ratzinger, however, seems to be more sensitive to the difficulty of trying to transpose concepts from hostile traditions. He seems to have a deeper appreciation of the principle that cultural forms and linguistic expressions *are not* distinguished from the thoughts and message they carry as accidents are distinguished from substance in Aristotelian philosophy. As was explained in Chapter 3, Francis George defines the fault line here as a difference between those who subscribe to an instrumentalist as against an expressivist view of language. Ratzinger is clearly more on the side of the expressivists, whereas John Paul II at least implicitly took a more instrumentalist approach, as did Paul VI and John XXIII.

A concrete example of this sensitivity to matters of form which was recently the subject of an article in the London *Daily Telegraph* is Ratzinger's stance on hosting a 1960s rock star to perform a concert in the presence of John Paul II. Ratzinger was opposed to the idea, however John Paul II listened to the concert and gave a homily using lyrics taken from some of the rock songs which he then restuffed with Christian meaning. John Paul was always prepared to try a strategy of sugar-coating the medicine, whereas Benedict tends to deliver it straight. Both, however, were in agreement about the cultural healing that is needed.

In conclusion, one could say that as a generalization Benedict has tended to rely more on language and symbols which are overtly Christian, unmutated, and directly scriptural, while John Paul applied his philosophical training to a programme of trying to purge the liberal idioms of their more odious content. As John Milbank concluded in an essay on *Deus Caritas Est*: 'There is no sign of a backing away from John Paul II's commitment to thinking through the moral and political issues of the day. One glimpses instead something like an accentuation of an insistence upon the relevance of the specific perspectives of faith to these issues, rather than just a reliance upon sound reason and natural law.'[21] The papacy of Benedict should therefore be seen in a harmonious contrast with John Paul II's in certain respects, but also as one which is in unison with his predecessor's on all the big issues, in particular, in union with John Paul II's call for the promotion of a civilization of love against the culture of death.

Finally, Benedict is in love with the Church which for him really is the mystical bride of Christ. He regards all models of the Church derived from the world of large corporations as completely defective and any suggestion that the Church's teachings might be decided by elected commissions as absurd. No doubt he is well aware that, as a matter of logic, unless the Catholic hierarchy was instituted by Christ to transmit and defend the deposit of the faith until the end of the world, then the Protestants are right to be critical of the Catholic hierarchy. Congregationalism has its own internal logic, as does Catholicism, but a Congregationalist Catholicism is absurd. The following is one of his favourite passages in literature taken from Joseph Roth's *The Radetzky March*, an elegiac account of life in the Austro-Hungarian empire in the twilight of Hapsburg glory. More than any other quotation this probably reaches to the heart of what animates the theology of Benedict XVI:

In this decaying world the Roman Church is the only thing left to give shape to life, to help life to keep its shape. Yes, we could even say that she dispenses shape . . . In instituting sin, she is already forgiving it. She does not allow the existence of any faultless human beings: this is the really human thing about her . . . Thereby the Roman Church demonstrates her most eminent characteristic, that of pardoning, of forgiving.[22]

APPENDIX I

The Subiaco Address[1]

The Permanent Significance of the Christian Faith

We are living in a time of great dangers and great opportunities for man and the world; a time which is also of great responsibility for us all. During the past century man's possibilities and his dominion over matter grew by truly unthinkable measures. However, his power to dispose of the world has been such as to allow his capacity for destruction to reach dimensions which at times horrify us. In this connection, the threat of terrorism comes spontaneously to mind, this new war without boundaries or fronts.

The fear that it might soon get a hold of nuclear or biological weapons is not unfounded, and has made it necessary for lawful states to adopt internal security systems similar to those that previously existed only in dictatorships. The feeling remains, nevertheless, that, in reality, all these precautions are not enough, as a global control is neither possible nor desirable.

Less visible, but no less disquieting, are the possibilities of self-manipulation that man has acquired. He has plumbed the depths of being, has deciphered the components of the human being, and is now capable, so to speak, of constructing man himself, who thus no longer comes into the world as a gift of the Creator, but as a product of our action, a product that, therefore, can also be selected according to the exigencies established by ourselves.

Thus, the splendour of being an image of God no longer shines over man, which is what confers on him his dignity and inviolability, and he is left only to the power of his own human capacities. He is no more than the image of man—of what man?

To this are added the great global problems: inequality in the distribution of the goods of the earth, growing poverty, and the more threatening impoverishment and exhaustion of the earth and its resources, hunger, sicknesses that threaten the whole world and the clash of cultures.

All this shows that the growth of our possibilities has not been matched by a comparable development of our moral energy. Moral strength has not grown

[1] Delivered by Cardinal Ratzinger at the Convent of Saint Scholastica, Subiaco, Italy, 1 April 2005.

together with the development of science; rather, it has diminished, because the technical mentality relegates morality to the subjective realm, while we have need, precisely, of a public morality, a morality that is able to respond to the threats that weigh down on the existence of us all. The real and gravest danger in these times lies, precisely, in this imbalance between technical possibilities and moral energy.

The security we need as a precondition of our freedom and our dignity cannot come, in the last analysis, from technical systems of control, but can, specifically, spring only from man's moral strength: whenever the latter is lacking or is insufficient, the power man has will be transformed increasingly into a power of destruction.

A new moralism

It is true that a new moralism exists today whose key words are justice, peace, and conservation of creation—words that call for essential moral values of which we are in real need. But this moralism remains vague and thus slides, almost inevitably, into the political-party sphere. It is above all a dictum addressed to others, and too little a personal duty of our daily life. In fact, what does justice mean? Who defines it? What serves towards peace?

Over the last decades we have amply seen in our streets and squares how pacifism can deviate toward a destructive anarchism and terrorism. The political moralism of the 70s, the roots of which are anything but dead, was a moralism that succeeded in attracting even young people full of ideals. But it was a moralism with a mistaken direction, in as much as it was deprived of serene rationality and because, in the last analysis, it placed the political utopia above the dignity of the individual man, showing itself even capable of arriving at contempt for man in the name of great objectives.

Political moralism, as we have lived it and are still living it, does not open the way to regeneration, and even more, also blocks it. The same is true, consequently, also for a Christianity and a theology that reduces the heart of Jesus' message, the 'kingdom of God', to the 'values of the kingdom', identifying these values with the great key words of political moralism, and proclaiming them, at the same time, as a synthesis of the religions.

Nonetheless, God is neglected in this way, notwithstanding the fact that it is precisely he who is the subject and cause of the kingdom of God. In his stead, great words (and values) remain, which lend themselves to all kinds of abuse.

This brief look at the situation of the world leads us to reflect on today's situation of Christianity and, therefore, on the foundations of Europe; that Europe which at one time, we can say, was the Christian continent, but which was also the starting point of that new scientific rationality which has given us great possibilities, as well as great threats. Christianity, it is true, did not start in Europe, and therefore it cannot even be classified as a European religion, the religion of the European cultural realm. But it received precisely in Europe its most effective cultural and intellectual imprint and remains, therefore, identified in a special way with Europe.

Furthermore, it is also true that this Europe, since the time of the Renaissance, and in a fuller sense since the time of the Enlightenment, has developed precisely that scientific rationality which not only in the era of the discoveries led to the geographic unity of the world, to the meeting of continents and cultures, but which today, much more profoundly, thanks to the technical culture made possible by science, imprints itself on the whole world, and even more than that, in a certain sense, gives it uniformity.

Godless society

And in the wake of this form of rationality, Europe has developed a culture that, in a manner unknown before now to humanity, excludes God from the public conscience, either by denying him altogether, or by judging that his existence is not demonstrable, uncertain, and, therefore, belonging to the realm of subjective choices, something, in any case, irrelevant to public life.

This purely functional rationality, so to speak, has implied a disorder of the moral conscience altogether new for cultures existing up to now, as it deems rational only that which can be proved with experiments. As morality belongs to an altogether different sphere, it disappears as a category unto itself and must be identified in another way, in as much as it must be admitted, in any case, that morality is essential.

In a world based on calculation, it is the calculation of consequences that determines what must or must not be considered moral. And thus the category of the good, as was clearly pointed out by Kant, disappears. Nothing is good or bad in itself, everything depends on the consequences that an action allows one to foresee.

If Christianity, on one hand, has found its most effective form in Europe, it is necessary, on the other hand, to say that in Europe a culture has developed that constitutes the absolutely most radical contradiction not only of Christianity, but of the religious and moral traditions of humanity.

From this, one understands that Europe is experiencing a true and proper 'test of tension'; from this, one also understands the radicalism of the tensions that our continent must face. However from this emerges also, and above all, the responsibility that we Europeans must assume at this historical moment — in the debate on the definition of Europe, on its new political shape. It is not a question of a nostalgic rearguard battle of history being played out, but rather a great responsibility for today's humanity.

Let us take a closer look at this opposition between the two cultures that have characterized Europe. In the debate on the Preamble of the European Constitution, this opposition was seen in two controversial points: the question of the reference to God in the Constitution and the mention of the Christian roots of Europe. Given that in article 52 of the Constitution the institutional rights of Churches are guaranteed, we can be at peace, it is said.

But this means that in the life of Europe, the Churches find a place in the realm of the political commitment, while, in the realm of the foundations of Europe, the imprint of their content has no place. The reasons that are given in the public debate for this clear 'no' are superficial, and it is obvious that more than indicating the real motivation, they conceal it. The affirmation that the mention of the Christian roots of Europe injures the sentiments of many non-Christians who are in Europe is not very convincing, given that it relates, first of all, to an historical fact that no one can seriously deny.

Naturally, this historical mention has a reference to the present. To mention the roots implies indicating as well the residual sources of moral orientation, which is a factor of Europe's identity. Who would be offended? Whose identity is threatened?

The Muslims, who in this respect are often and willingly brought in, do not feel threatened by our Christian moral foundations, but by the cynicism of a secularized culture that denies its own foundations. Neither are our Jewish fellow citizens offended by the reference to the Christian roots of Europe, in as much as these roots go back to Mount Sinai: they bear the sign of the voice that made itself heard on the mountain of God and unite with us in the great fundamental orientations that the Decalogue has given humanity. The same is true for the reference to God: it is not the mention of God that offends those who belong to other religions, but rather the attempt to build the human community absolutely without God.

The motivations of this twofold 'no' are more profound than one would think from the reasons offered. They presuppose the idea that only the radical Enlightenment culture, which has reached its full development in our time, could be constitutive for European identity. Next to this culture, then, different religious cultures can coexist with their respective rights, on the condition and to the degree in which they respect the criteria of the Enlightenment culture, and are subordinated to it.

Culture of rights

This Enlightenment culture is essentially defined by the rights of freedom; it stems from freedom as a fundamental value that measures everything: the freedom of religious choice, which includes the religious neutrality of the state; freedom to express one's own opinion, as long as it does not cast doubt specifically on this canon; the democratic ordering of the state, that is, parliamentary control on state organisms; the free formation of parties; the independence of the judiciary; and, finally, the safeguarding of the rights of man and the prohibition of discriminations. Here the canon is still in the process of formation, given that there are also rights of man that are in opposition, as for example, in the case of the conflict between a woman's desire for freedom and the right of the unborn to live.

The concept of discrimination is ever more extended, and so the prohibition of discrimination can be increasingly transformed into a limitation of the freedom of opinion and religious liberty. Very soon it will not be possible to state that homosexuality, as the Catholic Church teaches, is an objective disorder in the structuring of human existence. And the fact that the Church is convinced of not having the right to confer priestly ordination on women is considered by some up to now as something irreconcilable with the spirit of the European Constitution.

It is evident that this canon of the Enlightenment culture, less than definitive, contains important values which we, precisely as Christians, do not want and cannot renounce; however, it is also obvious that the ill-defined or undefined concept of freedom, which is at the base of this culture, inevitably entails contradictions; and it is obvious that precisely because of its use (a use that seems radical) it has implied limitations of freedom that a generation ago we could not even imagine. A confused ideology of freedom leads to dogmatism, which is showing itself increasingly hostile to freedom.

We must, without a doubt, focus again on the question of the internal contradictions of the present form of the Enlightenment culture. But we must first finish describing it. Since it is the culture of a reason that has finally achieved complete self-awareness, it naturally boasts of its claimed universality and imagines that it is complete in itself, without needing any other cultural factors to complement it.

Both these characteristics are clearly seen when the question is posed about who can become a member of the European community and, above all, in the debate about Turkey's entry into this community. It is a question of a state, or perhaps better, of a cultural realm, which does not have Christian roots, but which was influenced by the Islamic culture. Then, Ataturk tried to transform Turkey into a secular state, attempting to implant in Muslim terrain the secularism that had matured in the Christian world of Europe.

Universal culture?

We can ask ourselves if that is possible. According to the thesis of the Enlightenment and secular culture of Europe, only the norms and contents of the Enlightenment culture will be able to determine Europe's identity and, consequently, every state that makes these criteria its own, will be able to belong to Europe. It does not matter, in the end, on what plot of roots this culture of freedom and democracy is implanted.

And, precisely because of this, it is affirmed, that the roots cannot enter into the definition of the foundations of Europe, it being a question of dead roots that are not part of the present identity. As a consequence, this new identity, determined exclusively by the Enlightenment culture, also implies that God does not come in at all into public life and the foundations of the state.

Thus everything becomes logical and also, in some sense, plausible. In fact, what could we desire as being more beautiful than knowing that everywhere democracy and human rights are respected? Nevertheless, the question must be asked, if this secular Enlightenment culture is really the culture, finally proposed as universal, that can give a common cause to all men; a culture that should have access from everywhere, even though it is on a humus that is historically and culturally differentiated. And we also ask ourselves if it is really complete in itself, to the degree that it has no need of a root outside itself.

Let us address these last two questions. To the first, that is, to the question as to whether a universally valid philosophy has been reached which is finally wholly scientifically rational, which expresses the cause common to all men, we must respond that undoubtedly we have arrived at important acquisitions which can pretend to a universal validity. These include: the acquisition that religion cannot be imposed by the state, but that it can only be accepted in freedom; respect of the fundamental rights of man equal for all; the separation of powers and control of power.

It cannot be thought, however, that these fundamental values, recognized by us as generally valid, can be realized in the same way in every historical context. Not all societies have the sociological assumptions for a democracy based on parties, as occurs in the West; therefore, the total religious neutrality of the state, in the majority of historical contexts, has to be considered an illusion.

And so we come to the problems raised by the second question. But let us clarify first if the modern Enlightenment philosophies, considered as a whole, can contain the last word of the cause common to all men. These philosophies are characterized by the fact that they are positivist and, therefore, anti-metaphysical, so much so that, in the end, God cannot have any place in them. They are based on the self-limitation of rational positivism, which can be applied in the technical realm, but which when it is generalized, entails instead a mutilation of man. It succeeds in having man no longer admit any moral claim beyond his calculations and, as we saw, the concept of freedom, which at first glance would seem to extend in an unlimited manner, in the end leads to the self-destruction of freedom.

It is true that the positivist philosophies contain important elements of truth. However, these are based on imposed limitations of reason, character-istic of a specific cultural situation—that of the modern West—and therefore not the last word of reason. Nevertheless though they might seem totally rational, they are not the voice of reason itself, but are also identified culturally with the present situation in the West.

For this reason they are in no way that philosophy which one day could be valid throughout the world. But, above all, it must be said that this Enlightenment philosophy, and its respective culture, is incomplete. It consciously severs its own historical roots depriving itself of the regenerating forces from which it sprang, from that fundamental memory of humanity, so to speak, without which reason loses its orientation.

Knowing is doing

In fact, the principle is now valid, according to which, man's capacity is measured by his action. What one knows how to do, may also be done. There no longer exists a knowing how to do separated from a being able to do, because it would be against freedom, which is the absolute supreme value. But man knows how to do many things, and knows increasingly how to do more things; and if this knowing how to do does not find its measure in a moral norm, it becomes, as we can already see, a power of destruction.

Man knows how to clone men, and so he does it. Man knows how to use men as a store of organs for other men, and so he does it; he does it because this seems to be an exigency of his freedom. Man knows how to construct atomic bombs and so he makes them, being, in line of principle, also disposed to use them. In the end, terrorism is also based on this modality of man's self-authorization, and not on the teachings of the Koran.

The radical detachment of the Enlightenment philosophy from its roots becomes, in the last analysis, contempt for man. Man, deep down, has no freedom, we are told by the spokesmen of the natural sciences, in total contradiction with the starting point of the whole question. Man must not think that he is something more than all other living beings and, therefore, should also be treated like them, we are told by even the most advanced spokesmen of a philosophy clearly separated from the roots of humanity's historical memory.

We asked ourselves two questions: if rationalist (positivist) philosophy is strictly rational and, consequently, if it is universally valid, and if it is complete. Is it self-sufficient? Can it, or more directly must it, relegate its historical roots to the realm of the pure past and, therefore, to the realm of what can only be valid subjectively?

We must respond to both questions with a definitive 'no.' This philosophy does not express man's complete reason, but only a part of it, and because of this mutilation of reason it cannot be considered entirely rational. For this reason it is incomplete, and can only be fulfilled by re-establishing contact with its roots. A tree without roots dries up.

Removing God

By stating this, one does not deny all that is positive and important of this philosophy, but one affirms rather its need to complete itself, its profound deficiency. And so we must again address the two controversial points of the Preamble of the European Constitution. The banishment of Christian roots does not reveal itself as the expression of a higher tolerance, which respects all cultures in the same way, not wishing to privilege any, but rather as the absolutizing of a pattern of thought and of life that are radically opposed, among other things, to the other historical cultures of humanity.

The real opposition that characterizes today's world is not that between various religious cultures, but that between the radical emancipation of man from God, from the roots of life, on one hand, and from the great religious cultures on the other. If there were to be a clash of cultures, it would not be because of a clash of the great religions—which have always struggled against one another, but which, in the end, have also always known how to live with one another—but it will be because of the clash between this radical emancipation of man and the great historical cultures.

Thus, even the rejection of the reference to God, is not the expression of a tolerance that desires to protect the non-theistic religions and the dignity of atheists and agnostics, but rather the expression of a conscience that would like to see God cancelled definitively from the public life of humanity, and relegated to the subjective realm of residual cultures of the past.

Relativism, which is the starting point of all this, thus becomes a dogmatism which believes itself to be in possession of the definitive scope of reason, and with the right to regard all the rest only as a stage of humanity, in the end surmounted, and that can be appropriately relativized. In reality, this means that we have need of roots to survive, and that we must not lose sight of God, if we do not want human dignity to disappear.

Does this amount to a simple rejection of the Enlightenment and modernity? Absolutely not. From the beginning, Christianity has understood itself as the religion of the 'Logos', as the religion according to reason. In the first place, it has not identified its precursors in the other religions, but in that philosophical enlightenment which has cleared the path of traditions to turn to the search of the truth and towards the good, toward the one God who is above all gods.

In so far as religion of the persecuted, in so far as universal religion, beyond the different states and peoples, it has denied the state the right to regard religion as a part of state ordering, thus postulating the freedom of faith. It has always defined men, all men without distinction, as creatures and images of God, proclaiming for them, in terms of principle, although within the imperative limits of social ordering, the same dignity.

In this sense, the Enlightenment is of Christian origin and it is no accident that it was born specifically and exclusively within the sphere of the Christian faith, in places where Christianity, contrary to its own nature, had unfortunately become mere tradition and the religion of the state. Philosophy, as the investigation of the rational element (which includes the rational element in faith), had always been a positive element in Christianity, but the voice of reason had been too domesticated.

It was and is the merit of the Enlightenment to have again proposed these original values of Christianity and of having given back to reason its own voice. In the pastoral constitution, On the Church in the Modern World, Vatican Council II underlined again this profound correspondence between Christianity and the Enlightenment, seeking to come to a true conciliation between the Church and modernity, which is the great heritage that both sides must defend.

Given all this, it is necessary that both sides engage in self-reflection and be willing to correct themselves. Christianity must always remember that it is the religion of the 'Logos'. It is faith in the 'Creator Spiritus', in the Creator Spirit, from which proceeds everything that exists. It is precisely this that ought to give Christianity its philosophical power today, since the problem is whether the world comes from an irrational source, so that reason would be nothing but a 'by-product' of the development of the world, or whether the world comes from reason, so that its criterion and goal is reason.

The Christian faith inclines toward this second thesis, thus having, from the purely philosophical point of view, really good cards to play, despite the fact that many today consider only the first thesis as the only modern and rational one par excellence. However, a reason that springs from the irrational, and that is, in the final analysis, itself irrational, does not constitute a solution for our problems. Only creative reason, which in the crucified God is manifested as love, can really show us the way. In the so necessary dialogue between secularists and Catholics, we Christians must be very careful to remain faithful to this fundamental line: to live a faith that comes from the 'Logos', from creative reason, and that, because of this, is also open to all that is truly rational.

'As if God existed'

But at this point, in my capacity as believer, I would like to make a proposal to the secularists. At the time of the Enlightenment there was an attempt to understand and define the essential moral norms, saying that they would be valid 'etsi Deus non daretur', even in the case that God did not exist. In the opposition of the confessions and in the pending crisis of the image of God, an attempt was made to keep the essential values of morality outside the contradictions and to seek for them an evidence that would render them independent of the many divisions and uncertainties of the different philosophies and confessions. In this way, they wanted to ensure the basis of coexistence and, in general, the foundations of humanity. At that time, it was thought to be possible, as the great deep convictions created by Christianity to a large extent remained. But this is no longer the case.

The search for such a reassuring certainty, which could remain uncontested beyond all differences, failed. Not even the truly grandiose effort of Kant was able to create the necessary shared certainty. Kant had denied that God could be known in the realm of pure reason, but at the same time he had represented God, freedom and immortality as postulates of practical reason, without which, coherently, for him no moral behavior was possible.

Does not today's situation of the world make us think perhaps that he might have been right? I would like to express it in a different way: the attempt, carried to the extreme, to manage human affairs disdaining God completely leads us increasingly to the edge of the abyss, to man's ever greater isolation from reality. We must reverse the axiom of the Enlightenment and say: Even one who does not succeed in finding the way of accepting God, should, nevertheless, seek to live and to direct his life 'veluti si Deus daretur', as if God existed. This is the advice Pascal gave to his friends who did not believe. In this way, no one is limited in his freedom, but all our affairs find the support and criterion of which they are in urgent need.

Above all, that of which we are in need at this moment in history are men who, through an enlightened and lived faith, render God credible in this world. The negative testimony of Christians who speak about God and live against him, has darkened God's image and opened the door to disbelief. We need men who have their gaze directed to God, to understand true humanity. We need men whose intellects are enlightened by the light of God, and whose hearts God opens, so that their intellects can speak to the intellects of others, and so that their hearts are able to open up to the hearts of others.

Only through men who have been touched by God, can God come near to men. We need men like Benedict of Norcia, who at a time of dissipation and decadence, plunged into the most profound solitude, succeeding, after all the purifications he had to suffer, to ascend again to the light, to return and to found Montecassino, the city on the mountain that, with so many ruins, gathered together the forces from which a new world was formed

In this way Benedict, like Abraham, became the father of many nations. The recommendations to his monks presented at the end of his 'Rule' are guidelines that show us also the way that leads on high, beyond the crisis and the ruins.

'Just as there is a bitter zeal that removes one from God and leads to hell, so there is a good zeal that removes one from vices and leads to God and to eternal life. It is in this zeal that monks must exercise themselves with most ardent love: May they outdo one another in rendering each other honor, may they support, in turn, with utmost patience their physical and moral infirmities . . . May they love one another with fraternal affection . . . Fear God in love . . . Put absolutely nothing before Christ who will be able to lead all to eternal life' (Chapter 72).

APPENDIX II

The Regensburg Address

It is a moving experience for me to be back again in the university and to be able once again to give a lecture at this podium. I think back to those years when, after a pleasant period at the Freisinger Hochschule, I began teaching at the University of Bonn. That was in 1959, in the days of the old university made up of ordinary professors. The various chairs had neither assistants nor secretaries, but in recompense there was much direct contact with students and in particular among the professors themselves. We would meet before and after lessons in the rooms of the teaching staff. There was a lively exchange, with historians, philosophers, philologists, and, naturally, between the two theological faculties. Once a semester there was a *dies academicus*, when professors from every faculty appeared before the students of the entire university, making possible a genuine experience of *universitas*—something that you, too, Magnificent Rector, just mentioned—the experience, in other words, of the fact that, despite our specializations, which at times make it difficult to communicate with each other, we made up a whole, working in everything on the basis of a single rationality, with its various aspects, and sharing responsibility for the right use of reason. This reality became a lived experience.

The university was also very proud of its two theological faculties. It was clear, that, by inquiring about the reasonableness of faith, they too carried out a work which is necessarily part of the 'whole' of the *universitas scientiarum*, even if not everyone could share the faith which theologians seek to correlate with reason as a whole. This profound sense of coherence within the universe of reason was not troubled, even when it was once reported that a colleague had said there was something odd about our university: it had two faculties devoted to something that did not exist: God. That even in the face of such radical scepticism it is still necessary and reasonable to raise the question of God through the use of reason, and to do so in the context of the tradition of the Christian faith: this, within the university as a whole, was accepted without question.

I was reminded of all this recently when I read the edition by Professor Theodore Khoury (Münster) of part of the dialogue carried on—perhaps in

1391 in the winter barracks near Ankara—by the erudite Byzantine emperor Manuel II Paleologus and an educated Persian on the subject of Christianity and Islam, and the truth of both.[1] It was presumably the emperor himself who set down this dialogue, during the siege of Constantinople between 1394 and 1402; and this would explain why his arguments are given in greater detail than those of his Persian interlocutor.[2] The dialogue ranges widely over the structures of faith contained in the Bible and in the Quran, and deals especially with the image of God and of man, while necessarily returning repeatedly to the relationship between—as they were called—three 'Laws' or 'rules of life': the Old Testament, the New Testament, and the Quran. It is not my intention to discuss this question in the present lecture; here I would like to discuss only one point—itself rather marginal to the dialogue as a whole—which, in the context of the issue of 'faith and reason', I found interesting and which can serve as the starting point for my reflections on this issue.

In the seventh conversation (διάλεξις—controversy), edited by Professor Khoury, the emperor touches the theme of the holy war. The emperor must have known that Sura 2. 256 reads: 'There is no compulsion in religion'. According to some of the experts this is probably one of the Suras of the early period, when Mohammed was still powerless and under threat. But naturally the emperor also knew the instructions, developed later and recorded in the Quran, concerning holy war. Without descending to details, such as the difference in treatment accorded to those who have the 'Book' and the 'infidels', he addresses his interlocutor with a startling brusqueness—a brusqueness that we find unacceptable—on the central question about the relationship between religion and violence in general, saying: 'Show me just what Mohammed brought that was new, and there you will find things only evil and inhuman, such as his command to spread by the sword the faith he preached.'[3] The emperor, after having expressed himself so forcefully, goes on to explain in detail the reasons why spreading the faith through violence is

[1] Of the total number of twenty-six conversations (διάλεξις—Khoury translates this as 'controversy') in the dialogue ('Entretien'), T. Khoury published the seventh 'controversy' with footnotes and an extensive introduction on the origin of the text, on the manuscript tradition, and on the structure of the dialogue, together with brief summaries of the 'controversies' not included in the edition; the Greek text is accompanied by a French translation: 'Manuel II Paléologue, Entretiens avec un musulman. 7e Controverse', Sources chrétiennes, 115 (1966). In the meantime Karl Förstel published in Corpus Islamico–Christianum (Series Graeca, ed. A. T. Khoury and R. Glei) an edition of the text in Greek and German, with commentary: Manuel II Palaiologos, Dialoge mit einem Muslim, 3 vols. (Würzburg-Altenberge, 1993–6). As early as 1966 E. Trapp had published the Greek text with an introduction, as vol. ii of Wiener byzantinische Studien. I shall be quoting from Khoury's edition.

[2] On the origin and redaction of the dialogue cf. Khoury, 22–9; extensive comments in this regard can also be found in the editions of Förstel and Trapp.

[3] Controversy VII, 2 c: Khoury, 142–3; Förstel, vol. i, VII, Dialog 1.5, 240–1. In the Muslim world this quotation has unfortunately been taken as an expression of my personal position, thus arousing understandable indignation. I hope that the reader of my text can see immediately that this sentence does not express my personal view of the Quran, for

something unreasonable. Violence is incompatible with the nature of God and the nature of the soul. 'God', he says, 'is not pleased by blood—and not acting reasonably (σὺν λόγω) is contrary to God's nature. Faith is born of the soul, not the body. Whoever would lead someone to faith needs the ability to speak well and to reason properly, without violence and threats . . . To convince a reasonable soul, one does not need a strong arm, or weapons of any kind, or any other means of threatening a person with death . . . '[4]

The decisive statement in this argument against violent conversion is this: not to act in accordance with reason is contrary to God's nature.[5] The editor, Theodore Khoury, observes: For the emperor, as a Byzantine shaped by Greek philosophy, this statement is self-evident. But, for Muslim teaching, God is absolutely transcendent. His will is not bound up with any of our categories, even that of rationality.[6] Here Khoury quotes a work of the noted French Islamist R. Arnaldez, who points out that Ibn Hazm went so far as to state that God is not bound even by his own word, and that nothing would oblige him to reveal the truth to us. Were it God's will, we would even have to practise idolatry.[7]

At this point, as far as understanding of God, and thus the concrete practice of religion, is concerned, we are faced with an unavoidable dilemma. Is the conviction that acting unreasonably contradicts God's nature merely a Greek idea, or is it always and intrinsically true? I believe that here we can see the profound harmony between what is Greek in the best sense of the word and the biblical understanding of faith in God. Modifying the first verse of the Book of Genesis, the first verse of the whole Bible, John began the prologue of his Gospel with the words: 'In the beginning was the λόγος'. This is the very word used by the emperor: God acts, σὺν λόγω, with logos. Logos means both reason and word—a reason which is creative and capable of self-communication, precisely as reason. John thus spoke the final word on the biblical concept of God, and in this word all the often toilsome and tortuous threads of biblical faith find their culmination and synthesis. In the beginning was the logos, and the logos is God, says the Evangelist. The encounter between the biblical message and Greek thought did not happen by chance. The vision of Saint Paul, who saw the roads to Asia barred and in a dream saw a Macedonian man plead with him: 'Come over to Macedonia and help us!' (cf. Acts 16: 6–10)—this vision can

which I have the respect due to the holy book of a great religion. In quoting the text of the Emperor Manuel II I intended solely to draw out the essential relationship between faith and reason. On this point I am in agreement with Manuel II, but without endorsing his polemic.

[4] Controversy VII, 3 b–c: Khoury, 144–5; Förstel, vol. i, VII, Dialog 1.6, 240–3.

[5] It was purely for the sake of this statement that I quoted the dialogue between Manuel and his Persian interlocutor. In this statement the theme of my subsequent reflections emerges.

[6] Cf. Khoury, 144, n. 1.

[7] R. Arnaldez, *Grammaire et théologie chez Ibn Hazm de Cordoue* (Paris: Vrin, 1956), 13; cf. Khoury, 144. The fact that comparable positions exist in the theology of the late Middle Ages will appear later in my discourse.

be interpreted as a 'distillation' of the intrinsic necessity of a rapprochement between biblical faith and Greek inquiry.

In point of fact, this rapprochement had been going on for some time. The mysterious name of God, revealed from the burning bush, a name which separates this God from all other divinities with their many names, and simply asserts being, 'I am', already presents a challenge to the notion of myth, to which Socrates' attempt to vanquish and transcend myth stands in close analogy.[8] Within the Old Testament, the process which started at the burning bush came to new maturity at the time of the Exile, when the God of Israel, an Israel now deprived of its land and worship, was proclaimed as the God of heaven and earth and described in a simple formula which echoes the words uttered at the burning bush: 'I am'. This new understanding of God is accompanied by a kind of enlightenment, which finds stark expression in the mockery of gods who are merely the work of human hands (cf. Ps. 115). Thus, despite the bitter conflict with those Hellenistic rulers who sought to accommodate it forcibly to the customs and idolatrous cult of the Greeks, biblical faith, in the Hellenistic period, encountered the best of Greek thought at a deep level, resulting in a mutual enrichment evident especially in the later wisdom literature. Today we know that the Greek translation of the Old Testament produced at Alexandria—the Septuagint—is more than a simple (and in that sense really less than satisfactory) translation of the Hebrew text: it is an independent textual witness and a distinct and important step in the history of Revelation, one which brought about this encounter in a way that was decisive for the birth and spread of Christianity.[9] A profound encounter of faith and reason is taking place here, an encounter between genuine enlightenment and religion. From the very heart of Christian faith and, at the same time, the heart of Greek thought now joined to faith, Manuel II was able to say: Not to act 'with *logos*' is contrary to God's nature.

In all honesty, one must observe that in the late Middle Ages we find trends in theology which would sunder this synthesis between the Greek spirit and the Christian spirit. In contrast with the so-called intellectualism of Augustine and Thomas there arose with Duns Scotus a voluntarism which, in its later developments, led to the claim that we can only know God's *voluntas ordinata*. Beyond this is the realm of God's freedom, in virtue of which he could have done the opposite of everything he has actually done. This gives rise to positions which clearly approach those of Ibn Hazm and might even lead

---

[8] Regarding the widely discussed interpretation of the episode of the burning bush, I refer to my book *Introduction to Christianity* (London: Search Press, 1969), 77–93 (orig. pub. in German, as *Einführung in das Christentum* (Munich: Kasel, 1968); NB the pages quoted refer to the entire chapter entitled 'The Biblical Belief in God'). I think that my statements in that book, despite later developments in the discussion, remain valid today.

[9] Cf. A. Schenker, 'L'Écriture sainte subsiste en plusieurs formes canoniques simultanées', in *L'interpretazione della Bibbia nella chiesa. Atti del simposio promosso dalla congregazione per la dottrina della Fede* (Vatican City, 2001), 178–86.

to the image of a capricious God, who is not even bound to truth and goodness. God's transcendence and otherness are so exalted that our reason, our sense of the true and good, are no longer an authentic mirror of God, whose deepest possibilities remain eternally unattainable and hidden behind his actual decisions. As opposed to this, the faith of the Church has always insisted that between God and us, between his eternal Creator Spirit and our created reason, there exists a real analogy, in which—as the Fourth Lateran Council in 1215 stated—unlikeness remains infinitely greater than likeness, yet not to the point of abolishing analogy and its language. God does not become more divine when we push him away from us in a sheer, impenetrable voluntarism; rather, the truly divine God is the God who has revealed himself as *logos* and, as *logos*, has acted and continues to act lovingly on our behalf. Certainly, love, as Saint Paul says, 'transcends' knowledge and is thereby capable of perceiving more than thought alone (cf. Eph. 3: 19); none the less it continues to be love of the God who is *logos*. Consequently, Christian worship is, again to quote Paul—'λογικὴ λατρεία', worship in harmony with the eternal Word and with our reason (cf. Rom. 12: 1).[10]

This inner rapprochement between biblical faith and Greek philosophical inquiry was an event of decisive importance not only from the standpoint of the history of religions, but also from that of world history—it is an event which concerns us even today. Given this convergence, it is not surprising that Christianity, despite its origins and some significant developments in the East, finally took on its historically decisive character in Europe. We can also express this the other way around: this convergence, with the subsequent addition of the Roman heritage, created Europe and remains the foundation of what can rightly be called Europe.

The thesis that the critically purified Greek heritage forms an integral part of Christian faith has been countered by the call for a de-Hellenization of Christianity—a call which has more and more dominated theological discussions since the beginning of the modern age. Viewed more closely, three stages can be observed in the programme of de-Hellenization: although interconnected, they are clearly distinct from one another in their motivations and objectives.[11]

De-Hellenization first emerges in connection with the postulates of the Reformation in the sixteenth century. Looking at the tradition of scholastic theology, the Reformers thought they were confronted with a faith system totally conditioned by philosophy, that is to say an articulation of the faith based on an alien system of thought. As a result, faith no longer appeared as a

[10] On this matter I expressed myself in greater detail in my book *The Spirit of the Liturgy* (San Francisco: Ignatius, 2000), 44–50.

[11] Of the vast literature on the theme of de-Hellenization I would like to mention, above all: A. Grillmeier, 'Hellenisierung–Judaisierung des Christentums als Deuteprinzipien der Geschichte des kirchlichen Dogmas', in id. *Mit ihm und in ihm. Christologische Forschungen und Perspektiven* (Freiburg, 1975), 423–88.

living historical Word but as one element of an overarching philosophical system. The principle of *sola scriptura*, on the other hand, sought faith in its pure, primordial form, as originally found in the biblical Word. Metaphysics appeared as a premiss derived from another source, from which faith had to be liberated in order to become once more fully itself. When Kant stated that he needed to set thinking aside in order to make room for faith, he carried this programme forward with a radicalism that the Reformers could never have foreseen. He thus anchored faith exclusively in practical reason, denying it access to reality as a whole.

The liberal theology of the nineteenth and twentieth centuries ushered in a second stage in the process of de-Hellenization, with Adolf von Harnack as its outstanding representative. When I was a student, and in the early years of my teaching, this programme was highly influential in Catholic theology too. It took as its point of departure Pascal's distinction between the God of the philosophers and the God of Abraham, Isaac, and Jacob. In my inaugural lecture at Bonn in 1959, I tried to address the issue,[12] and I do not intend to repeat here what I said on that occasion, but I would like to describe at least briefly what was new about this second stage of de-Hellenization. Harnack's central idea was to return simply to the man Jesus and to his simple message, underneath the accretions of theology and indeed of Hellenization: this simple message was seen as the culmination of the religious development of humanity. Jesus was said to have put an end to worship in favour of morality. In the end he was presented as the father of a humanitarian moral message. Fundamentally, Harnack's goal was to bring Christianity back into harmony with modern reason, liberating it, that is to say, from seemingly philosophical and theological elements, such as faith in Christ's divinity and the triune God. In this sense, historical–critical exegesis of the New Testament, as he saw it, restored to theology its place within the university: theology, for Harnack, is something essentially historical and therefore strictly scientific. What it is able to say critically about Jesus is, so to speak, an expression of practical reason and, consequently it can take its rightful place within the university. Behind this thinking lies the modern self-limitation of reason, classically expressed in Kant's 'Critiques', but in the meantime further radicalized by the impact of the natural sciences. This modern concept of reason is based, to put it briefly, on a synthesis between Platonism (Cartesianism) and empiricism, a synthesis confirmed by the success of technology. On the one hand, it presupposes the mathematical structure of matter, its intrinsic rationality, which makes it possible to understand how matter works and how to use it efficiently: this basic premiss is, so to speak, the Platonic element in the modern understanding of nature. On the other hand, there is nature's capacity

[12] Newly published, with commentary, by Heino Sonnemans (ed.), *Joseph Ratzinger–Benedikt XVI, Der Gott des Glaubens und der Gott der Philosophen: Ein Beitrag zum Problem der theologia naturalis*, 2nd edn. (Leutesdorf: Johannes Verlag, 2005).

to be exploited for our purposes, and here only the possibility of verification or falsification through experimentation can yield decisive certainty. The weight between the two poles can, depending on the circumstances, shift from one side to the other. As strongly positivistic a thinker as J. Monod has declared himself a convinced Platonist/Cartesian.

This gives rise to two principles which are crucial for the issue we have raised. First, only the kind of certainty resulting from the interplay of mathematical and empirical elements can be considered scientific. Anything that would claim to be science must be measured against this criterion. Hence the human sciences, such as history, psychology, sociology, and philosophy, attempt to conform themselves to this canon of scientificity. A second point, which is important for our reflections, is that by its very nature this method excludes the question of God, making it appear an unscientific or pre-scientific question. Consequently, we are faced with a reduction of the radius of science and reason, one which needs to be questioned.

I will return to this problem later. In the meantime, it must be observed that from this standpoint any attempt to maintain theology's claim to be 'scientific' would end up reducing Christianity to a mere fragment of its former self. But we must say more: if science as a whole is this and this alone, then it is man himself who ends up being reduced, for the specifically human questions about our origin and destiny, the questions raised by religion and ethics, then have no place within the purview of collective reason as defined by 'science', so understood, and must thus be relegated to the realm of the subjective. The subject then decides, on the basis of his experiences, what he considers tenable in matters of religion, and the subjective 'conscience' becomes the sole arbiter of what is ethical. In this way, though, ethics and religion lose their power to create a community and become a completely personal matter. This is a dangerous state of affairs for humanity, as we see from the disturbing pathologies of religion and reason which necessarily erupt when reason is so reduced that questions of religion and ethics no longer concern it. Attempts to construct an ethic from the rules of evolution, or from psychology and sociology, end up being simply inadequate.

Before I draw the conclusions to which all this has been leading, I must briefly refer to the third stage of de-Hellenization, which is now in progress. In the light of our experience with cultural pluralism, it is often said nowadays that the synthesis with Hellenism achieved in the early Church was an initial inculturation which ought not to be binding on other cultures. The latter are said to have the right to return to the simple message of the New Testament prior to that inculturation, in order to inculturate it anew in their own particular milieux. This thesis is not simply false, it is coarse and lacking in precision. The New Testament was written in Greek and bears the imprint of the Greek spirit, which had already come to maturity as the Old Testament developed. True, there are elements in the evolution of the early Church which do not have to be integrated into all cultures. None the less, the fundamental decisions made about the relationship between faith and the use of human reason are part of the faith itself; they are developments consonant with the nature of faith itself.

And so I come to my conclusion. This attempt, painted with broad strokes, at a critique of modern reason from within has nothing to do with putting the clock back to the time before the Enlightenment and rejecting the insights of the modern age. The positive aspects of modernity are to be acknowledged unreservedly: we are all grateful for the marvellous possibilities that it has opened up for mankind and for the progress in humanity that has been granted to us. The scientific ethos, moreover, is—as you, yourself, mentioned, Magnificent Rector—the will to be obedient to the truth, and, as such, it embodies an attitude which belongs to the essential decisions of the Christian spirit. The intention here is not one of retrenchment or negative criticism, but of broadening our concept of reason and its application. While we rejoice in the new possibilities open to humanity, we also see the dangers arising from these possibilities and we must ask ourselves how we can overcome them. We will succeed in doing so only if reason and faith come together in a new way, if we overcome the self-imposed limitation of reason to the empirically falsifiable, and if we once more disclose its vast horizons. In this sense theology rightly belongs in the university and within the wide-ranging dialogue of sciences, not merely as a historical discipline and one of the human sciences, but precisely as theology, as inquiry into the rationality of faith.

Only thus do we become capable of that genuine dialogue of cultures and religions so urgently needed today. In the western world it is widely held that only positivistic reason and the forms of philosophy based on it are universally valid. Yet the world's profoundly religious cultures see this exclusion of the divine from the universality of reason as an attack on their most profound convictions. A reason which is deaf to the divine and which relegates religion into the realm of subcultures is incapable of entering into the dialogue of cultures. At the same time, as I have attempted to show, modern scientific reason with its intrinsically Platonic element bears within itself a question which points beyond itself and beyond the possibilities of its methodology. Modern scientific reason quite simply has to accept the rational structure of matter and the correspondence between our spirit and the prevailing rational structures of nature as a given, on which its methodology has to be based. Yet the question why this has to be so is a real question, and one which has to be remanded by the natural sciences to other modes and planes of thought—to philosophy and theology. For philosophy and, albeit in a different way, for theology, listening to the great experiences and insights of the religious traditions of humanity, and those of the Christian faith in particular, is a source of knowledge, and to ignore it would be an unacceptable restriction of our listening and responding. Here I am reminded of something Socrates said to Phaedo. In their earlier conversations, many false philosophical opinions had been raised, and so Socrates says: 'It would be easily understandable if someone became so annoyed at all these false notions that for the rest of his life he despised and mocked all talk about being—but in this way he would be deprived of the truth of existence and would suffer a great loss.'[13] The West has long been endangered by this aversion to the questions which underlie its rationality, and can only suffer great harm thereby. The courage to engage the whole breadth of reason, and not the denial of its grandeur—this is the programme with which a theology grounded in biblical faith enters into the debates of our time. 'Not to act reasonably, not to act with *logos*, is contrary to the nature of God', said Manuel II, according to his Christian understanding of God, in response to his Persian interlocutor. It is to this great *logos*, to this breadth of reason, that we invite our partners in the dialogue of cultures. To rediscover it constantly is the great task of the university.

---

[13] Cf. 90 c–d. For this text cf. also R. Guardini, *Der Tod des Sokrates*, 5th edn. (Mainz-Paderborn: Matthias-Grünewald Verlag, 1987), 218–21.

Notes

Introduction

1. J. Ratzinger, *Volk und Haus Gottes in Augustins Lehre von Der Kirche* (Munich: Karl Zink Verlag, 1954); id., *The Theology of History in St Bonaventure* (Chicago: Franciscan Herald Press, 1989).
2. A. Nichols, *Catholic Thought Since the Enlightenment* (London: Gracewing, 1998), 84.
3. Ratzinger, *Salt of the Earth: The Church at the End of the Millennium. An Interview with Peter Seewald* (San Francisco: Ignatius, 1996), 61.
4. Interview with Alfred Läpple by Gianni Valente and Pierluca Azzardo, *30 Days*, 1 (2006), 60.
5. Ratzinger, *Milestones: Memoirs 1927–1977* (San Franciso: Ignatius, 1998), 98.
6. Interview with Alfred Läpple by Gianni Valente and Pierluca Azzardo, *30 Days*, 1 (2006), 60.
7. Ratzinger, *Salt of the Earth*, 33 and 41.
8. Ibid. 33. The related Platonic–Augustinian idea to which he is also attracted is that the intellect is a kind of participation in the light of the divine mind. This theme of the Augustinian metaphysics of light and the ontology of participation also interested Gottlieb Söhngen, one of Ratzinger's professors in the theology faculty at Munich. These Platonic–Augustinian themes were often neglected in late nineteenth- and early twentieth-century Thomism but the mid-twentieth-century Italian Thomist, Cornelio Fabro (1911–1995), tried to address the neglect, and the contemporary Thomist, Rudi te Velde, from the University of Tilburg, is also drawing attention to the more Platonic dimensions of classical Thomism. Te Velde, *Participation and Substantiality in Thomas Aquinas* (Brill: Leiden, 1995); C. Fabro, *The Metaphysical Notion of Participation According to St Thomas Aquinas* (Turin: SEI, 1939); *Participation and Causality According to St Thomas Aquinas* (Turin: SEI, 1960).
9. Ratzinger, *Salt of the Earth*, 41.
10. Ibid. 60.
11. Id., Commentary on *Gaudium et Spes*, H. Vorgrimler (ed.), *Commentary on the Documents of Vatican II*, iii (New York: Herder and Herder, 1969), 155.
12. Ibid.
13. Id., *The Nature and the Mission of Theology: Approaches to Understanding its Role in the Light of Present Controversy* (San Francisco: Ignatius, 1993), 16–17.
14. Ibid. 22.

15. Benedict XVI, Angelus Address, St Peter's Square, 28 Jan. 2007.

16. Ratzinger, *Principles of Catholic Theology: Building Stones for a Fundamental Theology* (San Francisco: Ignatius, 1987), 160.

17. G. Kaplan, *Answering the Enlightenment: The Catholic Recovery of Historical Revelation* (New York: Herder and Herder, 2006), 99.

18. Interview with Alfred Läpple by Gianni Valente and Pierluca Azzardo, 62.

19. C. Fabro, 'Il Transcendentale tomistico', *Angelicum*, 60 (1983), 534–58; M. Jordan, 'The Grammar of *Esse*: Re-reading Thomas on the Transcendentals', *Thomist*, 44 (1980), 1–26 and id., 'The Evidence of the Transcendentals and the Place of Beauty in Thomas Aquinas', *International Philosophical Quarterly*, 29 (1989), 394–407.

20. A. A. Maurer, *About Beauty: A Thomistic Interpretation* (Houston, Tex.: Center for Thomistic Studies, 1983), 2–3.

21. R. Dodaro, *Christ and the Just Society in the Thought of St Augustine* (Cambridge: Cambridge University Press, 2004).

22. *Gaudium et spes*, 42 and *Lumen gentium*, 1.

23. Ratzinger, *Salt of the Earth*, 79.

24. F. S. Fiorenza, 'From Theologian to Pope: A Personal View Back, Past the Public Portrayals', *Harvard Divinity Bulletin*, 33 (2005).

25. Ratzinger, *The Spirit of the Liturgy* (San Francisco: Ignatius, 2000), 23.

26. J.-F. Lyotard, *The Post-Modern Condition: A Report on Knowledge* (Manchester: Manchester University Press, 1984).

27. Fiorenza, 'From Theologian to Pope', 56–62, at 56.

28. J. A. Komonchak, 'The Church in Crisis: Pope Benedict's Theological Vision', *Commonweal*, 3 June 2005, 11–14, at 13.

29. Ibid.

30. Benedict XVI, Christmas Message, *L'Osservatore Romano*, 4 Jan. 2006.

31. J. V. Schall, 'On Reading the Pope: Part II', 'Ignatius Insight' website, 20 Jan. 2006.

32. Ratzinger, 'The Church and Scientific Theology', *Communio: International Catholic Review*, 7 (1980), 332–42.

33. Fabro, *God in Exile* (Toronto: Newman, 1964), 69.

34. A. MacIntyre, 'The Specter of Communitarianism', *Radical Philosophy*, Mar./Apr. (1995), 34–5.

Chapter 1

1. For the most important works on the Leonine Thomist opposition to the *Ressourcement* project, see the following: R. Garrigou-Lagrange, 'La Théologie nouvelle: où va-t-elle?', *La Synthèse thomiste* (Paris: Desclée de Brouwer, 1946), 699–725; J. Guillet, *La Théologie catholique en France de 1914 à 1960* (Paris: Médiasèvres, 1988); M.-M. Labourdette, 'La Théologie et ses sources', *Revue thomiste*, 46 (1946); J. Daniélou, 'Les Orientations présentes de la pensée religieuse', *Études*, 249 Apr./May/June (1946), 5–21; A. Nichols, 'Thomism and the Nouvelle Théologie', *Thomist*, 64 (2000), 12; F. Kerr, *After Aquinas: Versions of Thomism* (Oxford: Blackwell, 2002), 134–49.

2. R. Peddicord, *The Sacred Monster of Thomism: An Introduction to the Life and Legacy of Reginald Garrigou-Lagrange OP* (South Bend, Ind.: St Augustine's Press, 2005), 2.

3. See e.g. the presentations of Leonine thought in Kerr, *After Aquinas: Versions of Thomism*; Nichols, *Catholic Thought Since the Enlightenment: A Survey* (Leominster: Gracewing, 1998); and A. MacIntyre, *Three Rival Versions of Moral Enquiry* (London: Duckworth, 1990).

4. E. Gilson, *Letters to Henri de Lubac* (San Francisco: Ignatius, 1988), 24.

5. M.-D. Chenu, 'L'Interprète de saint Thomas d'Aquin', in M. Courafier (ed.), *Étienne Gilson et Nous: la philosophie et son histoire* (Paris: Vrin, 1980), 43–4.

6. MacIntyre, *Three Rival Versions of Moral Enquiry*, ch. 3, esp. p. 70.

7. H. de Lubac, 'Nature and Grace', in T. Patrick Burke (ed.), *The Word in History: The St Xavier Symposium* (London: Collins, 1968), 33.

8. Kerr, *After Aquinas*, 134.

9. Ibid. 137.

10. R. Cessario, 'Cardinal Cajetan and his Critics', *Nova et Vetera*, 3 (2005), 115.

11. This work was published in English as *The Office of Peter and the Structure of the Church* (San Francisco: Ignatius, 1986).

12. A. Nichols, *The Word Has Been Abroad* (Edinburgh: T. & T. Clark, 1998), p. xix.

13. Ibid. p. ix.

14. K. Rahner, 'Concerning the Relationship between Nature and Grace', *Theological Investigations*, i (London: Darton, Longman and Todd, 1961); J. Milbank, *The Suspended Middle: Henri de Lubac and the Debate Concerning the Supernatural* (Grand Rapids, Mich.: Eerdmans, 2005); Nichols, 'Anonymous Christianity', *Beyond the Blue Glass: Catholic Essays on Faith and Culture*, i (London: St Austin Press, 2002), 107–28; K. Kilby, 'Balthasar and Karl Rahner', in Edward T. Oakes and David Moss (eds.), *The Cambridge Companion to Hans Urs von Balthasar* (Cambridge: Cambridge University Press, 2004), 256–69; K. D. Eberhard, 'Karl Rahner and the Supernatural Existential', *Thought* (1971), 537–63.

15. Milbank, *Theology and Social Theory: Beyond Secular Reason* (Oxford: Blackwell, 1990), 220–3.

16. Nichols, 'Anonymous Christianity', 112.

17. Ratzinger, *Principles of Catholic Theology: Building Stones for a Fundamental Theology* (San Francisco: Ignatius, 1987), 388.

18. For the most important accounts of Wojtyla's Lublin Thomism, see K. Wojtyla, *The Acting Person* (Dordrecht: D. Reidel, 1979); id., 'Person: Subject and Community', *Review of Metaphysics*, 33 (1979), 278–308; K. L. Schmitz, *At the Center of the Human Drama: The Philosophical Anthropology of Karol Wojtyla/Pope John Paul II* (Washington, DC: Catholic University of America Press, 1993); A. Dulles, *The Splendor of Faith: The Theological*

Vision of Pope John Paul II (London: Hodder and Stoughton, 1979); R. Duncan, 'Lublin Thomism', *Thomist* 51 (1987), 307–24.

19. Ratzinger, 'Concerning the Notion of Person in Theology', *Communio: International Catholic Review*, 17 (1990), 439–54.

20. Other scholars in the *Communio* school who rose to prominence during the pontificate of John Paul II include: Angelo Cardinal Scola, Rector of the Pontifical Lateran University from 1995 until his appointment as Patriarch of Venice in 2002; Marc Cardinal Ouellet, Archbishop of Quebec City; Roger Cardinal Etchegaray, Vice-Dean of the College of Cardinals; Walter Cardinal Kasper, appointed President of the Pontifical Council for Promoting Christian Unity; Péter Cardinal Erdő, Primate of Hungary; Philippe Cardinal Barbarin, Archbishop of Lyon; Professor Joseph Fessio SJ, founder of Ignatius Press and several institutions of Catholic higher education in the Americas; David L. Schindler, Dean of the John Paul II Institute for Marriage and Family, Washington, DC; Aidan Nichols OP, the first person to hold a lectureship in Roman Catholic theology in post-Reformation Oxford; Jean Duchesne, Condorcet College, Paris; Jean-Luc Marion, the Sorbonne and the University of Chicago; Olivier Boulnois, École Pratique des Hautes Études; Remi Brague, the Sorbonne; Jean Borella, University of Nancy; Robert Spaemann, Universities of Munich and Salzburg; Antonio Sicari OCD, general editor of the Italian edition of *Communio*; James Cardinal Stafford; Archbishop Xavier Martinez of Granada; and Christoph Cardinal von Schönborn, Archbishop of Vienna.

Of the neo-Thomists, so called because they do not take their Thomism neat, but mix it with dashes of modern philosophy, often elements from Immanuel Kant, the leaders were: John Finnis, Professor of Law and Legal Philosophy, University College, Oxford; Germain Grisez, Professor of Christian Ethics, Mount Saint Mary's College; Joseph Boyle, University of Toronto; and William E. May, John Paul II Institute for Marriage and Family, Washington, DC.

Other scholars associated with the Thomist tradition in some sense, and prominent defenders of the John Paul II pontificate, included: Carlo Caffara, Archbishop of Bologna, recently raised to the status of Cardinal by Benedict XVI; Cardinal Georges Cottier OP, Papal theologian under John Paul II; Ralph McInerny of Notre Dame University; Jude Dougherty, Catholic University of America; Russell Hittinger, University of Tulsa; John Hittinger, Sacred Heart Seminary, Detroit; Fr Augustine Di Noia OP, now with the Congregation for the Doctrine of the Faith; Fr Richard Schenk OP, University of San Francisco; Matthew Levering, Ave Maria University, Florida; Servais Pinckaers OP, University of Fribourg; Romanus Cessario OP, St John's Seminary, Boston; Fr James V. Schall SJ, Georgetown University; the late Elizabeth Anscombe, Cambridge University; Ryszard Legutko, the Jagiellonian University;

Monsignor Livio Melina, Pontifical Lateran University; Fr José Noriega Bastos, Pontifical Lateran University; Josef Seifert, Internationale Akademie für Philosophie, Liechtenstein; Serge-Thomas Bonino OP, Catholic University of Toulouse; Anthony Fisher OP, Foundation Director of the John Paul II Institute for Marriage and Family (Melbourne) and Auxiliary Bishop of Sydney; Dr Nicholas Tonti-Filipinni, John Paul II Institute for Marriage and Family (Melbourne); Professor Hayden Ramsay, University of Notre Dame (Sydney) and John Paul II Institute for Marriage and Family (Melbourne); and among the more intellectually inclined Cardinals who were not in any particular theological school, but who threw their intellectual weight behind the pontificate, there were the examples of Francis Cardinal George of Chicago, the late John Cardinal O'Connor of New York, and George Cardinal Pell of Sydney. The Centre for Faith and Culture in Oxford, under the direction of Stratford Caldecott, and the Lumen Christi Institute associated with the University of Chicago, under the direction of Thomas Levergood, brought together scholars who identified with a broad range of schools, including Thomists and members of *Communio* circles.

These lists are by no means exhaustive but serve to provide some concrete guide to the networks of academic support for the pontificate of John Paul II, especially in the Anglophone world.

21. Nichols, *Beyond the Blue Glass*, 33.
22. G. Valente, 'The Story of Joseph Ratzinger: 1969–1977', *30 Days*, 8 (2006), 65–6.
23. Notwithstanding the fact that Christof Maria Michael Hugo Damien Peter Adalbert Graf von Schönborn-Wiesentheid is associated with the German edition of *Communio*, he has equally strong claims to be labelled a Thomist given his Dominican formation and appointment at the Theology Faculty of the University of Fribourg, which is itself associated with the great Thomist names of Charles Cardinal Journet, Georges Cardinal Cottier OP, and Servais Pinckaers OP.
24. For excellent expositions of this position, see: de Lubac, 'Nature and Grace', and D. L. Schindler, 'Grace and the Form of Nature and Culture', *Catholicism and Secularisation in America* (Notre Dame, Ind.: Communio Books, 1990). For an example of the passion which this reading arouses in Thomists sympathetic to the tradition of Cajetan, see Cessario, 'Cardinal Cajetan and his Critics', 109–18.
25. J. Berkman, Introd., *The Pinckaer's Reader* (Washington, DC: Catholic University of America Press, 2005), 16.
26. J. Milbank, 'Post-modern Critical Augustinianism: A Short Summa in Forty-two Responses to Unasked Questions', *Modern Theology*, 7 (1991), 311–33.
27. P. Richardson, 'Explaining Benedict' <http://trushare.com/0121June05/TR121COVE.htm>.

28. K. Lee, Lecture notes <http//www.mirrorofjustice.com>.
29. The author is associated with both the Radical Orthodoxy and *Communio* circles but sides with the *Communio* scholars on anthropological issues. An acknowledgement that some Radical Orthodoxy scholars would not agree with Pope Benedict's reaffirmation of Catholic moral teaching on sexuality is therefore not an endorsement of this position on the part of the author, but simply an acknowledgement that an important intellectual fault line does exist here.

Chapter 2

1. K. Rahner, 'Towards a Fundamental Theological Interpretation of Vatican II', *Theological Studies*, 40 (1979), 716–28.
2. J. Ratzinger, *Theological Highlights of Vatican II* (New York: Paulist Press, 1966), 68.
3. Id., *The Ratzinger Report* (San Francisco: Ignatius, 1985), 35.
4. Id., *Theological Highlights of Vatican II*, 2.
5. Ibid.
6. Ibid. 40.
7. K. Barth, *Ad Limina Apostolorum* (Edinburgh: St Andrews Press, 1969), 20.
8. F. George, *Inculturation and Ecclesial Communion: Culture and Church in the Teaching of Pope John Paul II* (Rome: Urbaniana University Press, 1990).
9. Ratzinger, *Theological Highlights of Vatican II*, 100.
10. Id., *Principles of Catholic Theology: Building Stones for a Fundamental Theology* (San Francisco: Ignatius, 1987), 378.
11. J. O'Malley, *Tradition and Transition: Historical Perspectives on Vatican II* (Wilmington, Del.: Michael Glazier Books, 1989), 45.
12. H. de Lubac, *The Drama of Atheist Humanism* (San Francisco: Ignatius, 1995).
13. Ratzinger, 'The Dignity of the Human Person', in H. Vorgrimler (ed.), *Commentary on the Documents of Vatican II*, V (New York: Herder and Herder, 1969), 118.
14. Ibid. 126.
15. Ibid. 159.
16. D. L. Schindler, 'Christology and the *Imago Dei*: Interpreting *Gaudium et spes*', *Communio: International Catholic Review*, 23 (1996), 156–84; and W. Kasper, 'The Theological Anthropology of *Gaudium et spes*', ibid. 129–41.
17. Ratzinger, 'The Dignity of the Human Person', 121.
18. Ibid. 119.
19. Ibid.
20. Ibid.
21. Ibid. 120.
22. Ibid.
23. Ibid.

24. Id., 'The Current Situation of Faith and Theology', *L'Osservatore Romano*, 6 Nov. 1996, 4–6.
25. Id., 'Truth and Freedom', *Communio: International Catholic Review*, 23 (1996), 16–35, at 31.
26. Id., 'The Dignity of the Human Person', 119.
27. Ibid.
28. Kasper, *Faith and the Future* (London: Burns and Oates, 1985), 4.
29. Schindler, 'Trinity, Creation and the Order of Intelligence in the Modern Academy', *Communio: International Catholic Review*, 28 (2001), 407.
30. Ratzinger, *The Spirit of the Liturgy*, 32–3.
31. Id., *The End of Time* (Mahwah, NJ: Paulist Press, 2004), 20–1.
32. Id., 'The Dignity of the Human Person', 137–8.
33. Ibid. 138.
34. Id., *Das neue Volk Gottes: Entwürfe zur Ekklesiologie* (Düsseldorf, 1969), 146.
35. Id., *The Yes of Jesus Christ: Spiritual Exercises in Faith, Hope and Love* (New York: Crossroad, 1991), 41.
36. Ibid. 42.
37. Id., 'The Dignity of the Human Person', 136.
38. Ibid.
39. Ibid. 134–5.
40. Id., *Theological Highlights of Vatican II*, 167.
41. Id., 'The Dignity of the Human Person', 130–1.
42. L. Boeve, '*Gaudium et spes* and the Crisis of Modernity: The End of the Dialogue with the World', in M. Lamberigts and L. Kenis (eds.), *Vatican II and its Legacy* (Leuven: Leuven University Press, 2002), 90.
43. Here Boeve is not using 'neo-conservative' in the sense that it is commonly used in the United States to refer to a position which is liberal on economic policy but socially conservative on other areas of public policy. No one would regard Ratzinger as a 'neo-con' in the American sense. He has made too many criticisms of liberal economy theory to fit comfortably into that tradition.
44. Ibid.
45. N. Boyle, 'On earth, as in heaven', *Tablet*, 9 July 2005, 12–15.
46. Ibid. 14.
47. Ibid. 12.
48. J. A. Komonchak, 'Interpreting the Second Vatican Council', *Landas*, 1 (1987), 81–90.
49. Ratzinger, *Principles of Catholic Theology*, 382.
50. Ibid. 385.
51. Id., *Introduction to Christianity* (San Francisco: Ignatius, 1990), 41.
52. H. U. von Balthasar, 'The Fathers, the Scholastics and Ourselves', *Communio: International Catholic Review*, 24 (1997), 347–96, at 352.
53. Ibid. 349.

54. Ratzinger, *Das neue Volk Gottes*, 95–6; repr. in *Co-Workers of the Truth: Meditations for Every Day of the Year* (San Francisco: Ignatius, 1992), 341.
55. A. Dulles, 'Benedict XVI: Interpreter of Vatican II', Laurence J. McGinley Lecture, Fordham University, New York, 25 Oct. 2005, 19. Dulles quotes from Ratzinger, *Milestones: Cardinal Ratzinger's Memoirs (1927–1977)* (San Francisco: Ignatius, 1998), 128 in defending this judgement.

Chapter 3

1. Vatican I (1869–1870) had also produced a document on Revelation, known as *Dei filius*. It had been drafted by Joseph Kleutgen SJ (1811–1883) of the Gregorian University who was heavily influenced by the Thomism of the sixteenth-century Spanish Jesuit Francisco Suárez (1548–1617).
2. G. O'Shea, 'Historical Discontinuity in Contemporary Views on Revelation', Ph.D. diss., John Paul II Institute for Marriage and Family, Melbourne (2007).
3. J. Montag, 'Revelation: The False Legacy of Suárez', in J. Milbank, C. Pickstock, and G. Ward (eds.), *Radical Orthodoxy* (London: Routledge, 1999), 58.
4. Ratzinger, *On the Way to Jesus Christ* (San Francisco: Ignatius, 2005), 82.
5. Id., *Principles of Catholic Theology: Building Stones for a Fundamental Theology* (San Francisco: Ignatius, 1987), 185.
6. Id., *On the Way to Jesus Christ*, 64–5.
7. Id., *Principles of Catholic Theology*, 186.
8. H. U. von Balthasar and D. C. Schindler, *Love Alone is Credible* (San Francisco: Ignatius, 2005).
9. Ratzinger, 'Revelation Itself' in H. Vorgrimler (ed.), *Commentary on the Documents of Vatican II*, iii (New York: Herder and Herder, 1969), 170.
10. Ibid. 171.
11. Ibid. 177.
12. Id., 'The Church and Scientific Theology', *Communio: International Catholic Review*, 7 (1980), 339. In this context Ratzinger cites his reliance on the insights of Henri de Lubac in *Credo: Gestalt und Lebendigkeit unseres Glaubensbekenntnisses* (Einsiedeln: Johannes Verlag, 1975), 29–56.
13. Ratzinger, 'The Transmission of Divine Revelation', *Commentary on the Documents of Vatican II*, iii. 181.
14. Ibid. 182.
15. Ibid. 184.
16. Ibid. 185.
17. Vincent de Lérins, *Le Commonitorium par Saint Vincent de Lérins* (Namur: Éditions du soleil Levant, 1959).
18. Ratzinger, 'The Transmission of Divine Revelation', 187.
19. Id., *Principles of Catholic Theology*, 85.
20. Ibid. 91.

21. Id., *Introduction to Christianity* (San Francisco: Ignatius, 1990), 65.
22. Id., *Principles of Catholic Theology*, 86.
23. Ibid. 90.
24. Ibid. 93–4.
25. Ibid. 101.
26. Ibid.
27. Ibid.
28. Ibid. 98.
29. Id., *The Ratzinger Report* (San Francisco: Ignatius, 1985), 97.
30. Pontifical Biblical Commission, 'The Interpretation of the Bible in the Church' (Vatican City: Libreria Editrice Vaticana, 1994), 9–10.
31. Ibid. 36.
32. Ratzinger, 'Biblical Interpretation in Crisis: On the Question of the Foundations and Approaches of Exegesis Today', in R. J. Neuhaus (ed.), *Biblical Intepretation in Crisis: The Ratzinger Conference on Bible and Church* (Grand Rapids, Mich.: Eerdmans, 1989).
33. Ibid.
34. Ibid.
35. Ibid.
36. Ibid.
37. A. MacIntyre, *Three Rival Versions of Moral Enquiry* (London: Duckworth, 1990), 200–1; see also T. Rowland, *Culture and the Thomist Tradition: After Vatican II* (London: Routledge, 2003), 124.
38. International Theological Commission, 'Memory and Reconciliation: The Church and the Faults of the Past', *Pope Speaks*, 45 (2000), 208–49, at 224.
39. Ratzinger, 'Biblical Interpretation in Crisis', 2.
40. Id., Preface to 'The Interpretation of the Bible in the Church'.
41. Benedict XVI, *Jesus of Nazareth* (New York: Doubleday, 2007), p. xii.
42. K. Rahner, 'Die Forderung nach einer "Kurzformel" des christlichen Glaubens', *Schriften*, 8 (1967), 153–64; trans. into English as 'The Need for a "Short Formula" of Christian Faith', in Graham Harrison, *Theological Investigations*, 9 (London: Darton, Longman and Todd, 1972), 117–26.
43. Ratzinger, *Principles of Catholic Theology*, 122.
44. Ibid. 128.
45. Ibid.
46. Ibid.
47. St Bonaventure, *The Journey of the Mind to God*, trans. P. Boehner (Cambridge: Hackett, 1993), 21.
48. Ratzinger, *Principles of Catholic Theology*, 23.
49. Ibid. 24.
50. Ibid. 23.
51. Ibid. 87.
52. Ibid. 88.

53. 'Sapir–Whorf' hypothesis in *Cambridge Encyclopedia of Language* (Cambridge: Cambridge University Press, 1987).

54. F. George, *Inculturation and Ecclesial Communion: Culture and Church in the Teaching of Pope John Paul II* (Rome: Urbaniana University Press, 1990), 88.

55. F. Kerr, *Theology after Wittgenstein* (Oxford: Blackwell, 1986), 11.

56. Ratzinger, *On the Way to Jesus Christ*, 72.

57. Ibid. 73.

58. Ibid. 66.

59. Id., *Introduction to Christianity*, 95–6.

60. Ibid. 139.

61. Id., *Truth and Tolerance* (San Francisco: Ignatius, 2004), 170.

62. Id., *The Nature and Mission of Theology* (San Francisco: Ignatius, 1995), 15.

63. Id., *Introduction to Christianity*, 140–1.

64. Id., Sorbonne Address: 'The Truth of Christianity', 25–7 Nov. 1999, trans. Maria Klepacka.

65. Ibid. 183.

66. Ibid.

67. Id., Sorbonne Address. For the same idea expressed in different words see Benedict XVI, *Deus Caritas Est*, art. 10.

68. Ratzinger, 'The Transmission of Divine Revelation', 188.

69. G. O'Shea, 'Historical Discontinuity in Contemporary Views on Revelation', Ph.D. diss., John Paul II Institute for Marriage and Family, Melbourne (2007).

Chapter 4

1. J. Ratzinger, *What it Means to be a Christian* (San Francisco: Ignatius, 2006), 47.

2. L. Albacete, 'The Pope Against Moralism and Legalism', *Anthropotes* (1994), 85.

3. Ibid.

4. H. U. von Balthasar and D. C. Schindler, *Love Alone is Credible* (San Francisco: Ignatius, 2005). First pub. 1963 in German.

5. Ratzinger, 'Homily for Msgr Luigi Giusanni', *Communio: International Catholic Review*, 31 (2004), 685–7, at 685.

6. H. U. von Balthasar, *Convergences to the Source of Christian Mystery* (San Francisco: Ignatius, 1983), 34.

7. P. Henrici, 'Modernity and Christianity', *Communio: International Catholic Review*, 17 (1990), 140–51.

8. Ibid. 150–1.

9. Jansenism is notoriously difficult to define. The term was coined by Jesuits in the 1640s to refer to those influenced by the ideas of Cornelius Jansen, Bishop of Ypres (1510–1576). William Doyle has suggested that 'many difficulties are avoided if we look at Jansenism not as a body of doctrine but as a series of historical situations'. See W. Doyle, *Jansenism:*

Catholic Resistance to Authority from the Reformation to the French Revolution (London: Palgrave Macmillan, 2000), 87. Cardinal Giovanni Bona (1609–1674) suggested that a Jansenist is a Catholic who did not like Jesuits. Their general orientation was to resist practices which aroused the senses and to foster a lopsided emphasis on the fallen condition of human nature. Although the movement had for a time Gallican rather than ultramontanist orientations, it took a more ultramontanist orientation when planted in Irish soil by French émigrés fleeing the Revolution and Irish priests trained in France who staffed Maynooth seminary at its foundation in 1795. In particular the Irish diaspora in the countries of the New World tended to define itself in opposition to a Protestant establishment rather than against the Roman curia; and thus loyalty to the Papacy was strengthened as a key characteristic distinguishing Catholic from Protestants.

10. For a treatment of this, see J. Milbank, *The Suspended Middle: Henri de Lubac's Debate Concerning the Supernatural* (Grand Rapids, Mich.: Eerdmans, 2005).

11. Ratzinger, *What it Means to be a Christian*, 49.

12. Ibid. 54.

13. Ibid. 75.

14. Id., *Principles of Catholic Theology: Building Stones for a Fundamental Theology* (San Francisco: Ignatius, 1987), 77.

15. Ibid.

16. Id., 'The Renewal of Moral Theology: Perspectives on Vatican II and *Veritatis Splendor*, *Communio: International Catholic Review*, 32 (2005), 357–69, at 358.

17. Ibid.

18. Ibid.

19. Ibid. 363.

20. Ibid. 368.

21. I. Markham, *Truth and the Reality of God: An Essay in Natural Theology* (Edinburgh: T. & T. Clark, 1998), 115.

22. Ratzinger, *Images of Hope: Meditations on Major Feasts* (San Francisco: Ignatius, 2006), 88.

23. A. Scola, 'The Unity of Love and the Face of Man: An Invitation to Read *Deus Caritas Est*', *Communio: International Catholic Review*, 33 (2006), 316–46, at 325.

24. Ratzinger, *The Yes of Jesus Christ: Spiritual Exercises in Faith, Hope and Love* (New York: Crossroad, 1991), 73.

25. Id., *The Ratzinger Report* (San Francisco: Ignatius, 1985), 87.

26. K. Wojtyla, *Person and Community: Selected Essays* (New York: Peter Lang, 1993), 183.

27. Ibid. 301–15.

28. M. Waldstein, *Man and Woman He Created Them: A Theology of the Body* (Boston, Mass.: Daughters of St Paul, 2006).
29. Ibid. 96.
30. J. Ratzinger and M. Pera, *Without Roots* (New York: Basic Books, 2006), 125–6.
31. Id., *Behold the Pierced One* (San Francisco: Ignatius, 1986), 58.
32. Id., *The Yes of Jesus Christ*, 81.
33. Id., *What it Means to be a Christian*, 78.
34. G. Bernanos, in *We the French*, quot. von Balthasar in *Bernanos: An Ecclesial Existence* (San Francisco: Ignatius, 1996), 298.
35. Ratzinger, *The Yes of Jesus Christ*, 82.
36. Id., *Co-Workers of the Truth: Meditations for Every Day of the Year* (San Francisco: Ignatius, 1992), 67.
37. Benedict XVI, Homily at his Inauguration Mass, 24 Apr. 2005.
38. Vatican Radio, 7 Mar. 1997, quot. M. Bardozzi, *In the Vineyard of the Lord: The Life, Faith and Teachings of Joseph Ratzinger/Benedict XVI* (New York: Rizzoli, 2005), 111–12.
39. Ratzinger, *The Ratzinger Report*, 91.
40. Ibid. 97.
41. Id., *Values in a Time of Upheaval* (San Francisco: Ignatius: 2006), 148.
42. Id., 'The Spiritual Roots of Europe Speech', quot. *In the Vineyard of the Lord*, 121.
43. D. L. Schindler, 'Catholic Theology, Gender and the Future of Western Civilisation', *Heart of the World, Center of the Church* (T. & T. Clark: Edinburgh, 1996), 237–75; A. Scola, 'The Dignity and Mission of Women: The Anthropological and Theological Foundations', *Communio: International Catholic Review*, 25 (1998), 42–56.
44. Schindler, 'Catholic Theology', 237–75.
45. Ratzinger, *Behold the Pierced One*, 60.
46. Ibid. 51.
47. Id., *God and the World* (San Francisco: Ignatius, 2000), 83.
48. Ibid. 82.
49. Id., *On the Way to Jesus Christ* (San Francisco: Ignatius, 2005), 8.
50. Id., *Eschatology: Death and Eternal Life* (Washington, DC: Catholic University of America Press, 1988), 215.
51. Ibid. 229.
52. Ibid. 230.
53. Ibid. 233.
54. Ibid.
55. Ibid. 257.
56. Id., *Values in a Time of Upheaval*, 76.
57. Ibid. 85.
58. Ibid. 91.
59. Ibid.

60. Ibid.
61. Ibid.
62. Ibid. 97.
63. Ibid. 80.
64. Ibid. 97, n. 19.
65. Id., *Behold the Pierced One*, 51.
66. Id., 'Cardinal Frings's Speeches during the Second Vatican Council: Apropos A. Muggeridge's *The Desolate City*', *Communio: International Catholic Review*, 15 (1988), 130–47, at 147.

Chapter 5

1. J. Ratzinger, *Theological Highlights of Vatican II* (New York: Paulist Press, 1966), 90–1.
2. Id., 'The Ecclesiology of Vatican II', Aversa Congress, 15 Sept. 2001.
3. P. McPartlan, 'The Eucharist, the Church and Evangelisation: The Influence of Henri de Lubac', *Communio: International Catholic Review*, 23 (1996), 776–85.
4. Ratzinger, *Co-Workers of the Truth: Meditations for Every Day of the Year* (San Francisco: Ignatius, 1992), 324.
5. Id., *Principles of Catholic Theology: Building Stones for a Fundamental Theology* (San Francisco: Ignatius, 1987), 50.
6. Id., 'Announcements and Prefatory Notes of Explanation on the Dogmatic Constitution on the Church', in H. Vorgrimler (ed.), *Commentary on the Documents of Vatican II*, i (London: Burns and Oates, 1966), 297–307, at 301–2.
7. J. Ratzinger and K. Rahner, *The Episcopate and the Primacy* (New York: Herder and Herder, 1962), 45.
8. 'Letter to the Bishops of the Catholic Church on Some Aspects of the Church Understood as Communion', Document of the Congregation for the Doctrine of the Faith, 28 May 1992, art. 4.
9. In this he was following the critical commentary by G. Alberigo, which he described as one of the best pieces of critical writing on the problems of the Pastoral Constitution. See his 'Die Konstitution in Beziehung zur gesamten Lehre des Konzils', in G. Baraúna and V. Schurr, *Die Kirche in der Welt von heute* (Salzburg: Müller, 1967), cited Ratzinger, 'The Dignity of the Human Person', *Commentary on the Documents of Vatican II* (New York: Herder and Herder, 1969), v. 119 n. 2.
10. Ratzinger, *The Ratzinger Report* (San Francisco: Ignatius, 1985), 47.
11. Id., 'The Dignity of the Human Person'.
12. Id., 'Letters to the Austrian Bishops' Conference', June 1997.
13. 'Letter to the Bishops of the Catholic Church on Some Aspects of the Church Understood as Communion', art. 1.
14. Ratzinger, *Many Religions—One Covenant* (San Francisco: Ignatius, 1998), 19.

15. Id., *Daughter Zion* (San Francisco: Ignatius, 1983), 31.

16. Id., 'On the Position of Mariology and Marian Spirituality within the Totality of Faith and Theology', in *The Church and Women: A Compendium* (San Francisco: Ignatius, 1988), 67–81, at 72.

17. Id., *The Ratzinger Report*, 49.

18. Id., *Salt of the Earth: The Church at the End of the Millenium. An Interview with Peter Seewald* (San Francisco: Ignatius, 1996), 271.

19. H. Küng, *Structures of the Church*, trans. Salvator Attanasio (New York: Thomas Nelson and Sons, 1964); id., *Global Responsibility: In Search of a New World Ethic* (New York: Crossroad, 1991); id., *A Global Ethic for Global Politics and Economics* (Oxford: Oxford University Press, 1997).

20. Benedict XVI, *Images of Hope: Meditations on Major Feasts* (San Francisco: Ignatius, 2006), 34.

21. Ratzinger, *Church, Ecumenism and Politics* (New York: Crossroad, 1988), 128–9.

22. Id., *The Nature and Mission of Theology: Approaches to Understanding its Role in the Light of Present Controversy* (San Francisco: Ignatius, 1993), 84.

23. H. U. von Balthasar, *Thérèse of Lisieux: The Story of a Mission* (London: Sheed & Ward, 1953), pp. xii–xiii.

24. 'Letter to the Bishops of the Catholic Church on Some Aspects of the Church Understood as Communion', art. 15.

25. Ratzinger, 'The Theological Locus of Ecclesial Movements', *Communio: International Catholic Review*, 25 (1998), 480–504, at 481.

26. Id., *The Yes of Jesus Christ: Spiritual Exercises in Faith, Hope and Love* (New York: Crossroad, 1991), 38.

27. Id., 'The Theological Locus of Ecclesial Movements', 485.

28. Ibid. 484.

29. Ibid. 503.

30. Ibid.

31. Ibid. 'Ecclesial Movements', 480–505, at 503.

32. Id., *Images of Hope*, 26.

33. Id., *The Episcopate and the Primacy*, 61. See also Ratzinger's article on the origins of papalism: 'Der Einfuss des Bettelordensstreites auf die Entwicklung der Lehre vom päpstlichen Universalprimat', in J. Auer and H. Volk (eds.), *Theologie in Geschichte und Gegenwart* (Munich, 1957), 697–724.

34. 'Letter to the Bishops of the Catholic Church on Some Aspects of the Church Understood as Communion', art. 13.

35. Ratzinger, *Theological Highlights*, 112–13.

36. Id., *The Ratzinger Report*, 59–60.

37. Ibid. 61.

38. Id., 'The Ecclesiology of the Constitution on the Church, Vatican II, *Lumen gentium*', *L'Osservatore Romano*, 19 Sept. 2001, 5.

39. Ibid.

40. H. de Lubac, *The Motherhood of the Church* (San Francisco: Ignatius, 1982), 199.
41. Ibid. 200.
42. Ratzinger, *On the Way to Jesus Christ* (San Francisco: Ignatius, 2005), 133.
43. Ibid. 137.
44. W. Kasper, 'On the Church', *America*, 23–30 Apr. 2001; Ratzinger, 'The Local Church and the Universal Church: A Response to Walter Kasper', ibid., 19 Nov. 2001.
45. *Dominus Iesus*, 16.
46. Ibid.
47. Ibid. 17.
48. Ratzinger, *Theological Highlights*, 71.
49. Id., 'Dialogue, Communion and Martyrdom: Thoughts on the Relation between Intra-ecclesial and Inter-religious Dialogue', *Communio: International Catholic Review*, 27 (2000), 816–24, at 817.
50. Id., *On the Way to Jesus Christ*, 77.
51. Quot. John L. Allen Jnr, 'Ratzinger credited with saving Lutheran pact', *National Catholic Reporter*, 10 Sept. 1999.
52. Ratzinger, *Theological Highlights of Vatican II*, 24.
53. Ibid. 73.
54. Ibid.
55. At the time of writing this group is seeking Uniate Rite status within the Catholic Church.
56. Ratzinger, *Church, Ecumenism and Politics*, 91.
57. Id., *Principles of Catholic Theology*, 199.
58. Ibid.
59. Id., *Truth and Tolerance* (San Francisco: Ignatius, 2004), 45.
60. J. Hick, *An Interpretation of Religion: Human Responses to the Transcendent* (London: Macmillan, 1989), 171; id., *The Metaphor of God Incarnate* (London: SCM, 1993).
61. Ratzinger, 'Inter-religious Dialogue and Jewish–Christian Relations', *Communio: International Catholic Review*, 25 (1998), 29–41, at 33.
62. Ibid. 35.
63. J. Ratzinger, H. U. Balthasar, et al., *Principles of Christian Morality* (San Francisco: Ignatius, 1986), 54.
64. Ratzinger, *Truth and Tolerance*, 107–9.
65. Id., *Introduction to Christianity* (San Francisco: Ignatius, 2004), 22.
66. See Appendix II.

Chapter 6

1. A. MacIntyre, *Three Rival Versions of Moral Enquiry* (London: Duckworth, 1990).
2. J. Ratzinger, 'Christ, Faith, and the Challenge of Cultures', Address to the presidents of the Asian bishops' conference, 2–5 Mar. 1993.
3. Id., *Values in a Time of Upheaval* (San Francisco: Ignatius, 2006), 17.

4. C. Dawson, 'The Christian View of History', *Blackfriars*, 32 (1951), 312–27, at 313.

5. J. Pieper, *The End of Time: A Meditation on the Philosophy of History* (Indiana: St Augustine's Press, 1998), 16 and 19–20.

6. H. U. von Balthasar, *A Theology of History* (San Francisco: Ignatius, 1994), 39–40.

7. Ratzinger, *Principles of Catholic Theology: Building Stones for a Fundamental Theology* (San Francisco: Ignatius, 1987), 155–6.

8. Id., *The Yes of Jesus Christ: Spiritual Exercises in Faith, Hope and Love* (New York: Crossroad, 1991), 46.

9. Id., 'Prepolitical Moral Foundations of a Free Republic', in *Political Theologies: Public Religions in a Post-Secular World*, ed. Hent de Vries and Lawrence E. Sullivan (New York: Fordham University Press, 2006), 261.

10. Id., *'In the Beginning . . . ': A Catholic Understanding of the Story of Creation and the Fall* (Grand Rapids, Mich.: Eerdmans, 1986), 83.

11. Ibid. 84.

12. Ibid.

13. Ibid.

14. Ibid. 89; see also R. Buttiglione and A. Scola, 'Von Abraham zu Prometheus: Zur Problematik der Schöpfung innerhalb des modernen Denkens', *Internationale katholische Zeitschrift*, 5 (1976), 30–41.

15. Ibid. 89.

16. Ratzinger, *The Spirit of the Liturgy* (San Francisco: Ignatius: 2000), 16.

17. Id., *'In the Beginning . . . '*, 28.

18. Ibid. 32.

19. Benedict XVI, 'The Regensburg Address', *L'Osservatore Romano*, 20 Sept. 2006. See Appendix II.

20. John Paul II, *Fides et Ratio* (72).

21. Ratzinger, *Church, Ecumenism and Politics* (New York: Crossroad, 1988), 213–14.

22. Ibid. 218.

23. Ibid. 219.

24. Ibid. 226.

25. O. O'Donovan, *The Desire of the Nations: Rediscovering the Roots of Political Theology* (Cambridge: Cambridge University Press, 1996), 251. O'Donovan argues that the possibilities open to contemporary societies and peoples with a history and memory of the Gospel proclamation do not include naive malevolence, but only a formation that is demonic to the extent that it is not redeemed and redemptive. For O'Donovan, 'the redemptive reality within history becomes the occasion for a disclosure of the historical possibilities of evil, an evil shaped in imitation and replication of the redemptive good'.

26. *La Repubblica*, 19 Nov. 2003. Quot. Sandro Magister in 'The Church is Under Siege. But Habermas, the Atheist, Is Coming to its Defense' <http://chiesa.espresso.repubblica.it>.

27. Ratzinger, 'Dialogue, Communion, and Martyrdom: Thoughts on the Relation between Intra-ecclesial and Inter-religious Dialogue', *Communio: International Catholic Review*, 27 (2000), 816–24, at 817.

28. Ratzinger, *The Yes of Jesus Christ*, 76. Note: this work was published initially in German in 1989 and the first English translation was published in 1991 and titled *To Look on Christ* (New York: Crossroad).

29. Id., *Values in a Time of Upheaval*, 156–7.

30. Ratzinger endorses the ideas of Robert Spaemann in 'Ist eine nicht-missionarische Praxis universalistischer Religionen möglich?', in *Theorie und Praxis*, Festschrift N. Lobkowicz zum 65. Geburtstag (Berlin, 1996).

31. On the problems associated with the 'world ethos' postulated by Küng, see Spaemann, 'Weltethos als "Projekt"', *Merkur*, 50 (1996), 893–904.

32. Ratzinger, 'Prepolitical Moral Foundations of a Free Republic', 267.

33. Id., 'Truth and Freedom', *Communio: International Catholic Review*, 23 (1996), 16–35, at 31.

34. Id., 'Europe in the Crisis of Cultures', *Communio: International Catholic Review*, 32 (2005), 345–56, at 346–7.

35. Id., *Truth and Tolerance* (San Francisco: Ignatius, 2003), 356–8.

36. Id., *Church, Ecumenism and Politics*, 151.

37. Id., *Values in a Time of Upheaval*, 23.

38. Ibid. 69–71.

39. Id., 'The Church and Economics', *Communio: International Catholic Review*, 13 (1986), 199–204.

40. Id., *On the Way to Jesus Christ* (San Francisco: Ignatius, 2005), 121.

41. Ibid., 123–4.

42. Interview with the Italian Catholic agency SIR, Rome, 7 May 2004.

43. Ibid.

44. Ratzinger, *On the Way to Jesus Christ*, 124.

45. J. Haldane, *Faithful Reason: Essays Catholic and Philosophical* (London: Routledge, 2004), 150.

46. J. V. Schall, *Jacques Maritain: The Philosopher in Society* (Lanham, Md.: Rowman and Littlefield, 1998), 95.

47. Ibid. 213.

48. Ratzinger, *Values in a Time of Upheaval*, 38–9.

49. Ibid. 40.

50. Id., 'Prepolitical Moral Foundations of a Free Republic', 267.

51. Ibid. 268.

52. *Deus Caritas Est*, 34.

53. Ibid. 40.

54. Ibid.

55. Ratzinger, 'Europe in the Crisis of Cultures', *Communio: International Catholic Review*, 32 (2005), 345–56, at 348.

56. Ibid. 349.

57. Id., *Church, Ecumenism and Politics*, 224.
58. Ibid.
59. Schall, 'An Interview with Justin Murray', 9 Nov. 2006. See 'Ignatius Insight' website.
60. Ratzinger, *Salt of the Earth: The Church at the End of the Millennium. An Interview with Peter Seewald* (San Francisco: Ignatius, 1996), 244.
61. Id., *Church, Ecumenism and Politics*, 162.

Chapter 7

1. Ratzinger was strongly influenced by Romano Guardini's *Liturgische Bildung: Versuche* (Rotenfels: Quickbornhaus, 1923). A revised edition was published under the title *Liturgie und liturgische Bildung* (Würzburg: Werkbund, 1966).
2. For summaries of *Sacrosanctum Concilium*, see L. Bouyer, *The Liturgy Revived: A Doctrinal Commentary of the Conciliar Constitution on the Liturgy* (London: Darton, Longman and Todd, 1965); G. Tattersall, '*Pasch* and *Eschaton* in *Ecclesia*: Joseph Ratzinger's Theology of the Liturgy', *Priest*, 11 (2007), 12–15.
3. A. Nichols, 'A Tale of Two Documents', *A Pope and a Council on the Sacred Liturgy* (Farnborough: St Michael's Abbey Press, 2002), 12.
4. Ibid. 25.
5. Ratzinger, *Theological Highlights of Vatican II* (New York: Paulist Press, 1966), 88.
6. For an extensive analysis of Lercaro's contributions to liturgical change in the 1960s, see A. Reid, *The Organic Development of the Liturgy*, 2nd edn. (San Francisco: Ignatius Press, 2005).
7. 'The Fall of a Progressive', *Tablet*, 6 Apr. 1968, 335.
8. Ratzinger, Preface to Reid, *The Organic Development of the Liturgy*, 11.
9. John XXIII, *Veterum Sapientia*, Feb. 1962, art. 2.
10. Ibid. art. 3.
11. Ibid. arts. 6, 7, and 8.
12. Paul VI, Wednesday Audience Address, 26 Nov. 1969, *L'Osservatore Romano*, 4 Dec. 1969, 12.
13. Ibid. 1.
14. Ibid. 12.
15. Ibid.
16. Ibid.
17. R. Scruton, *The Philosopher on Dover Beach* (Manchester: Carcanet, 1990), 115.
18. Ratzinger, Preface to Reid, *The Organic Development of the Liturgy*, 10.
19. Ibid.
20. Id., *On the Way to Jesus Christ* (San Francisco: Ignatius, 2005), 155.
21. Ibid. 158.
22. Id., *The Spirit of the Liturgy* (San Francisco: Ignatius, 2000), 23.
23. Id., *Principles of Catholic Theology* (San Francisco: Ignatius, 1987), 389–90.

24. Id., *God and the World* (San Francisco: Ignatius, 2000), 416.
25. Reid, 'Looking Again at the Liturgical Reform: Some General and Monastic Considerations', *Downside Review*, 124 (2006), 255–6, n. 16.
26. Ratzinger, *The Feast of Faith* (San Francisco: Ignatius, 1986), 74.
27. Id., *The Spirit of the Liturgy*, 170.
28. Id., Speech delivered on the 10th anniversary of the *Motu Proprio Ecclesia Dei*, 24 Oct. 1998, Rome.
29. Id., *Co-Workers of the Truth: Meditations for Every Day of the Year* (San Francisco: Ignatius, 1992), 130 from *Das neue Volk Gottes*, 139–40.
30. Ratzinger, *God and the World*, 418.
31. *Sacramentum caritatis*, Mar. 2007, para. 62.
32. Francis Arinze, 'Language in the Roman Rite Liturgy: Latin and the Vernacular', Keynote address at Gateway liturgical conference, St Louis, Mo., 11 Nov. 2006.
33. Ratzinger, *The Feast of Faith*, 81.
34. Ibid. 82.
35. *Sacramentum caritatis*, para. 41.
36. Ibid. para. 35.
37. Ibid.
38. Ibid.
39. Ratzinger, *The Feast of Faith*, 100.
40. Ibid. 111. Significantly, Aquinas was relying on the authority of Augustine here, but Ratzinger may argue that Augustine's position was more nuanced. St Thomas himself acknowledges the statement of Augustine that 'when it happens that I am more moved by the voice than by the words sung, I confess to have sinned, and then I would rather not hear the singer'. The following publications have also influenced Ratzinger's position on this point: W. Kurzschenkel, *Die theologische Bestimmung der Musik* (Trier: Paulinus, 1971); K. G. Fellerer (ed.) *Geschichte der katholischen Kirchenmusik*, i (Kassel: Bärenreiter, 1972); ii (Kassel: Bärenreiter, 1976); H. J. Burbach, *Studien zur Musikanschauung des Thomas von Aquin* (Regensburg: Bosse, 1966); id., 'Thomas von Aquin und die Musik', *Musica sacra*, 94 (1974), 80–2; D. Sertillanges, 'Prière et musique', *Vie Spirituelle*, 7 (1930), 130–64; F. Haberl, 'Zur Theologie der Kirchenmusik', *Musica sacra*, 91 (1971), 213–19; id., 'Die humane und sakrale Bedeutung der Musik', in H. Lonnendonker, *In caritate et veritate. Festschift für Johannes Overath* (Saarbrücken: Minerva—Verlag, Thinnes and Nolte, 1973), 17–23; H. J. Burbach, 'Sacro-Pop', *Communio: International Catholic Review*, 3 (1974), 91–4 (German edn.); J. Overath, 'Kirchenmusik im Dienst des Kultes', *Internationale katholische Zeitschrift*, 13 (1984), 355–68. See also Ratzinger, 'Theologische Probleme der Kirchenmusik', ibid. 9 (1980), 148–57.
41. Ratzinger, *The Feast of Faith*, 118–19.
42. Ibid. 119.

43. Id., *A New Song for the Lord* (New York: Crossroad, 1996), 124.
44. Id., *The Feast of Faith*, 120–1.
45. Ibid. 124–5.
46. Id., *Co-Workers of the Truth*, 129–30.
47. Id., *The Feast of Faith*, 66–7.
48. Ibid.
49. Ibid. 68.
50. Id., *The Spirit of the Liturgy*, 168.
51. Id., *The Feast of Faith*, 67.
52. Id., *The Spirit of the Liturgy*, 168–9.
53. Id., *Co-Workers of the Truth*, 135; id., *The Feast of Faith*, 127–31.
54. P. Johnson, 'When High Mass was sung with a king's escort and fixed bayonets', *Spectator*, 22 (2003), 28.
55. Ratzinger, *The Ratzinger Report* (San Francisco: Ignatius, 1985), 130.
56. Scholarly discussion of this was advanced in the 2007 Holy Thursday Homily of Benedict XVI.
57. Ratzinger, *The Spirit of the Liturgy*, 79.
58. Id., 'Theology of the Liturgy'. Lecture delivered at the *Journées liturgiques de Fontgombault* Conference, 22–4 July 2001, pub. *Oriens*, 7 (2002), spec. suppl. insert, 2.
59. John Carmel Cardinal Heenan, 'Letter to Evelyn Waugh, August 28, 1964', in S. M. P. Reid (ed.), *A Bitter Trial: Evelyn Waugh and Cardinal Heenan on the Liturgical Changes* (Curdridge: St Austin Press, 1996), 48.
60. Ratzinger, *Co-Workers of the Truth*, 303.
61. Id., *The Spirit of the Liturgy*, 69.
62. Ibid. 78.
63. Id., *God is Near Us* (San Francisco: Ignatius, 2003), 37.
64. Ibid., 70–1.
65. Id., *The Spirit of the Liturgy*, 194.
66. Ibid. 185.
67. Id., *God is Near Us*, 93.
68. Id., *The Spirit of the Liturgy*, 198.
69. Ibid.
70. A. Bugnini, *The Reform of the Liturgy, 1948–1975* (Collegeville, Minn.: Liturgical Press, 1990), 377.
71. Ratzinger, *The Spirit of the Liturgy*, 170.
72. *Sacramentum caritatis*, para. 49.
73. Ibid. paras. 52 and 53.
74. Ratzinger, *God is Near Us*, 37.
75. Id., *A New Song for the Lord*, 32.
76. Ibid.
77. Ibid. 75.
78. A. Nichols, *Looking at the Liturgy: A Critical View of its Contemporary Form* (San Francisco: Ignatius, 1996), 21.

79. C. Pickstock, *After Writing: On the Liturgical Consummation of Philosophy* (Oxford: Blackwell, 1998), 176.

80. Ratzinger, Speech delivered on the 10th anniversary of the *Motu Proprio Ecclesia Dei*.

81. John Paul II, Wednesday Audience Address, 26 Feb. 2003, *Adoremus Bulletin*, 9 (2003).

82. T. Bertone, *Le Figaro* interview, Easter 2007, 56–60.

83. Ratzinger, 'Klaus Gamber: L'Intrépidité d'un vrai témoin', trans. S. Wallon, *La Réforme liturgique en question* (Le Barroux: Éditions Sainte-Madeleine, 1992), 6–8. This statement was originally published in German and then translated into French. It is the French translation which is most often cited. There is no official English translation. The French is as follows: 'après le concile ... à la place de la liturgie fruit d'un développement continu, on a mis une liturgie fabriquée. On est sorti du processus vivant de croissance et de devenir pour entrer dans la fabrication. On n'a plus voulu continuer le devenir et la maturation organiques du vivant à travers les siècles, et on les a remplacés – à la manière de la production technique – par une fabrication, produit banal de l'instant.'

84. Tattersall, '*Pasch* and *Eschaton* in *Ecclesia*', 12.

Conclusion

1. D. Tracy, 'The Uneasy Alliance Reconceived: Catholic Theological Method, Modernity and Postmodernity', *Theological Studies*, 50 (1989), 548–71.

2. K. L. Schmitz, 'Postmodernism and the Catholic Tradition', *American Catholic Philosophical Quarterly*, 73 (1969), 223–53, at 235.

3. C. Taylor, 'Two Theories of Modernity', *Hastings Center Report*, Mar.–Apr. 1995, 24–7.

4. J. Ratzinger, *Principles of Catholic Theology* (San Francisco: Ignatius, 1987), 56.

5. Id., *On the Way to Jesus Christ* (San Francisco: Ignatius, 2005), 46.

6. Ibid.

7. J. A. Komonchak, 'The Church in Crisis: Pope Benedict's Theological Vision', *Commonweal*, 3 June 2005.

8. R. A. Krieg (ed.), *Romano Guardini: A Precursor of Vatican II*, (Notre Dame, Ind.: University of Notre Dame Press, 1997), 69.

9. Ratzinger, *Co-Workers of the Truth* (San Francisco: Ignatius, 1992), 265.

10. Benedict XVI, *L'Osservatore Romano*, 27 July 2005.

11. N. Biggar, 'Karl Barth and Germain Grisez on the Human Good: An Ecumenical Rapprochement', N. Biggar and R. Black (eds.), *The Revival of Natural Law: Philosophical, Theological and Ethical Responses to the Finnis–Grisez School* (Aldershot: Ashgate, 2000), 178.

12. Ratzinger, 'The Dignity of the Human Person', in H. Vorgrimler (ed.), *Commentary on the Documents of Vatican II*, v (New York: Herder and Herder, 1969), 115–64, at 118.

13. Id., *Salt of the Earth: The Church at the End of the Millenium. An Interview with Peter Seewald* (San Francisco: Ignatius, 1996), 282.

14. Ibid. 27.

15. Id., *A New Song for the Lord* (Crossroad: New York, 1986), 124.

16. Id., *Faith and the Future* (Chicago, Ill.: Franciscan Herald Press, 1971), 75.

17. J. Thornhill <http://www.catalyst-for-renewal.com.au/john_thornhill. htm>, 26 Sept. 2003.

18. John Paul II, *Tertio Millennio Adviente*, Art. 10.

19. Ratzinger, *The Spirit of the Liturgy* (San Francisco: Ignatius, 2000), 20.

20. John Paul II, 'General Audience Homily of November 24, 1999', *L'Osservatore Romano*, 25 Sept. 1994, 5.

21. J. Milbank, 'The Future of Love: A Reading of Pope Benedict XVI's Encyclical', *Communio: International Catholic Review*, 33 (2006), 368–75, at 369.

22. Joseph Roth, *The Radetzky March*, quot. J. Ratzinger in *God and the World* (San Francisco: Ignatius, 2000), 67.

Bibliography

Primary Sources: Publications by Joseph Ratzinger

Chapter 1

'The Changeable and the Unchangeable in Theology', *Theological Digest, 10* (1962), 71–6.

'Homily at the Funeral Liturgy for Hans Urs von Balthasar', *Communio: International Catholic Review*, 15 (1988), 512–16.

Introduction to Christianity (San Francisco: Ignatius, 1990).

'*Communio*: A Program', *Communio: International Catholic Review*, 19 (1992), 436–49.

'God in Pope John Paul II's Crossing the Threshold of Hope', *Communio: International Catholic Review*, 22 (1995), 107–12.

'Relativism: The Central Problem for the Faith Today', Address to the presidents of the doctrinal commissions of the bishops' conference of Latin America, Guadalajara, Mexico, May 1996.

Chapter 2

Theological Highlights of Vatican II (New York: Paulist Press, 1966).

'Das Menschenbild des Konzils in seiner Bedeutung für die Bildung in Christliche Erziehung nach dem Konzil', *Berichte und Dokumentationen*, 4, ed. Kulturbeirat beim Zentralkomitee der deutschen Katholiken (Cologne, 1967), 33–65.

'Kommentar zu Art. 11–22 der Pastoralkonstitution über die Kirche in der Welt von heute', *Lexikon fur Theologie und Kirche*, suppl. vol. iii (Freiburg, 1968), 313–54.

'The Dignity of the Human Person': Commentary on Chapter I, Part I of *Gaudium et spes*, in H. Vorgrimler (ed.), *Commentary on the Documents of Vatican II* (New York: Herder and Herder, 1969).

The Ratzinger Report (San Francisco: Ignatius, 1985).

'Cardinal Frings' Speeches during the Second Vatican Council: Apropos of A. Muggeridge's *The Desolate City*', *Communio: International Catholic Review*, 15 (1988), 131–47.

'The Current Situation of Faith and Theology', *L'Osservatore Romano*, 6 Nov. 1996.

Salt of the Earth: The Church at the End of the Millennium. An Interview with Peter Seewald (San Francisco: Ignatius, 1996).

Chapter 3

Der Gott des Glaubens und der Gott der Philosophen (Munich, 1960).

'Die Heilige Schrift und die Tradition', *Theologische-praktische Quartalschrift*, 3 (1963), 224–7.

Das Problem der Dogmengeschichte in der Sicht der katholischen Theologie (Cologne and Opladen, 1966).

Rahner, K. and Ratzinger, J., *Revelation and Tradition* (New York: Herder and Herder, 1966).

'Commentary on the Dogmatic Constitution on Divine Revelation', in H. Vorgrimler (ed.), *Commentary on the Documents of Vatican II*, iii (New York: Herder and Herder, 1969).

'The "Brief Formulas of Faith" Question Again. Some Comments', *Communio: International Catholic Review*, 2 (1973), 164–8.

'The Church and Scientific Theology', *Communio: International Catholic Review*, 7 (1980), 332–42.

'Sources and Transmission of the Faith', *Communio: International Catholic Review*, 10 (1983), 17–34.

'Faith, Philosophy and Theology', *Communio: International Catholic Review*, 11 (1984), 350–63.

'Problems in Catechesis Today: An Interview with Joseph Cardinal Ratzinger', *Communio: International Catholic Review*, 11 (1984), 145–56.

'On Hope', *Communio: International Catholic Review*, 12 (1985), 71–84.

'Interpretation–Contemplation–Action', *Communio: International Catholic Review*, 13 (1986), 139–55.

Principles of Catholic Theology: Building Stones for a Fundamental Theology (San Francisco: Ignatius, 1987).

'Biblical Interpretation in Crisis: On the Question of the Foundations and Approaches of Exegesis Today': Lecture delivered on 27 January 1988 at Saint Peter's Church, New York.

'Jesus Christ Today', *Communio: International Catholic Review*, 17 (1990), 68–87.

'The Catechism of the Catholic Church and the Optimism of the Redeemed', *Communio: International Catholic Review*, 20 (1993), 469–84.

The Nature and Mission of Theology: Approaches to Understanding its Role in the Light of Present Controversy (San Francisco: Ignatius, 1993).

'The Interpretation of the Bible in the Church', Preface by Card. Joseph Ratzinger, Pontifical Biblical Commission, 18 Mar. 1994.

Gospel, Catechesis and Catechism: Sidelights on the Catechism of the Catholic Church (San Francisco: Ignatius, 1997).

'The Jewish People and their Sacred Scriptures in the Christian Bible', Preface by Card. Joseph Ratzinger, Pontifical Biblical Commission, 24 May 2001.

Introduction to Christianity (San Francisco: Ignatius, 2004).

On the Way to Jesus Christ (San Francisco: Ignatius, 2005).

'Lectio Divina will Bring to the Church a New Spiritual Springtime', Address to the International Congress on 'Sacred Scripture in the Life of the Church', 14–18 Sept. 2005, Rome.

Handing on the Faith in an Age of Disbelief (San Francisco: Ignatius, 2006).

Jesus of Nazareth (New York: Doubleday, 2007).

Chapter 4

'Beyond Death', *Communio: International Catholic Review*, 1 (1974), 157–65.

'Preaching about God Today', *Communio: International Catholic Review*, 1 (1974), 450–62; *Theological Digest*, 22 (1974), 196–201.

Behold the Pierced One (San Francisco: Ignatius, 1986).

'Letter to the Bishops of the Catholic Church on the Pastoral Care of Homosexual Persons', Congregation for the Doctrine of the Faith, 1 Oct. 1986.

Principles of Christian Morality, with H. U. von Balthasar, et al. (San Francisco: Ignatius, 1986).

'Freedom and Liberation: The Anthropological Vision of the Instruction *Libertatis Conscientia*', *Communio: International Catholic Review*, 14 (1987), 55–72.

Auer, J and Ratzinger, J., *Dogmatic Theology: Eschatology, Death and Eternal Life* (Catholic University of America Press: Washington, DC, 1988).

'Man Between Reproduction and Creation', *Communio: International Catholic Review*, 16 (1989), 197–211.

'Peace and Justice in Crisis: The Task of Religion', *Communio: International Catholic Review,* 16 (1989), 540–51.

The Yes of Jesus Christ: Spiritual Exercises in Faith, Hope and Love (New York: Crossroad, 1991).

'Conscience in Time', *Communio: International Catholic Review*, 19 (1992), 647–57.

'Christian Faith as "the Way"': An Introduction to *Veritatis Splendor*', *Communio: International Catholic Review*, 21 (1994), 199–207.

'Christian Universalism: On Two Collections of Papers by Hans Urs von Balthasar', *Communio: International Catholic Review*, 22 (1995), 545–57.

'The New Covenant: A Theology of Covenant in the New Testament', *Communio: International Catholic Review*, 22 (1995), 635–51.

'Funeral Homily for Msgr Luigi Giussani', *Communio: International Catholic Review*, 31 (2004), 685–7.

'The Renewal of Moral Theology: Perspectives of Vatican II and *Veritatis Splendor*', *Communio: International Catholic Review*, 32 (2005), 357–68.

Deus Caritas Est: God is Love, First Encyclical Letter (London: Catholic Truth Society, 2006).

On Conscience (San Francisco: Ignatius, 2006).

What it Means to be a Christian (San Francisco: Ignatius, 2006).

Chapter 5

Volk und Haus Gottes in Augustins Lehre von der Kirche (Munich: Karl Zink Verlag, 1954).

The Episcopate and the Primacy (New York: Herder and Herder, 1962).

Das neue Volk Gottes: Entwürfe zur Ekklesiologie (Düsseldorf, 1969).

Demokratie in der Kirche: Moglichkeiten, Grenzen, Gefahren (Limburg, 1970).

'Unity of the Church—Unity of Mankind: A Congress Report', *Communio: International Catholic Review*, 1 (1974), 53–7.

'What Unites and Divides Denominations? Ecumenical Reflections', *Communio: International Catholic Review*, 1 (1974), 115–18.

'The Future of Ecumenism', *Theological Digest*, 25 (1977).

'Observations on the final report of Anglican–Roman Catholic International Commission (ARCIC), *Animadversiones quas Sacra Congregatio pro Doctrina Fidei, de mandato SS.mi super enuntiatis ultimis Commissionis vulgo ARCIC cognominatae, de Eucharistica doctrina, de sacris Ordinibus atque de subiecto auctoritatis in Ecclesia, exaravit et omnibus Conferentiis Episcoporum die 2 Aprilis transmisit*', 27 Mar. 1982.

Daughter Zion (San Francisco: Ignatius, 1983).

'Luther and the Unity of the Churches: An Interview with Joseph Cardinal Ratzinger', *Communio: International Catholic Review*, 11 (1984), 210–26.

'On the Position of Mariology and Marian Spirituality within the Totality of Faith and Theology', *The Church and Women: A Compendium* (San Francisco: Ignatius, 1988), 67–81.

'You are Full of Grace: Elements of Biblical Devotion to Mary', *Communio: International Catholic Review*, 16 (1989), 54–68.

'Biblical Foundations of Priesthood', *Communio: International Catholic Review*, 17 (1990), 617–27.

Co-Workers of the Truth: Meditations for Every Day of the Year (San Francisco: Ignatius, 1992).

'Letter to the Bishops of the Catholic Church on Some Aspects of the Church Understood as Communion', Document of the Congregation for the Doctrine of the Faith, 28 May 1992.

'The Holy Spirit as *Communio*: Concerning the Relationship of Pneumatology and Spirituality in Augustine', *Communio: International Catholic Review*, 25 (1998), 324–39.

'Inter-religious Dialogue and Jewish–Christian Relations', *Communio: International Catholic Review*, 25 (1998), 29–41.

Many Religions—One Covenant (San Francisco: Ignatius, 1998).

'The Primacy of the Successor of Peter in the Mystery of the Church', Reflections of the Congregation for the Doctrine of the Faith, 1998.

'The Theological Locus of Ecclesial Movements', *Communio: International Catholic Review*, 25 (1998), 480–504.

'Answers to Main Objections to *Dominus Iesus*', orig. pub. *Frankfurter Allgemeine Zeitung*, 22 Sept. 2000.

'Declaration "*Dominus Iesus*" on the Unicity and Salvific Universality of Jesus Christ and the Church', Congregation for the Doctrine of the Faith, 2000.

'Dialogue, Communion, and Martyrdom: Thoughts on the Relation between Intra-ecclesial and Inter-religious Dialogue', *Communio: International Catholic Review*, 27 (2000), 816–24.

'The Ecclesiology of the Constitution on the Church, Vatican II, *Lumen gentium*', *L'Osservatore Romano*, 19 Sept. 2001.

'The Ecclesiology of Vatican II', Address at the opening of the Pastoral Congress of the Diocese of Aversa, Italy, 15 Sept. 2001.

'The Local Church and the Universal Church: A Response to Walter Kasper', *America*, 19 Nov. 2001.

'Letting God Work: An Article by Cardinal Joseph Ratzinger on the Occasion of the Canonization of Josemarìa Escrivà', *L'Osservatore Romano* (spec. suppl.), Oct. 2002.

Pilgrim Fellowship of Faith: The Church as Communion (San Francisco: Ignatius, 2002).

God is Near Us: The Eucharist, the Heart of Life (San Francisco: Ignatius, 2003).

'Thoughts on the Place of Marian Doctrine and Piety in Faith and Theology as a Whole', *Communio: International Catholic Review*, 30 (2003), 147–60.

Truth and Tolerance (San Francisco: Ignatius, 2003).

'Common Declaration of Pope Benedict XVI and the Archbishop of Canterbury, His Grace Rowan Williams', Vatican City, 23 Nov. 2006.

'The Mystery of the Relationship between Christ and the Church: Reflections from the Experience of the Apostles', Wednesday Audience Addresses, 2006, pub. in *L'Osservatore Romano* throughout 2006.

Chapter 6

Christian Brotherhood (London: Sheed & Ward, 1966).

Faith and the Future (Chicago: Franciscan Herald Press, 1971).

'Eschatology and Utopia', *Communio: International Catholic Review*, 5 (1978), 211–27.

'Europa: Erstanden aus dem christlichen Glauben', in R. Hammerschmid (ed.), *Eine Pilgerreise durch Polen* (Kevelaer, 1980), 55–64.

'Technological Security as a Problem of Social Ethics', *Communio: International Catholic Review*, 5 (1982), 238–46.

'Instruction on Certain Aspects of the "Theology of Liberation"', Sacred Congregation for the Doctrine of the Faith, 1984.

'Church and Economy', *Communio: International Catholic Review*, 13 (1986), 199–204.

'In the Beginning . . . ': A Catholic Understanding of the Story of Creation and the Fall (Grand Rapids, Mich.: Eerdmans, 1986).

'Instruction on Christian Freedom and Liberation', Sacred Congregation for the Doctrine of the Faith, 1986.

Church, Ecumenism and Politics (New York: Crossroad, 1988).

The Theology of History in St Bonaventure (Chicago: Franciscan Herald Press, 1989).

'Christ, Faith, and the Challenge of Cultures', Address to the presidents of the Asian bishops' conference, 2–5 Mar. 1993.

'Truth and Freedom', *Communio: International Catholic Review*, 23 (1996), 16–35.

'Culture and Truth: Some Reflections on the Encyclical Letter *Fides et Ratio*', Address given by Card. Joseph Ratzinger, on Saturday, 13 Feb. 1999 in the Chapel at St Patrick's Seminary, *Patrician* (1999).

God and the World (San Francisco: Ignatius, 2000).

'Doctrinal Note on Some Questions Regarding the Participation of Catholics in Political Life', Congregation for the Doctrine of the Faith, 2003.

The End of Time?: The Provocation of Talking about God, with J. B. Metz, et al. (Mahwah, NJ: Paulist Press, 2004).

'Homily of Card. Joseph Ratzinger during the Mass for the Pontifical Academy of Sciences Celebrated in Montecassino, 7 Nov. 2004'.

'Introduction to Christianity: Yesterday, Today, and Tomorrow', *Communio: International Catholic Review*, 31 (2004), 481–95.

'Reason Separated From God is Obstacle to Peace' (zenit.org., 7 Nov. 2004). Address delivered 4 June 2004 on the 60th anniversary of the Normandy invasion, pub. *Vita e Pensiero*, journal of the Catholic University Sacro Cuore, Rome.

Christianity and the Crisis Cultures (San Francisco: Ignatius, 2005).

'Europe in the Crisis of Cultures', *Communio: International Catholic Review*, 32 (2005), 345–56.

The Dialectics of Secularisation: On Reason and Religion, with Jürgen Habermas as co-author (San Francisco: Ignatius, 2006).

'Prepolitical Moral Foundations of a Free Republic', *Political Theologies: Public Religions in a Post-Secular World*, ed. Hent de Vries and Lawrence E. Sullivan (New York: Fordham University Press, 2006).

Values in a Time of Upheaval (San Francisco: Ignatius, 2006).

Without Roots, with M. Pera as co-author (New York: Basic Books, 2006).

Chapter 7

'Zur theologischen Grundlegung der Kirchenmusik', *Gloria Deo: pax hominibus, Festschrift zum 100-jährigen Bestehen der Kirchenmusikschule Regensburg* (Regensburg, 1974), 39–62.

The Feast of Faith (San Francisco: Ignatius, 1986).

'Liturgy and Sacred Music', *Communio: International Catholic Review*, 3 (1986), 377–91.

'Remarks to the Bishops of Chile Regarding the Lefebvre Schism', 13 July 1988, Santiago, Chile.

'The Meaning of Sunday', *Communio: International Catholic Review*, 21 (1994), 5–26.

A New Song for the Lord (New York: Crossroad, 1996).

The Spirit of the Liturgy (San Francisco: Ignatius, 2000).

'The Feeling of Things, the Contemplation of Beauty', Message to the Communion and Liberation (CL) meeting, Rimini, 24–30 Aug. 2002.

'Theology of the Liturgy', Paper delivered at a congress on the liturgy held at the Benedictine monastery, Fontgombault, France, 22–4 July 2001, *Oriens: Journal of the Ecclesia Dei Society*, 1 (2002).

Forward to U. M. Lang, *Turning Towards the Lord: Orientation in Liturgical Prayer* (San Francisco: Ignatius, 2003).

'Remarks by Card. Ratzinger at the beginning of the Concert of the Mitteldeutscher Rundfunk from Leipzig, for the 25th Anniversary of the Pontificate of John Paul II, 17 Oct. 2003'.

Preface to A. Reid, *The Organic Development of the Liturgy* (2nd edn., Farnborough: St Michael's Abbey Press, 2004).

'Gregorian Chant and Choral Polyphony in the Liturgy', Address for the blessing of the new organ of the *Alte Kapelle*, Regensburg, 13 Sept. 2006, *Adoremus Bulletin*, 12 (2006), 12.

Images of Hope: Meditations on Major Feasts (San Francisco: Ignatius, 2006).

Sacramentum caritatis: Post-Synodal Apostolic Exhortation on the Eucharist as the Source and Summit of the Church's Life and Mission, Mar. 2007.

Summorum Pontificum, 7 July 2007.

Secondary Sources

Arinze, F., 'Language in the Roman Rite Liturgy: Latin and the Vernacular', Keynote address at Gateway liturgical conference, St Louis, Mo., 11 Nov. 2006.

—— et al., *Cardinal Reflections: Active Participation in the Liturgy* (Chicago: Hillenbrand, 2005).

Bardozzi, M., *In the Vineyard of the Lord: The Life, Faith and Teachings of Joseph Ratzinger/Benedict XVI* (New York: Rizzoli, 2005).

Boeve, L., 'Europe in Crisis: A Question of Belief or Unbelief? Perspectives from the Vatican', *Modern Theology*, 23 (2007), 205–27.

Bogle, J., *The Pope Benedict Code* (Leominster: Gracewing, 2006).

Boyle, N., 'On earth, as in heaven', *Tablet*, 9 July 2005.

Chapp, L., '*Deus Caritas Est* and the Retrieval of Christian Cosmology', *Communio: International Catholic Review*, 33 (2006), 449–73.

Chaput, C., 'Reflections on Cardinal Kasper's "On the Church"', *America*, 30 July 2001.

Congar, Y., *The Meaning of Tradition* (San Francisco: Ignatius, 2004).

Daniélou, J., *The Lord of History: Reflections on the Inner Meaning of History* (London: Longman, 1958).

Dodaro, R., *Christ and the Just Society in the Thought of Augustine* (Cambridge: Cambridge University Press, 2004).

Dupré, L., *Passage to Modernity: An Essay in the Hermeneutics of Nature and Culture* (New Haven, Conn.: Yale University Press, 1993).

Dupré, L., *The Enlightenment and the Intellectual Foundations of Modern Culture* (New Haven, Conn.: Yale University Press, 2004).

Dulles, A., 'Benedict XVI: Interpreter of Vatican II', Laurence J. McGinley Lecture, Fordham University, New York, 25 Oct. 2005.

Fischer, H. J., *Pope Benedict XVI: A Personal Portrait* (New York: Crossroad, 2005).

Hanby, M., *Augustine and Modernity* (London: Routledge, 2003).

—— 'The Logic of Love and the Unity of Catholic Truth: Reflections on *Deus Caritas Est*', *Communio: International Catholic Review*, 33 (2006), 400–23.

John XXIII, '*Veterum Sapientia*: Apostolic Constitution on the Promotion of the Study of Latin, 22 Feb. 1962'.

John Paul II, *Apostolos Suos*, Apostolic Letter on the Theological and Juridical Nature of Episcopal Conferences, 1998.

—— 'Give Praise through Beauty of Music', Wednesday Audience Address, 26 Feb. 2003, *Adoremus Bulletin*, 9 (2003).

Kaplan, G., *The Catholic Recovery of Historical Revelation* (New York: Crossroad, 2006).

Kasper, W., 'On The Church: A Friendly Reply to Cardinal Ratzinger', *America*, 23–30 Apr. 2001, trans. Ladislas Orsy, SJ. Orig. pub. *Stimmen der Zeit*, Dec. 2000.

Kerr, F., *After Aquinas: Versions of Thomism* (Oxford: Blackwell, 2002).

—— *Twentieth-Century Catholic Theologians* (Oxford: Blackwell, 2007).

Komonchak, J. A., 'Interpreting the Second Vatican Council', *Landas*, 1 (1987), 81–90.

—— 'The Church in Crisis: Pope Benedict's Theological Vision', *Commonweal*, 3 June 2006, 11–14.

Lamberigts, M., and Kenis, L., *Vatican II and its Legacy* (Leuven: Leuven University Press, 2002).

de Lubac, H., *The Motherhood of the Church* (San Francisco: Ignatius, 1982).

—— *A Brief Catechesis on Nature and Grace* (San Francisco: Ignatius, 1984).

—— *The Splendor of the Church* (San Francisco: Ignatius, 1986).

—— *Catholicism, Christ and the Common Destiny of Man* (San Francisco: Ignatius, 1988).

—— *Theology in History* (San Francisco: Ignatius, 1996).

—— *Augustinianism and Modern Theology* (New York: Crossroad, 2000).

—— *Scripture in the Tradition* (New York: Crossroad, 2000).

MacIntyre, A., *After Virtue* (London: Duckworth, 1981).

—— *Whose Justice? Which Rationality?* (London: Duckworth, 1988).

—— *Three Rival Versions of Moral Enquiry* (London: Duckworth, 1990).

Milbank, J., et al., *Radical Orthodoxy* (London: Routledge, 1999).

—— 'The Future of Love: A Reading of Pope Benedict XVI's Encyclical *Deus Caritas Est*', *Communio: International Catholic Review*, 33 (2006), 368–75.

Nichols, A., 'Joseph Ratzinger's Theology of Political Ethics', *New Blackfriars*, 68. 808 (1987), 380–93.

Nichols, A., *The Theology of Joseph Ratzinger: An Introductory Study* (Edinburgh: T. & T. Clark, 1988).

—— *Looking at the Liturgy: A Critical View of its Contemporary Form* (San Francisco: Ignatius, 1996).

—— *Catholic Thought Since the Enlightenment: A Survey* (Leominster: Gracewing, 1998).

—— *Christendom Awake: On Re-energising the Church in Culture* (Edinburgh: T. & T. Clark, 1999).

—— *Beyond the Blue Glass: Catholic Essays on Faith and Culture*, i (London: St Austin Press, 2002).

—— 'A Tale of Two Documents', *A Pope and a Council on the Sacred Liturgy* (Farnborough: St Michael's Abbey Press, 2002).

Paul VI, 'Changes in Mass for Greater Apostolate', Address to a general audience, 26 Nov. 1969.

Pieper, J., *The End of Time: A Meditation on the Philosophy of History* (San Francisco: Ignatius, 1980).

Pickstock, C., *After Writing: On the Liturgical Consummation of Philosophy* (Oxford: Blackwell, 1998).

Reid, A., *The Organic Development of the Liturgy*, 2nd edn. (Farnborough: St Michael's Abbey Press, 2004).

—— '*Sacrosanctum concilium* and the Organic Development of the Liturgy', Eleventh International Colloquium on the Liturgy, Centre International d'Etudes Liturgiques, Merton College, Oxford, Sept. 2006.

Reid, S. M. P. (ed.), *A Bitter Trial: Evelyn Waugh and Cardinal Heenan on the Liturgical Changes* (Curdridge: St Austin Press, 1996).

Schindler, D. L., *Heart of the World, Center of the Church: Communio Ecclesiology, Liberalism and Liberation* (Edinburgh: T. & T. Clark, 1996).

—— 'Truth, Freedom and Relativism in Western Democracies: A Comment on Pope Benedict XVI's Contributions to *Without Roots*', *Communio: International Catholic Review*, 32 (2005), 669–81.

—— 'The Redemption of *Eros*: Philosophical Reflections on Benedict XVI's First Encyclical', *Communio: International Catholic Review*, 33 (2006), 375–400.

Schall, J. V., *At the Limits of Political Philosophy* (Washington, DC: Catholic University of America Press, 1996).

—— 'Ratzinger on the Modern Mind', *Homiletic and Pastoral Review* (1997), 6–14.

—— *Roman Catholic Political Philosophy* (Lanham, Md.: Lexington, 2004).

—— *The Regensburg Lecture* (South Bend, Ind.: St Augustine's Press, 2007).

Scola, A., 'The Dignity and Mission of Women: The Anthropological and Theological Foundations', *Communio: International Catholic Review*, 23 (1998), 42–56.

—— *The Nuptial Mystery* (Cambridge: Eerdmans, 2005).

Scola, A., 'The Unity of Love and the Face of Man: An Invitation to
    Read *Deus Caritas Est*', *Communio: International Catholic Review*, 33 (2006),
    316–46.
Spaemann, R., 'Weltethos als "Projekt" ', *Merkur*, 50 (1996), 893–904.
Tattersall, G., '*Pasch* and *Eschaton* in *Ecclesia*: Joseph Ratzinger's Theology of
    the Liturgy', *Priest*, 11 (2007), 12–15, 21–23.
Tracy, D., 'The Uneasy Alliance Reconceived: Catholic Theological
    Method, Modernity and Postmodernity', *Theological Studies*, 50 (1989),
    548–71.
Valente, G., 'The Story of Joseph Ratzinger', *30 Days* (2006).
von Balthasar, H. U., 'The Fathers, the Scholastics and Ourselves', *Communio:
    International Catholic Review*, 24 (1997), 347–96.
Walsh, C. J., 'De Lubac's Critique of the Post-conciliar Church', *Communio:
    International Catholic Review*, 19 (1992), 404–32.

Index

CABRINI COLLEGE LIBRARY
610 KING OF PRUSSIA ROAD
RADNOR, PA 19087-3699

DEMCO